HEALING COMMUNITIES IN CONFLICT

HEALING COMMUNITIES
IN CONFLICT

INTERNATIONAL ASSISTANCE IN **COMPLEX EMERGENCIES**

Kimberly A. Maynard

Columbia University Press, New York

Columbia University Press
Publishers Since 1893
New York   Chichester, West Sussex

Copyright © 1999 Columbia University Press
All rights reserved
Library of Congress Cataloging-in-Publication Data
Maynard, Kimberly A.
    Healing communities in conflict : international assistance in
complex emergencies / Kimberly A. Maynard.
        p.   cm.
    Includes bibliographical references and index.
    ISBN   0-231-11278-5 (cloth : alk. paper). —
    ISBN   0-231-11279-3   (pbk. : alk. paper)
        1. International relief. 2. Humanitarian assistance.
    3. Refugees. I. Title.
    HV553.M39   1999
    362.8'7526—dc21   98-46125

For My Parents
Bob and Andrea Priscilla Maynard

CONTENTS

PREFACE

We are too fast to react, and too slow to see. The international community wants to close its eyes and ears.

—Relief worker in Burundi

As I drove through the small Rwandan town, it looked much like other parts of this conflict-ridden country: poor and dilapidated but bustling with life. Twelve-year-old street vendors sold vegetables from aluminum bowls carried on their heads, barefoot children ran along the street, and women sitting next to roadside stands offered cigarettes and penny candy. Everything that wasn't green was a muted gray and brown, save for flashes of red bare earth between clumps of vegetation.

Cresting a hill, however, I entered another world. At the top stood what looked at first like a moon base. Four round white medical tents were clustered incongruously in an open field. Throngs of people pressed against the surrounding fence, but a guard stationed at the opening diligently kept them at bay. My white face was enough to allow me immediate entrance, which I accepted as the crowd stared and parted.

Once inside, I wandered among the aberrant structures posing as medical rooms. One contained three elderly women and two young girls, each sitting or lying on a mat on the spotless white floor of the tent. Another housed small children, similarly spread out on the floor, some being cradled by their mothers. A third was filled with supplies. Upon closer examination, I discovered that large portions of the supplies were not catheters, gauze, or drugs, but piles of M&Ms, granola bars, and orange Tang. In the middle of the circle of tents was a covered area where Anglos sporting gray-blue operating gowns complete with pants and masks performed triage and outpatient care on plastic tables. A local woman cleaned up, retrieved supplies, and translated for the patients.

None of the foreign physicians or nurses I met spoke French or the local language. Each was only in country for a couple of weeks before being replaced. I learned that initially the clinic had had few patients, in part because those who had not fled the wave of widespread killings were using a local health center in a neighboring town. Gradually, however, the numbers began to increase as previously displaced citizens returned and word of the new medical service spread. Now, one of the nurses told me with an air of importance, people who weren't even sick flocked to be admitted.

The clinic, I was informed, was nearly self-sufficient; the relief organization had arrived intact (replete with supplies and skills), had selected a likely location, and begun operation. Hiring or training local personnel was therefore unnecessary. When I asked what would become of the local population when the organization—along with its tents, nurses, and supplies—left at the end of the year, one physician admitted to having thought about this question but offered no solution. Later I learned that local tensions along ethnic lines were increasing over who would fill the gap and control the area when the foreigners departed.

On the other side of the globe, twenty thousand U.S. troops were on a year-long peacekeeping mission in Bosnia and Herzegovina. News media in the United States inundated the public with stories of the enmity between the Bosnian Serbs, Croats, and Muslims, the fear that pervaded the region, and the trepidation among the soldiers that the Dayton Agreement would not hold. Still, by the end of 1996, one year and several months after the ceasefire began, five years from the beginning of the brutal ethnic conflict, and hundreds of years from the rise of animosity, the U.S. soldiers were scheduled to depart, under the expectation that peace would prevail.

These examples of the shortsightedness that accompanies foreign involvement in countries torn by civil strife are not unique. On many occasions, humanitarians around the world have observed as well-intended but misguided activities have exacerbated local hostilities. Over my years of work with nongovernmental organizations, United Nations agencies, the U.S. government, private foundations, and international organizations in various foreign disasters, I have watched these patterns of error become more vivid and the consequences more profound.

Perhaps in reluctant recognition of its inappropriate expectations, the United States has since twice extended its peace operations in Bosnia, admitting to an unrealistic timeframe. Nevertheless, field practitioners await what is unfolding there with the same apprehension felt for other strife-torn regions in the years following the Cold War. Grateful for the time bought with the continued presence of peacekeeping forces in Bosnia, we participate and watch as the international community repeatedly reveals its limited perspective in its reaction to other such complex emergencies.[1] While accomplishing some immediate goals, such shortsighted responses often contribute to increased tension and preparations for a return to violence. It seems time, therefore, for the international community to rethink its response to complex emergencies and to develop a more comprehensive and effective approach.

The Need to Revisit International Assistance

By virtue of their complexity, situations of internal conflict and massive suffering render any single international aid approach imperfect. However, the lack of conceptual depth common to such fast-response, short-term approaches (as illustrated in the examples of Bosnia and Rwanda) is avoidable. There are four areas in particular in which international actions often miss the mark.

Prevailing Environment

First, international reactions are rarely adequately tailored to existing conditions. One might gather from initial U.S. diplomatic and military actions in the former Yugoslavia, for example, that we are still thinking in terms that preceded even the Cold War era—that is, a time when the typical conflict occurred among nation-states, victory was clearcut, surrender terms were given, and each side complied with the ceasefire agreement. During that period, the victors ensured that the terms of the agreement were carried out. But contemporary strife does not lend itself to sustainable peace in this manner. Today's conflicts seem to grow from a much deeper root than political ideology or state will and are therefore able to sustain themselves over longer periods. Addressing the immediate outward manifestations of the problem simply ignores the internal motivation, which resurfaces over time. This has proved true in Rwanda, as the region witnesses the reemergence of interethnic brutality.

Narrow Focus

Second, the narrow focus of much of the international response on single actions, such as food distribution, refugee repatriation, or vaccination campaigns, often negates consideration of other interwoven issues. The intricacy of complex emergencies implies that multiple factors may have serious effects on the outcome of a disaster. Our task-oriented programs, however, often ignore the bigger picture, and thus not only may flounder but sometimes backfire, causing larger and even more critical problems. The mass exodus of Rwandans into Zaire in July 1994 offers a good example. In the rush to provide conventional aid, the international community neglected the fact that a large percentage of the refugees were members of the military and militia who had carried out the genocide. Later, these same people turned their rancor and violence on fellow refugees in powerful intimidation campaigns that successfully prevented hundreds of thousands from returning home for over two years (Kumar et al. 1996).

In addition, in our efforts to resolve some of these disputes, we tend to focus on immediate ends, ignoring the sustainability of peace. Through years of practice and research, conflict negotiation and mediation have evolved into sophisticated methodologies for reaching agreement. Much less is understood, however, about how to sustain the agreement, or what is required to continue a peace process. In the same vein, we have also focused the majority of our work in conflict management at the formal leadership level. Again, the Dayton Agreement for Bosnia offers an example. The agreement centered on the terms of the ceasefire and the ensuing distribution of authority among the leaders of the three factions. It thus ignored many of the more fundamental ingredients of the conflict and the Agreement's longer-term implications for the citizens of the region.

Limited Range

Third, the scope of the international community's involvement is generally limited to certain disciplines. Although recent years have seen greater incorporation of psychology, human rights law, conflict management, environmental issues, and even a bit of anthropology into the response equation, the range of activity is still limited. Some of the psychological recovery programs in Rwanda, for instance, had minimal anthropological or sociological information about the indigenous cultural mechanisms for coping with trauma. Humanitarian operations attempting to provide aid without stimulating further violence rarely draw on specialists in conflict management. As a result, a well-intentioned and even innovative policy that genuinely attempts to address root causes may still fall far short of what's needed.

Restricted Discussion

Fourth, a dearth of vertical—as well as horizontal—communication often leads to a breakdown in information-sharing and discourse on international assistance, both within and between organizations and interest groups. Field input into agency policy is rarely given the attention it deserves. At the same time, headquarters decision-makers seldom spend adequate time in the field and thus often lack an appreciation of the consequences of their decisions. As a result, programs and policies directed from the center may not be appropriate to existing conditions or, worse, they may even prove harmful.

Perhaps more importantly, the triadic relationship between donor organization policymakers, academics, and implementers has been unduly limited. Innovation at the practical and research levels too rarely converges to inform decision-makers about appropriate action. As a result, actions at the policy level can exacerbate already precarious conditions. Witness the media-centered U.S. Marines' siege of Mogadishu, which drew thousands of people into the capital in anticipation of the expected incoming food, or the continued massive and unquestioning assistance to Rwandan refugees in Zaire between 1994 and 1996 as leaders gathered arms and strength in admitted preparation for an invasion. These well-intentioned actions were not adequately based on an understanding of the local reality. Better communication with those working at the ground level might have made the situation clearer: the inevitability of massive population displacement and the urbanization that resulted from focusing international assistance on Mogadishu. It might have exposed the nefarious activities of certain Rwandan refugees and revealed how the international community was unwittingly contributing to a potential new round of conflict.

These four shortcomings, I believe, lead the international community as a whole toward sometimes inappropriate, overly dramatic, or superficial actions that constitute a dangerously limited approach to internal turmoil and complex emergencies. The fundamental issues that created the crisis in the first place are often overlooked, impeding progress toward a sustainable peace. In my estimation, much of the error and ineffectiveness comes from ignorance. Some scholars and practitioners may argue that the greatest lack is not knowledge but rather the political will to engage in foreign troubles. Indeed, politics interjects itself into even the most altruistic agenda, impedes reactions, and often distorts potentially helpful activities. Nevertheless, I believe that an inability to think through the larger consequences of our actions—or inaction—constitutes much of the basis for the failure of political will as well as for most of the errors committed when we *do* respond to foreign crises.

My experiences in the field and at headquarters lead me to conclude that our actions are not so much misdirected as lacking in scope. Effective efforts require a much broader vision, one that incorporates a wider time span, a range of disciplines, an understanding of the spectrum of factors bearing on the situation, and input from field practitioners, policymakers, senior organizational staff, and academicians. My hope in writing this book is to contribute one section to a bridge that will span the gap between those living in country and involved daily with refugees, combatants, victims of violence, deteriorating governments, resident citizens, and conditions of conflict and those informing and making decisions about how to respond to these crises.

Ultimately, what seems to be required is a new paradigm for foreign involvement in complex emergencies. The international community needs an operational strategy based on a long-term perspective that will direct its collective will toward the most appropriate action leading to a self-sustaining peace. Such a vision of holistic collaboration should guide our conduct, in the realistic knowledge that by striving for the ideal, we may reach a much-improved midpoint. This study attempts to speak to that need.

Organization of the Book

This text covers a wide territory. It not only engages several scholarly disciplines, such as international law, political science, and human rights, but also contains areas not generally explored in academic research, such as community reception of returning refugees. It combines fields that are not typically connected, such as psychology and community development. I do not presume expertise in each field; rather, I hope to show how each relates to effective international assistance.

Approach

The primary focus of this book is upon conditions at the grassroots level particularly during the return home of uprooted populations. Today's conflicts, more so than those of the past, directly involve all levels of society. It is the citizen who is the combatant, who is the subject of human rights abuse, and who receives food distributions. Returning populations ultimately settle in some community-like setting, bringing with them all the issues of contention. A close look at the conditions, situations, and attitudes of those involved in the violence and those receiving international assistance may lead to new conclusions about how best to support a sustainable peace. The community-level experience of conflict is an area seldom examined in academic or even policy circles. Thus, while much can be said about larger problems of society under these same conditions, I've left that to the work of other scholars. Similarly, much can (and has) been written on the problem of population migration. While touching on the motivation to flee and the experience of displacement, however, this study focuses primarily on the return phase. The experience of return, as opposed to the technical orchestration of repatriation, has received little scholarly attention. It is my assumption that this process can ultimately affect the sustainability of peaceful coexistence.

Many citizens of donor countries, and some in positions of significant authority, argue that foreign assistance ought not to be a priority among Western nations. Its effectiveness over the long run is dubious at best, they contend, and the focus should be on our own needy people. Others maintain that international aid—particularly when uninvited, massive, and inappropriate—disrupts local culture, causing greater havoc than the original conflict, and therefore should cease.

These valid arguments notwithstanding, it is inevitable that Western assistance will continue. As long as television shows images of starvation and suffering, the will to respond will persist in some form at some level. For this reason, I believe it is our duty as donors to learn to provide the most effective and least disruptive assistance. As an active participant in providing international aid, I furthermore view it as our responsibility to control and be accountable for our own actions, particularly when operating in foreign countries.

For these reasons, this book addresses my Western colleagues and focuses on our collective actions of international assistance. It attempts to appeal to participants at all three points of the triad—academicians, policymakers, and practitioners—as well as to general readers no matter what their level of knowledge about the subject. Scholars whose specialty is in international relations, refugee affairs, human rights, or conflict studies may be experts in specific sections of this volume, while policymakers may be highly familiar with several of the topics discussed here but unfamiliar with the overall perspective. Practitioners, as a group, are likely to understand the particular implications and applications of examples and suggestions in the text, but may not be acquainted with the larger theory. Therefore, aspects of this book may appear too simplistic to some, and novel to others.

This work is offered as a contribution to the ongoing discussion on effective response to complex emergencies and their ultimate resolution. The hope is to provide some broad-based perspectives and ideas that might stimulate further interaction. Rather than aiming to be definitive or magisterial, I seek to be suggestive and propositional. As a consultant in conflict situations, where I have operated between the theoretician and the implementer, devising, revising, and advocating action, I endeavor to base my judgments in reality, while appealing to broader knowledge. This study attempts to distill the reflective practitioner's internal dialogue between theory and practice. The concepts offered here will ultimately require field validation, experimentation, and peer-discussion.

Internal Organization

This book is divided into two parts. The first five chapters establish the issues involved, setting the stage for the last three chapters, which explore possible approaches. Chapter 1 introduces the post–Cold War global context and its distinct influence on contemporary conflict, complex emergencies, and subsequent international reaction. It offers a broad political, economic, and social foundation for considering the complex and unique factors bearing on these situations.

Chapter 2 examines the evolution of armed violence in the twentieth century, presenting a new construct for modern-day conflicts. It then explores conditions that could foster such outbreaks of violence and considers factors involved in bringing them to an end. Finally, it discusses complex emergencies as outgrowths of violence and the resulting repercussions on all aspects of society.

Chapter 3 looks at the conditions of conflict and complex emergencies that spawn displacement, as well as the social change that occurs among the uprooted, eventually affecting other aspects of society. This chapter first examines the phenomenon of displacement, including different types, the motivation and stages of migration, and life in asylum. Then it explores the repercussions of displacement on the region, the home country, the community and the individual, and the particular impact of internally displaced persons on society as a whole.

The focus of chapter 4 is the return of refugees and internally displaced persons to their strife-ravaged communities. The discussion covers the options displaced populations face, the decision-making process, and the influences on the family and the individual in the decision to return. Lastly, it explores the problems facing both the community and the returnees upon their reunification.

Chapter 5 delves into the other side of armed violence, that of the largely unexplored experience of the community and the conflict's effect on everyday life. It explores the implications of the experience for the common citizen and the challenges facing the community as a whole. Thus, the first half of the book depicts the setting for international humanitarian involvement: communities devastated by civil conflict and wracked by the results of a complex emergency, which receive returnees under extremely contentious and fragile circumstances.

The second half of the book turns toward approaches for managing these situations. Chapter 6 addresses the conceptual process of healing, investigating the necessary elements of rehabilitating intergroup relationships. It offers a comprehensive theoretical approach to community-level reintegration and rebuilding cohesion.

Next, chapter 7 examines the role of the international community in this rehabilitation process, touching on the negative impacts of outside assistance on communities recovering from complex emergencies. It then provides an operational framework in which international agencies can promote community healing. The final section describes selected activities along the spectrum of international assistance.

Chapter 8 sets the approaches outlined thus far into an agenda for future action. It brings the discussion back full circle to the global perspective, summarizing the findings and reviewing possible means for improving the response of the international community to future emergencies.

Tribute to Fred Cuny

Frederick C. Cuny was an exceptional person. For nearly thirty years, his extensive experience in disasters throughout the world made him arguably the foremost expert in humanitarian operations. At the same time, his tenacious mind continued to produce books, papers, and concepts that illuminated aspects of the field and answered larger questions of policy with startling academic acumen. He was one of the earlier writers on the impact of disasters and humanitarian intervention in *Disasters and Development* (1983). Though a staunch critic of virtually all bureaucratic establishments, he provided advice to the highest levels of the U.S. government, offered innovative strategies to United Nations agencies, and was a key figure in formulating U.S. military policy on humanitarian operations.

Fred's contribution to humanitarian operations covered subjects including military involvement, practical disaster planning, political strategies for dealing with opposition leaders, helping civilians caught in conflict, repatriation of refugees, and operating in war zones. Among many accomplishments, beginning with working on the airlift to Biafra in 1969, Fred led the U.S. humanitarian response to Iraq, designed a comprehensive plan for Somalia, and saved the lives of thousands of Bosnians in his three-year-long effort to establish and maintain gas, electricity, and water for Sarajevo. His last effort was an attempt to arrange a ceasefire in Chechnya, where he was abducted and presumably killed in April 1995.

I met Fred in Russia where we collaborated on a three-month assessment of Central Asia and the Caucasus, examining the prospects for potential humanitarian disaster in the newly independent republics. We traveled throughout the region in a whirlwind of interviews, visits to small communes, stays and dinners with people in their homes, and late-night sessions with local authorities. Fred and I peered into the crevices of the life in this relatively remote region of the world, walked through the markets, talked with old women selling flowers, and sat in dachas drinking tea and discussing the implications of our findings.

Since that trip we remained fast friends. He provided insight and advice on my business, and I worked for him at his consulting firm, Intertect, and crewed for him while he flew sail planes. Fred was a consultant on my Ph.D. committee until his death. His work is an example of the potential for interaction between field practice and theory. His life was an example of a person dedicated to improving the methodology of helping others.

ACKNOWLEDGMENTS

Because a book like this bears the mark of many hands, there are numerous scholars, colleagues, friends, and family members I would like to thank for their direct and indirect contributions. I am particularly indebted to John Tallmadge who, from conception to publication, provided wise and gentle counsel and undeviating belief in my ideas and experience. I also profited from his scholarship and grace with the English language: whatever perspicuity exists in these pages is due, in part, to his careful regard for the written word. To Joseph Jordan, Helena Meyer-Knapp, and Renee Roberts I owe my deepest appreciation for their close scrutiny and invaluable critique during the development of this study.

The seed of this book was born in a series of discussions with Hal Saunders. It is his investment in me that inspired, encouraged, and helped me formulate the thoughts developed in these chapters. Gil Loescher provided astute guidance throughout the study, and expert professional knowledge that greatly improved the book. Both were key to developing my relationship with Columbia University Press and to both I give my profound thanks.

I cannot express enough gratitude to George D'Angelo who shared the journey with me, who spent endless hours scrutinizing every word, sometimes repeatedly, and who deep into the night or at a moment's notice, listened to my ideas with unwavering regard. Krishna Kumar first engaged me in a critical discussion of complex emergencies, then invited me to explore their implications in Rwanda and publish with him. He continues to challenge the international community to think outside the box in our response to humanitarian crises. Special thanks to Rozana Olaya, who not only meticulously organized and formatted major sections of the manuscript, but fed me lunch when it was most required. My appreciation also goes to my editor at Columbia University Press, Kate Wittenberg, for her patience and outstanding guidance in seeing this to print. I wish also to thank the Union Institute for its intellectual support and recognition of my ideas.

I am deeply indebted to my parents Andrea and Bob, and my siblings Chris, Robin, and Lisa Maynard, whose foundation of love has sustained me throughout the years and maintained my heart's home while I was away. Lastly, I'd like to thank Al Charters for his continued understanding and patience during this attention- and time-consuming process. Indeed, your acceptance allows me to follow that roving ambition. It is to you that I owe the future.

Finally, to the Angolan, Bosnian, Georgian, Liberian, Somali, Kosovar, and Tajik who unwittingly bears the brunt of our mistakes, and perhaps unwillingly is the subject of our good intentions, I offer hope as we continue to learn and evolve in our international exploits.

ABBREVIATIONS

Now one other annoying thing about scholars is that they are always using Big Words that some of us can't understand.

—*The Tao of Pooh* (p. 28)

CDIE	Center for Development Information and Evaluation
CWA– ACIST	Church World Action–African Community Initiatives Support Teams
DFID	Department for International Development (UK)
DHA	Department of Humanitarian Affairs (UN)
DP	Displaced Person
DPKO	Department of Peacekeeping Operations (UN)
ECHO	European Community Humanitarian Office
GAD	Gender and Development
ICRC	International Committee of the Red Cross
ICVA	International Council of Voluntary Agencies
IDP	Internally Displaced Person
IFRC	International Federation of Red Cross and Red Crescent Societies
IOM	International Organization for Migration
IRC	International Rescue Committee
ISSVR	International Study of Spontaneous Voluntary Repatriation
LIC	Low-Intensity Conflict
MSF	Médecins Sans Frontières
NGO	Nongovernmental Organization
OAU	Organization of African Unity
OAS	Organization of American States
OCHA	Office for the Coordination of Humanitarian Affairs
ODA	Overseas Development Administration (UK)

OECD	Organization for Economic Cooperation and Development
OFDA	Office of U.S. Foreign Disaster Assistance
OTI	Office of Transition Initiatives
QIP	Quick Impact Project
SCF	Save the Children Federation
SIPRI	Stockholm International Peace Research Institute
SRSG	Special Representative to the Secretary General
UNDP	United Nations Development Program
UNDRO	United Nations Disaster Response Organization
UNESCO	United Nations Educational, Scientific, and Cultural Organization
UNHCR	United Nations High Commissioner for Refugees
UNHCHR	United Nations High Commissioner for Human Rights
UNICEF	United Nations Children's Fund
UNOSOM	United Nations Operation in Somalia
USAID	United States Agency for International Development
USCR	United States Committee for Refugees
USIP	United States Institute of Peace
WFP	World Food Program (UN)
WHO	World Health Organization (UN)
WID	Women in Development

HEALING COMMUNITIES IN CONFLICT

PART ONE

COMPLEX EMERGENCIES SINCE THE COLD WAR

CHAPTER ONE **THE INTERNATIONAL HUMANITARIAN CONTEXT**

The gist of the new internal conflicts is that the ethnic pieces put together by colonial glue and reinforced by the old world order are now pulling apart and reasserting their autonomy. Old identities, rendered dormant by the structures and values of the nation-state system, are reemerging and redefining the standards of political participation, distribution of goods and services, and government legitimacy.

—Francis M. Deng (1993:115)

In July 1994 the world watched as hundreds of thousands of Rwandans fled across the Zaire border in a human migration reminiscent of biblical times. On the other side of the globe, Serb, Croat, and Bosnian Muslims viciously battled for ethnic dominance in Bosnia and Herzegovina. Soon thereafter, in yet another corner of the world, Chechens and Russians launched endless, gruesome attacks against each other. Such conflicts, though not unique in history, reached unprecedented proportions that year, causing immense humanitarian catastrophe.

My experience in these kinds of crises has led me to reevaluate the explanations for and possible responses to such events. Around the world, study of international relationships has illuminated patterns in the seemingly chaotic and ever-changing global scenario. An exploration of these relationships provides insight into the more specific context of humanitarian crises. This first chapter examines conditions as we emerge from the Cold War era of the past fifty years and how the accompanying changes in the nature of violent conflict have contributed to the growth of complex emergencies. It then looks at the character and implications of these crises and the ensuing international response, including the rights and methods of foreign involvement.

The Post–Cold War World

The breakup of the Soviet bloc and the end of communist rule has conceivably been the most significant political change in twentieth-century history. Not long ago, in the early 1980s, the Cold War checkerboard globe was clearly divided between black and red, and superpowers moved, took positions, and plotted strategies in proxy wars of ideology. Governments, opposition parties, and insurgent groups all knew where their allegiance lay, who would supply them with armaments and training, and to whom they could turn should they need assistance if turmoil erupted in their region. But by the mid-1980s the crisp colors and clear lines were fading, and by the end of the decade the game was no longer being played the same way.

The period following the Cold War not only saw the emergence of twenty new states (Rotfeld 1997:4), but has brought dramatic shifts in international relationships. Though the world has not yet begun to understand the implications of an end to dual superpower dominance, two trends appear to have particular impact.

Growing Global Connectivity

First, global interaction seems to be increasingly based on linkages across borders among all elements of society, not simply through official channels. Whole sections of the world have opened up to foreign goods, tourism, business, cultural and professional exchanges, and civic institutions. The dramatic impact of the crash in Asia's financial systems on Western economies is a glaring example of our global connectivity. Communications technology and the growth of the information age further enhance globalization, as once-isolated societies gain access to greater international information through computers, satellite systems, and the media.

Though governments continue to engage in diplomacy, unofficial contacts are playing a greater part in influencing individual and national attitudes toward other countries. Foreign travel, for example, brings greater contact between peoples and cultures, joint ventures foster ongoing partnerships, professional organizations develop cross-national interests, and people-to-people exchanges offer close contact with other cultures. Most of us have been affected by the rise in independent television, as well as by international media such as CNN and the BBC, which brings events affecting the lives of people across the globe into the homes of ordinary citizens.

The arts, film, literature, and even fashion, now internationally intermingled, offer further insight into foreign cultures. Components of civil society—that is, those nonstate individuals and organizations that influence or have the potential to influence relations between government and citizens, such as human rights advocates, environmental or women's groups, charities, the media, business associations, academic institutions, religious affiliations, non-governmental organizations (NGOs), or professional associations—have similar international counterparts. On the insidious side, drug cartels, mafia rings, terrorist groups, and religious extremists also find easier access abroad and have greater representation all over the world.

Increasing Decentralization

Second, a trend toward decentralization appears to be weakening the role of governments and distributing a portion of the power among a broader base. One can observe this trend from the grand view of the global scale all the way down to the local community level. The breakup of the communist bloc, for example, involved the transfer of power from several large central command structures to many smaller republics. Russia once served as the economic nucleus for all of the Soviet Union, collecting and distributing goods to and from the other regions. Now, each republic has established import and export agreements, and goods no longer pass freely across their borders.

In the United States, as another example, the federal government has given the states more fiscal and regulatory control over domains such as public assistance and speed limits. The world has watched the old, colonial-style, centrally governed commonwealths of Somalia and Sierra Leone meet their demise as local leaders assumed decision-making roles in a continuous struggle for greater control. In China, economic decentralization has given the growing middle class greater control over its own resources. In the larger, worldwide arena the nearly four-fifths of the global population in the third world has grown concerned about foreign domination. As a result, the heretofore less advantaged countries are demanding greater access to resources and power through such avenues as the North-South dialogue and stronger regional coalitions. In effect, this is decentralization on the largest scale.

As a result of these trends, the world seems to be shifting its allegiance from powerful central governments toward smaller individual entities. Trend forecaster John Naisbitt contends that, increasingly, "the world is about the individual, not the state" or even the corporation (1994:45). In this new phase, Naisbitt claims, the strongest power is fast becoming the smallest entity—more mobile, flexible, and innovative, and no longer dependent upon a mammoth support system. Consequently, coordination and networking among the entities have assumed some of the functions of monolithic governments, which at one time more stringently controlled communication and oversaw interactions among elements of civil society.

The trend toward individualization and public participation in political affairs is also causing tremendous turmoil. Logically, the presence of more numerous, smaller entities multiplies the problems of communication and potentially increases contention for power. The conflict in the former Yugoslavia is a prominent illustration of newly established states fighting for power as they struggle to understand and establish their self-identity.

Although the breakup of the communist bloc has recast the international power structure, the emerging global dynamics have other causes as well. The world has witnessed, for instance, a growing debate over the redefinition of sovereignty, upsurges in religious extremism, the globalization of economics, the proliferation of weapons technology and accessibility, and environmental devastation. In addition, general changes in the world's population seem to influence many developments. Changing demographics, including huge population increases, are overwhelming the financial and administrative capacity of governments. Similarly, a redistribution of resources and power may encourage civilian populations to become politically, economically, and culturally empowered. Citizens appear less willing to grant categorical control to an omnipotent and distant leader as the era of absolute governmental authority wanes.

This small but significant transformation in the global power structure radically affects the way groups interact. Political scientist James Rosenau contends that "the more rapid the rate of social change, the greater the likelihood of intra-societal violence" (Dougherty and Pfaltzgraff 1981:344). Indeed, these tumultuous times have escalated the intensity and altered the character of violence (chapter 2 explores this transformation in more detail). Its important role in the context of global affairs, however, deserves brief scrutiny here as a foundation for later discussion.

The New Face of Contemporary Conflict and Its Implications

Much of today's armed violence is born of intense animosity among identity groups based on ethnicity, language, culture, race, religion, regional roots, or other fundamentally differentiating factors and hence can be labeled *identity conflict*. Extreme brutality, widespread citizen involvement, and societal implosion characterize such hostilities. Many of the transitional governments evolving out of communism have been overrun by social enmity among their highly diverse populations and subsequently embroiled in identity conflicts. Joseph Montville, a scholar in conflict studies at the Center for Strategic and International Studies, speaks for a number of his colleagues about the importance of identification with a larger group and the contribution of this identification to aggressive behavior (1995). The number of people affected is considerable, largely as a function of their indiscriminate nature. Although identity conflict has appeared in the past, its emergence in the 1990s as the prevalent form of violence has produced such notable trouble spots as Rwanda, Burundi, Somalia, Bosnia and Herzegovina, the Caucasus, Tajikistan, Chechnya, and Kosovo.

At the end of the Cold War, the world was shocked to discover the force of animosity among many of the world's five to eight thousand ethnic groups, sparking pockets of internal armed violence around the globe. Although the world has experienced a decrease in the total number of major armed conflicts since 1990, the vast majority, unlike the previous era, have been of an internal nature. According to the Stockholm International Peace Research Institute, in 1989, the last year of the Cold War, there were thirty-six major conflicts—that is, those resulting in more than one thousand deaths—and of these, five were international (Stolenberg and Wallensteen 1997:17). A few years later, in 1993, there were thirty-two major armed conflicts, and all of them were internal (Wallensteen and Axell 1993:7). Then, in 1995 the number declined to thirty conflicts, all of which, again, were within states (SIPRI 1996:15).[1] Although the total continued to decrease in 1996 to twenty-seven conflicts, one—that between India and Pakistan over Kashmir—was international (SIPRI 1997:17).

Another change in the nature of conflict is the proportion of civilian casualties. Now nine out of ten deaths from armed violence are noncombatant victims of massacres, personal vendettas, indiscriminate attacks, or collateral killings in cross-fires. In World War I this figure was between 5 and 14 percent (Independent Commission on International Humanitarian Issues 1986:25; Ahlström 1991:8).

The abundance of weapons left over from the superpower legacy and the vast machinery of international small arms exports no doubt contribute to the easy access to firepower and the ensuing deaths. I believe, however, that a significant reason for the number of people affected by today's identity conflicts lies in the grassroots nature of these conflicts, which defines virtually all humans and all areas as fair game. The players involved are both state and nonstate actors of all levels, types, and authority. The results include massive casualties and social disruption, which undermine even the basic means of survival, sending the country into a terminal tailspin. The outcome is a complex emergency.

Repercussions of Modern Conflict: The Complex Emergency

Complex emergencies are so termed because of the breadth of variables involved and their complicated pattern of interactions. With the emergence of identity conflicts at the turn of the decade, the world witnessed a significant rise in this kind of disaster. The period between 1978 and 1985 saw an average of five complex emergencies[2] per year; in 1995 there were twenty-three. At that point, however, the number began to decline, and in 1996 there were twenty complex emergencies (U.S. Mission 1995:1; U.S. Mission 1997:5). The hardest-hit area has been sub-Saharan Africa, followed by the regions bordering Russia (Rotfeld 1997:9). Most of these disasters are the result of identity conflicts. By virtue of their convoluted nature and extensive damage, complex emergencies also seem to have long recovery periods. The number of these emergencies and their duration has a significant impact on national, regional, and international resources.

A direct consequence of complex emergencies is the need for humanitarian relief. As both the intensity and number of emergencies began to decline in the mid-1990s (Sollenberg and Wallensteen 1997:19), so too did the number of "people at risk," that is, those who require emergency aid to avoid malnutrition and death. That figure worldwide declined 13 percent, from approximately 41.5 million in 1996 to around 36.2 million in early 1997, according to the United States Mission to the United Nations' 1997 compilation of statistics. Nevertheless, that figure is still three times the number of people in need of similar aid in the early 1980s (1997:5). In 1995 the sub-Saharan region of Africa alone had over 24 million citizens requiring humanitarian assistance (U.S. Mission 1995:4). While this number decreased in 1997 to between 16.9 and 17.9 million, the region still represents almost half those in need worldwide (U.S. Mission 1997:8).

Another fallout from complex emergencies is economic devastation. During the course of a crisis, national financial resources are usually depleted through expanded military expenditures, looting, corruption, and, in some cases, humanitarian assistance to citizens. Complex emergencies also undermine domestic economic production by destroying livelihoods, discouraging investment, disrupting trade and commerce, and hindering capital formation. Ultimately, this process ruins individual and national economic solvency and undermines the country's ability to sustain itself.

From the global perspective, a serious consequence of complex emergencies is the regional instability they generate. This is caused by large numbers of refugees[3] fleeing to neighboring countries to escape violence; an upsurge in regional arms trade to support the conflict; increased drug trafficking; the rise of antisocial networks as means of collecting revenue; and the export of violence to neighboring nations. It is important to note the particular destabilizing influence of refugees upon the region. Though similar in many ways to past migrations, population movements emanating from identity conflicts tend to generate greater resistance to those seeking asylum, to result in protracted stays in exile as well as increased violence and social disruption, and, therefore, to cause larger problems for regional and home country governments. Furthermore, the number of refugees has escalated substantially since the 1970s. Although their numbers have begun to decline most recently, there are still anywhere from 13 to 15 million refugees and between 10 and 24 million internally displaced persons (IDPs) and "others of concern"[4] in the world today (UNHCR 1996:11; USCR 1996:4–6). This compares to twenty years ago in the 1970s, when there were about 2.5 million refugees and IDPs were not even a consideration (UNHCR 1993b; U.S. Mission 1995:3).

The intense animosity inherent in identity conflicts accompanies refugees across borders and creates a more volatile asylum scene. Refugee camps have been used as home bases for pursuing personal vendettas through cross-border raids from the safety of an internationally sanctioned asylum. In addition, camps often constitute a haven for criminal activities that breed trouble and normalize antisocial behavior. Floods of refugees, moreover, often financially and politically destabilize countries of first asylum. Despite international aid to refugee camps, the large number of people using local resources and seeking employment inevitably disrupt the economies of host countries and communities (Chambers 1993). This disruption can increase tension between regional and local populations. By 1998, for example, Guinea Conakry's years of hosting Liberian and Sierra Leonine refugees has arguably taken its toll on the country's economic and political stability. International resources, moreover, are dwindling, and the likelihood is remote that the seemingly inexhaustible coffer will remain as generous. Thus, today's protracted refugee situations may become increasingly precarious.

Complex emergencies stemming from identity conflicts caught the world off guard. In a state-centered system designed for national defense, the kind of internal implosion caused by identity conflicts goes beyond past experience, even in humanitarian circles. Since the old allegiances are no longer valid, and new ones are still forming, it is difficult for us in the donor community to determine which groups deserve support. Moved to take action, we sometimes make decisions based on such insubstantial or incongruous grounds as old colonial ties, control of natural resources, or media appeal. The international response to complex emergencies has frequently been ad hoc, using short-term relief aid to address long-term political crises. Sadly, such largely inappropriate responses are draining the diminishing pot of global resources for international assistance. The lack of a comprehensive analysis and global plan of action creates a surge reaction to fight spot fires, rather than a concerted and coordinated approach to addressing the larger conflagration.

Humanitarian Intercession: A Comprehensive Concept

The international community still appears to be at odds over the definition and parameters of humanitarian response. The conventional term, *humanitarian intervention*, for example, despite its benevolent connotations, has been tainted by such cases as Japan's invasion of Manchuria in 1931 to protect Japanese settlers, Hitler's takeover of Czechoslovakia in 1938 to protect ethnic Germans from mistreatment, and the United States aid to the Contras during the 1980s to provide tents, communications equipment, and boots, all under the name of humanitarianism (Minear and Weiss 1993b:9, 24).

In UN matters and international law, humanitarian intervention usually has a narrow meaning, referring to foreign involvement in a country to improve poor humanitarian conditions, that is, suffering, malnourishment, homelessness, injuries, or sickness. Such involvement generally appears to be a reaction to the demise in human rights or physical circumstances. Kimberly Stanton of the MacArthur Foundation states that previously "in international law, humanitarian intervention has meant the use of force to end genocide or other massive atrocities. As the practice of intervention has evolved during the twentieth century, the phrase also has come to mean the provision of assistance to threatened populations, especially victims of war. Intervention in this sense is designed not to get at the root causes of a crisis but to relieve the worst of its effects" (Stanton 1993:14).

More specifically, international involvement is conventionally divided into forcible and nonforcible actions. (As is evident in Stanton's statement, further ambiguity rests in what characterizes each, and more importantly, which constitutes humanitarian intervention.) Although there is an abundance of recent analysis on the issue by international relations and legal specialists, there is little agreement on specifics. The word *intervention* itself implies invasive interference in the domestic affairs of a foreign state *against its will*. Many activities along the spectrum of humanitarian action, however, may be welcomed. For that reason, I believe that "intervention" is essentially an inaccurate usage when referring to the broad context. Furthermore, although the term *humanitarian intervention* entails activities along a broad spectrum, it has come to be viewed as specifically relating to the deployment of armed forces, such as in Iraq, Somalia, and Bosnia-Herzegovina.

The term *humanitarian intercession* might better denote the range of possible activities when foreign entities attempt to stop human rights abuses or correct conditions that contribute to human suffering.[5] I will use "humanitarian intercession" to signify all actions from outside that have the potential to halt the escalation of conflict in a growing complex emergency. This includes, but is not limited to, diplomacy, conflict resolution, human rights promotion, humanitarian assistance, deployment of armed forces, and not least, utilization of the media. I use "intervention" only to refer to specific invasive actions that run contrary to the will of the government, or within the context of specific international law that still uses this terminology. "Military intervention," in this context, means the invasive use of foreign armed forces for humanitarian purposes under Chapter VII of the UN Charter but against the will of the government involved.

International legal experts continue to debate whether humanitarian intercession necessarily involves forcible actions. Stanton (1993), for example, maintains that intercession is coercive, and that the coercive aspect is in fact central to the notion. Nancy Arnison (1993), law professor of international human rights, on the other hand, holds intercession could entail both forcible and nonforcible actions. According to Arnison, nonforcible actions include diplomacy, UN resolutions, or cross-border food delivery. They may further include bilateral or UN-sponsored high-level peace negotiations, special rapporteurs, observer missions, or conventional peacekeeping forces. Forcible action, on the other hand, may involve use of foreign military units, sanctions, medium- and lower-level conflict resolution teams, unbidden relief assistance, or human rights commissions (Arnison 1993; Stanton 1993).

These categories are themselves controversial. UN resolutions, for example, may be considered both forcible and nonforcible actions. Their collective origin implies a collaborative effort, although certain resolutions specifically outline coercive actions against the state in question. In addition, nonforcible mechanisms, such as observer missions, can recommend or instigate forcible action such as military or legal interference to prevent or suppress acts of genocide (Genocide Convention Article 8). In a stateless society, moreover, factions controlling a portion of the country may welcome and invite peacekeeping forces, while those in another section adamantly oppose such foreign involvement.

Although these ambiguities have been the object of much academic discourse in recent years, the obscurities have only deepened. A legalistic definition of humanitarian response appears far too confining, and, as Stanton notes, its application does not necessarily address either the root matters involved, related human rights issues, or even the full extent of humanitarian assistance. In fact, not only have the conditions outgrown the terminology, but humanitarianism itself has expanded beyond its conventional form. On the basis of these arguments and my own observations, I suggest that humanitarian intercession is no longer only the process of saving lives and reducing suffering. Indeed, in identity conflicts and complex emergencies, it may also be an integrated response to the entire range of factors causing physical and non-physical human pain.

My experience, furthermore, shows that affecting the physical condition of human beings does not necessarily ameliorate their situation nor does it eliminate the potential to inflict greater pain. Rather, such amelioration is something akin to the Band-Aid approach on a much larger wound. Some of the greatest suffering I have witnessed results from separation from one's family, the destruction of community solidarity, an inability to create an adequate livelihood, continual fear of abuse, deep resentment against former friends, physical torture, personal remorse and guilt, the death of one's spouse, or homelessness.

The operational persistence of the old model of relief has created a fundamental gap between conventional methods of humanitarian assistance and the realities of modern disasters. The crises are being played out in the complex interdependence of today's international relationships, described by Harold Saunders, director of International Affairs at the Kettering Foundation, as "whole bodies politic." "Whole bodies politic" refers to the notion that international environments are shaped by the continuous interaction of relationships on the full range of human experience and on many levels of society across permeable borders (Saunders 1990, 1993a). Therefore, not only do all sectors and echelons of society affect a crisis, but ameliorating the situation over the course of its development also requires the full range of influences. I suggest that to confine by definition the options, levels, or players involved is to limit the range of potential solutions. Rather, a *complex* emergency inherently requires an equally diverse and multilevel reaction. A larger conceptual framework seems necessary to address the full spectrum of humanitarian issues inherent in today's disasters.

Such a structure for humanitarian intercession should include an expanded time frame from pre- to postcrisis phases, should embrace the complete range of interconnecting problems, and should consider the entire array of mechanisms available to address the issues. This coincides with former UN Secretary-General Boutros Boutros-Ghali's *An Agenda for Peace* (1992a), in which he suggested a more comprehensive approach to international peace and security, outlining a continuum of steps from preventive diplomacy, to peacemaking, to peacekeeping, to peacebuilding.

Consider the following five-phase response to a developing complex emergency. The first step might include preventive and continual education and training as well as concerted intergroup dialogue, forums for discussion of contentious issues, and continued support of civil society. Second, early-warning mechanisms could be expanded to include international, interagency, intragovernmental information-sharing from all sources of whole bodies politic, including NGOs, government agencies, corporations, media, UN organizations, religious institutions, travel exchanges, scholars, observer missions, international associations, educational institutions, and businesses. Today's extensive communication networks could enhance this potential. Critical is a proactive and well-defined approach to data collection, followed by organization and dissemination of the information. (While early knowledge of a looming crisis can be improved, such knowledge does not necessarily inhibit the evolution of the emergency. More useful in this regard, perhaps, is the fact that better information-gathering mechanisms can contribute to the overall understanding of the emergency's context.)

A third phase in the conceptual framework would entail early reaction. For this phase, the tools in the proverbial toolbox may need to be augmented to include such options as targeted training, elicitive conflict mitigation, diplomatic intercession, human rights alerts, economic incentives, mediation, development of specific elements of civil society, peacekeeping missions, and constructive media campaigns. I believe, however, that international intercession should not be the only option available at this stage. A potentially viable response might very well be to do nothing. This option should be selected after careful scrutiny of the situation and comprehensive understanding of the potential repercussions have produced the conviction that to do nothing is the most beneficial choice for the populations involved in the long run.

The fourth phase employs a wide spectrum of resources in the response to an existing complex emergency. These could include human rights monitoring, humanitarian assistance, sanctions, regional political and humanitarian support, refugee aid, diplomatic pressure, conflict mediation, arms embargoes, foreign military intervention, zones of tranquillity, and other measures to alleviate the hardship and halt the violence. The fifth and final phase addresses the postcrisis situation, employing such tactics as encouraging refugees and IDPs to return, reintegration of displaced populations, (re)building civil society, war crimes tribunals, sustained dialogue, peace education, building plurality in government, conciliatory media programs, infrastructure reconstruction, collaborative community development, psychological assistance, economic development, truth commissions, and (re)constructing a civilian police force and fair legal system.

Many of these activities in all five phases occur independently. However, contributing to a sustainable peace, not merely alleviating the pain of violence, requires a broader conceptual framework, which must be reflected in the operational strategy. In the past, international responses have rested chiefly in the fourth phase. In this larger conceptual framework, phases one through three and five form an expanded focus. The broader picture allows international players to see the signs of developing complex emergencies and the broader operational framework allows us to respond more effectively at each stage.

Such a view creates a link between social health and sustainable stability, placing an emphasis on healing the damaged relationships between individuals and groups. This latter phase, then, requires long-term and comprehensive strategies for economic development, rebuilding violence-torn communities, strengthening community cohesion, and developing civil society, all of which are interrelated. (Chapter 7 explores some of these prospects in more detail.) In sum, of top importance in humanitarian intercession (no matter its avowed benevolent intentions) is the appropriateness of the aid and legitimacy of the action inside the sovereign host nation.

The Right of International Humanitarian Intercession

Until recently, the "sovereignty" of a nation, a term originating in the sixteenth century, was considered to be virtually absolute. Over the centuries the international system has vehemently upheld the right of a government to control the activities and resources within its borders (Roberts 1993). Strict sovereignty, however, appears to be gradually succumbing to the infiltration of high technology and the pressure of massive populations. Under present conditions of expansive transportation, international communication, and global economics, state boundaries no longer seem sacrosanct, and government dominion no longer absolute. It is against this backdrop that humanitarian intercession is apparently becoming more plausible and ultimately more acceptable.

Nevertheless, as a pillar of international law, state sovereignty still poses a formidable obstacle to humanitarian intercession, particularly when the latter involves military units. The United Nations Charter, for one, explicitly prohibits intervention in a country's internal affairs except when there is a threat to international peace and security. The "threat to peace" provision under UN Charter Article 2 (VII) reads:

> Nothing contained in the present Charter shall authorize the United Nations to intervene in matters which are essentially within the domestic jurisdiction of any state or shall require the Members to submit such matters to settlement under the present Charter; but this principle shall not prejudice the application of enforcement measures under Chapter VII.

In fact, nearly every international instrument developed over the past century—a period in which the number of states subject to international law has tripled (Rotfeld 1997:4)—is rooted in the notion of strict domestic jurisdiction. The majority of international laws were founded during the bipolar period when conflicts were primarily between states. In today's struggles, however, the source of violence more often lies within a single country, diminishing the relevance of many previous legal precepts. Consequently, the application of international law to current conditions is under intense scrutiny in diplomatic circles, particularly vis-à-vis humanitarian intercession.

As a result, in the post–Cold War era, the notion of inviolability appears to be gradually waning in favor of international efforts to intercede in deteriorating human rights and humanitarian conditions (Arnison 1993). As complex interdependence displaces state-centric politics, one can observe the multivariate aspects of whole bodies politic, including the various levels, categories, and modes of interaction beginning to emerge in the form of humanitarian actions.

Since 1991, the United Nations has selectively intervened in multiple cases of mass suffering, regardless of the home government's approval or lack thereof. These actions launched a new phase of debate over sovereignty and the right of collective intercession, provoked by each new UN resolution. The first move was made on April 5, 1991, when the Security Council passed Resolution 688, prevailing over Iraq's affirmation of sovereignty and demanding that it allow humanitarian access to its population. The proclamation specifies that, "as a contribution to removing the threat to international peace and security in the region, [Iraq must] immediately end this repression." The proclamation thus draws a link between human rights violations and ensuing massive displacement, and threats to international peace. This established a precedent for future interventions under Chapter VII's "threat to peace" provision of the UN Charter.

Later that year, on December 17, 1991, the General Assembly further eroded the dominion of sovereignty in humanitarian crises with the passage of a resolution that strengthens the ability of the UN to respond to humanitarian emergencies when a government denies access (Arnison 1993:39). According to Arnison, this action changed the prerequisite for humanitarian intercession from a *request* by the affected country to "*the consent* of the affected country," falling just short of recognizing a collective right to intercede for humanitarian purposes (1993:39).

It was not until 1992 that foreign military force was formally linked to humanitarian intercession, and then only by inference. The Security Council passed Resolution 770, which called on states to facilitate the relief effort in Bosnia-Herzegovina by "all necessary measures," a phrase taken to include military force (Arnison 1993:39). The right of military intervention was further expanded with the UN operation in Somalia at the end of 1992. In this case, which included six UN resolutions, the use of foreign military forces rested on the (albeit contentious) international legal premise that an interna-

tional military presence in a collapsed state could help restore order, thus jus-
tifying the intervention on the "threat to peace" basis (Roberts 1993:440).
Security Council Resolution 794 authorizing Operation Restore Hope this
time explicitly sanctioned massive military intervention without government
invitation.

The UN justified these military interventions on the grounds that internal
conflict constitutes a threat to the peace for two fundamental reasons. First, the
destabilizing influence of large refugee flows and potential subsequent cross-
border raids and arms trade arguably compromises security in the region.
Second, massive human rights abuses can jeopardize political stability.
Whereas previously, individuals were considered objects of state action, more
recently the internationalization of human rights recognizes the extensive
rights of the individual under international law, including some procedural
capacity to act (Pease and Forsythe 1993). In this respect, the rights of the individual have gained over the rights of the state. In 1998 the strength of these
arguments drove the debate over international military intervention in Kosovo.

In addition, humanitarian relief efforts themselves have contributed to the
erosion of state sovereignty by prevailing over governments attempting to block
relief operations. Aid agencies all over the world have brokered humanitarian
ceasefires, established corridors of tranquillity, and implemented no-fire zones
for the safe passage of relief supplies to affected populations. Despite such successes, it is my experience that the safety of supplies and personnel is far from
guaranteed in many complex emergencies, and this fact continues to play a
major part in the sovereignty debate.

As Arnison explains, however, the controversy over intercession in the
diplomatic arena goes further than the debate over sovereignty in several
respects. First, some, mostly Southern countries, argue that the absence of
agreed-upon guidelines for intercession permits stronger nations to arbitrarily
meddle in the affairs of other states, particularly former colonies, under the pre-
text of humanitarianism. Second, since international intercessions have (thus
far) been conducted under the umbrella of the United Nations, sanctioned by
the Security Council, they strengthen the control and interest of those countries
with a seat on the Council (which also supply a good portion of the funding for
such ventures). Third, many developing countries with limited representation
in the UN do not want to rely on Security Council votes for intercession. Fourth,
in collective responses, foreign governments can hide under the cloak of the
UN as an excuse for not taking earlier action, clearly an issue for several years
in the case of Bosnia. Fifth, such action may mask an unwillingness of states to
grant asylum to victims. Sixth, humanitarian intercession may hold people
in place who need asylum from the threat of persecution. And finally, the

presence of foreign entities can either suppress *or* exacerbate persecution of individuals or targeted groups (Arnison 1993).

Clearly, the question over the appropriateness of intercession, whether collectively under the auspices of the UN, or independently in the name of an NGO, is far from decided. "Many argue justifiably, that refusing to act with imperfect means in an imperfect world is an inappropriate nicety representing an attempt to achieve moral purity at the expense of other's suffering," claims Mary Anderson of the Collaborative for Development Action and its Local Capacities for Peace Project (Anderson 1994:16). Some appeal for new international laws to override the sovereignty argument in favor of intercession in cases of massive human suffering. Others claim new interpretations of current international law could allow the "threat to international peace" justification to include widespread internal displacement, even if the threat is not yet apparent (Arnison 1993). Still others, such as Eftihia Voutira and Shaun Brown, in "A Cautionary Tale: A Review of Some Non-governmental Practices in Conflict Resolution" (1995), contend that the greatest public good should be the deciding factor and that outsiders have no right to determine what constitutes the collective good within a country.

Ultimately, however, advocates of strict sovereignty are in a losing battle as the complex interdependence of global interaction becomes less confinable and whole bodies politics weaves its way into virtually all aspects of society, including humanitarian intercession. I believe that the task remains to evolve a full range of tools within an integrated strategy with which to address complex emergencies at every stage of development. Only with a wide variety of options, including that of noninvolvement, can the complete spectrum of issues have the possibility of being appropriately considered and addressed.

Tools for Humanitarian Intercession

Those of us involved in contemporary complex emergencies face an enormous challenge: to assess, plan, and respond to a multitude of rapidly changing conditions. Moreover, the means at our disposal do not necessarily address the needs of today's situations. In response, as practitioners, researchers, and policymakers, we are attempting to keep pace with the new requirements by adapting conventional tools and developing new options. The bulk of the efforts, however, remain within the standard arenas of diplomacy, conflict resolution, human rights, humanitarian relief, and armed intervention; only modest attempts at innovation have sought to exercise other components of whole bodies politic.

Those working in the field admit that the range of options available may be further restricted or otherwise altered by mandates, finances, experience, available personnel, or the time frame of particular institutions. This includes the United Nations and its individual agencies, independent representatives and member states, national governments, inter- and nongovernmental organizations, "experts" (both academic and practitioners), and "transnational" organizations such as the Red Cross family.

The following is a brief review of some of the mechanisms to provide a basis for assessing the potential for humanitarian intercession to affect complex emergencies.

Diplomacy

The diplomatic arena offers individual or combined efforts aimed at resolving differences. The United Nations alone has a number of avenues of intercession using its "good offices." For example, Chapter VI of the UN Charter outlines diplomatic and nonforcible measures for the settlement of disputes. Under a Chapter VI deployment, the rules of engagement for peacekeeping forces restrict the use of force solely to self-defense. The Rwanda peacekeeping intercession, for instance, was initially under Chapter VI. In contrast, Chapter VII allows "whatever means necessary" when there is a threat to the peace. This implies overt use of force and offensive action to carry out humanitarian operations, such as was used in Somalia. In today's conflicts, however, the 1945 rulings often fail to address the complexity of contemporary conditions. Consequently, the Security Council in recent years has expanded the rules of engagement occasionally to include protection of humanitarian convoys or relief workers, under what is commonly called "Chapter VI and a half."

Boutros Boutros-Ghali's *An Agenda for Peace* (1992a) defined specific tactics for addressing global conflicts, beginning with the concept of preventive diplomacy. The Secretary-General can send fact-finding missions for the purpose of collecting information and may designate a Special Envoy as an emissary to the country. A stronger option is to establish a Special Representative to the Secretary-General (SRSG). Unlike the Special Envoy, the SRSG resides in country and becomes the primary official link between the country's authorities and the United Nations.

Either delegate can request contact with leaders and government authorities in an attempt to resolve the dispute and promote peace. They can further request diplomatic initiatives by regional organizations- and member states. Furthermore, if conditions warrant, the SRSG or the Special Envoy can recommend that the Secretary-General advocate to the Security Council severing diplomatic relations with the country involved (Chapter VII, Article 41). The SRSG has the benefit of long-term interaction and has access to a whole spectrum of individuals and organizations including peacekeeping forces, humanitarian assistance, resident ambassadors, and conflict resolution teams. SRSGs are common in areas of ongoing or increasing tension such as Burundi, Somalia, and Bosnia.

A second UN diplomatic intercession mechanism is through the Security Council. The Security Council, for example, can pass resolutions requiring regional organizations to assist in the termination of a member's domestic conflict, or recommend terms of settlement (Chapter VI, Article 33). More powerful resolutions under Chapter VII can impose sanctions (Article 41) or, as has been the case several times since 1991, it can impose foreign military forces. As a membership organization, the UN, however, generally works with the recognized government of the country. The UN has the access and mandate to persuade high-level authorities to desist from aggressive actions and take steps leading toward peace. For precisely the same reason, its conduct is limited, since it may not have regular contact with opposition leaders.

Bilateral diplomatic missions may also try to bring about a peaceful resolution to the fighting. Usually conducted by Western donor governments, these missions are made up of high-level negotiators, country specialists, and even psychologists, whose aim is to develop a mutually acceptable settlement on the most visibly contentious issues. Prominent examples are the various Middle East peace accords and the 1998 efforts by U.S. Ambassador Richard Holbrooke to broker an agreement in Kosovo.

Similarly, regional organizations may send diplomatic missions or representatives to mediate peace settlements. The Organization of African Unity (OAU), for example, has recently begun to develop its own conflict resolution capacity. Finally, individuals and independent organizations may attempt diplomatic measures to help settle contentious issues. Former President Carter and the Carter Center are notable examples of this type of diplomacy.

Not quite as visible perhaps are the efforts of academic institutions and private foundations that often intervene at the leadership level via conferences and meetings with representatives of the disputing sides. As noted, the diplomatic efforts of various entities may be combined to bring about a joint settlement. The SRSG potentially has contact with many sources of political and international pressure that may be brought to bear in tandem. Regional organizations may work closely with the UN or private negotiators, such as occurred in the first Bosnian peace mission, which was conducted jointly by the UN and the European Community.

Nevertheless, the level at which it takes place and the fact that its objective is to come to a settlement, not to resolve the root problems, limits diplomacy.

Conflicts based on long-held, broad-based animosities are not easily resolved by top-level, diplomatic negotiations, which generally ignore the source of the conflict and, often, public sentiment. Hizkias Assefa, director of the Nairobi Peace Initiative, explains that the level of mutual participation in search of a solution correlates directly with the effectiveness and sustainability of the agreement. The less depth sought in addressing the root cause of the conflict, the lower the effectiveness and the shorter the life span of the agreement (Assefa 1993).

Conflict Management

A second instrument in today's intercession toolbox, and one that overlaps with diplomatic efforts, is conflict management. Used here in the broad sense to include resolution, transformation, and mitigation, conflict management can be largely distinguished by the level at which it is directed—whether upper, middle, or grassroots.[6] (A range of activities is possible at each level and will be discussed in chapter 7.) High-level efforts include diplomatic attempts to reach a settlement. Additionally, NGOs or transnational organizations may be involved in larger peace negotiations, such as engagement by the World Council of Churches and the All Africa Conference of Churches in brokering the Addis Ababa Accords of 1972, which ended Sudan's seventeen-year civil war (Minear and Weiss 1993a:60).

Middle-level conflict management involves civic and religious leaders, professionals, intellectuals, mid-range officials, and intermediate-level leadership of opposition groups. Conflict management specialists, including NGOs, foundations, and professional groups, are usually the principal actors at this level. Activities include training in conflict resolution skills or short meetings between the contending sides. A few notable exceptions offer hands-on, long-term interaction aimed at abating fundamental animosities. The grassroots level essentially addresses public opinion and occasionally ordinary citizens. The few international players involved at this level generally focus on conflict management skills training and improving cross-identity exposure and information flow.

Human Rights

Advancing human rights principles is yet a third avenue through which the international community can intercede under the humanitarian cloak. The assemblage of international and UN conventions and resolutions have set the standards for the treatment of human beings. The Geneva Conventions specifically apply to wartime protection and are the mandate of the International

Committee of the Red Cross (ICRC). The ICRC conducts prison visits, provides humanitarian assistance, oversees prisoner exchanges, exercises a protection role for internally displaced persons, and generally attempts to ensure that international law is being followed by all sides (UNHCR 1993a). For their part, NGOs deploy fact-finding missions all over the world to ascertain the human rights status of countries. They publicize their findings worldwide, warn of serious violations, and confront perceived offenders with their allegations.

The UN itself has various human rights mechanisms with which to intervene in a state's conduct, including special rapporteurs, monitoring committees, working groups, the 1503 confidential procedure system, and human rights monitoring missions such as those conducted in Guatemala, El Salvador, Cambodia, and Haiti. In March 1994 the Secretary-General designated a United Nations High Commissioner for Human Rights (UNHCHR), which in turn deployed human rights field officers to Rwanda as a first mission of its kind. Though the deployment was initially fraught with problems, the establishment of UNHCHR and its first operational effort are indications of the new priorities of the post–Cold War era and the change in attitude toward intercession and human rights compliance.

Here again, the issue of sovereignty comes to play, as illustrated when the Democratic Republic of Congo successfully refused to allow a human rights team to investigate allegations of gross abuse in mid-1997. Human rights protection instruments function definitively better for refugees and commonly disintegrate upon repatriation. They are generally weaker for victims of noninternational—that is, internal—armed conflict and are basically nonexistent for individual targets of human rights abuse (Stafford 1993). However, as the color of state sovereignty grows more muted, individual human rights have gained some leverage over domestic jurisdiction. Concurrently, international organizations are increasingly perceived as having the responsibility to protect these rights.

Humanitarian Assistance

Humanitarian assistance offers a fourth tool in intercession. The institutional pillars of the relief system are UN agencies, NGOs, donor relief agencies, the ICRC, and the International Federation of the Red Cross and Red Crescent Societies. UN agencies such as the High Commissioner for Refugees (UNHCR), the World Food Program (WFP), and the new Office for the Coordination of Humanitarian Affairs (OCHA), again, generally work through host governments (the United Nations Children's Fund [UNICEF; formerly the United Nations International Children's Emergency Fund] is a possible exception). UNHCR assists conventional refugees, although it is increasingly also caring for several other types of forced migrants. In addition to physical assistance, UNHCR provides security protection for refugees, aids in voluntary repatriation, and negotiates safe passage for returnees. UNICEF typically assists in the areas of childhood immunizations, health facilities, sanitation, and supplementary feeding programs, among others, under its mandate of caring for children, while the WFP provides food aid and logistics. OCHA is a new organization, replacing the Department of Humanitarian Affairs (DHA) under the UN reform measures instigated by Secretary-General Kofi Annan. Its mandate is to coordinate among all entities working in an emergency, as well as to collect and disseminate information and provide general oversight in the development of response mechanisms.

Besides these standard UN relief agencies, other UN organizations are increasingly engaging in emergency operations. The United Nations Development Program (UNDP), for example, maintains a resident representative in most developing countries, who may be appointed Resident Coordinator responsible for the UN response in the early stages of a disaster, before a Humanitarian Coordinator is appointed. UNDP further interfaces with relief operations in the throes of a disaster through its own emergency response branch. Moreover, in recognizing the serious disruption in development that disasters cause, UNDP promotes crisis mitigation and prevention strategies through its development programs. Despite the prophylactic efforts, 40 percent of UNDP's budget currently is spent on emergencies.[7]

Nongovernmental organizations make up the largest number of players in a complex emergency, and their proportion is continuing to grow. They offer a range of expertise and a variety of policies and orientations. Each has its own mandate in terms of specific tasks, parameters, and methodologies. For example, some might work in the emergency phase only and are quick to respond, while others may arrive on the scene later and continue through the reconstruction period. Some NGOs require the close participation of government structures, while others operate virtually independent of any local authority. Religious denomination is the foundation and support of many NGOs. Several have their own funding sources, others rely on UN or donor country support, while still others refuse government financing altogether. NGOs often specialize in target populations such as refugees or children, particular world regions, or specific sectors such as water and sanitation, medical assistance, or food delivery.

NGOs often appear uninvited into a country during these emergencies. At times, there may be no legitimate government to authorize relief aid and specify types and providers of assistance. Other times, however, NGOs may circumvent or neglect interaction with authorities about needs, locations, and procedures, and simply arrive on the scene with good intentions. In my view, this constitutes a breach of professionalism and is one of the more serious issues the NGO community faces.

Nevertheless, the past decade has seen substantial progress in the field of humanitarian aid as a whole. The level of individual and organizational professionalism has risen significantly, leading to dramatic improvements in the conduct of relief operations. In addition, relief agencies are replacing or augmenting conventional methods of response with new techniques specific to complex emergencies, which present a host of concerns and considerations unknown in natural disasters. (Chapter 2 will delve more deeply into these issues.)

Military Forces

Military units may be used to intervene in humanitarian crises as another option in the toolbox. Traditionally, this has meant the use of UN peacekeeping forces under a Chapter VI mandate to monitor peace agreements. One of the longest-standing such forces has been the Palestinian mission. Recently, however, foreign militaries have intervened under much stronger rules of engagement to protect humanitarian principles. Former UN Secretary-General Boutros-Ghali remarked, "The 1990s have given peacekeeping another new task: the protection of the delivery of humanitarian supplies to civilians caught up in a continuing conflict" (1992b:91). These have all been joint international operations conducted under the auspices of the United Nations and Security Council resolutions. The recent peacekeeping engagements have had four major objectives: (1) to protect relief efforts and reverse deteriorating humanitarian conditions, as in the United Nations Operation in Somalia (UNOSOM), and the protection of Kurdish peoples in Iraq; (2) to provide logistical assistance through the use of military aircraft, communication, and transportation, as was the case in Rwanda after the ceasefire; (3) to enforce a ceasefire long enough for peace to take hold, as is currently the situation in Bosnia; and (4) to serve as a deterrent force in an effort to prevent the deterioration of stability, as is the case in Macedonia, the only one of its kind. In Zaire in late 1996 a slight variation for military use was proposed: to use highly technical equipment and personnel to locate and help the return escort of hundreds of thousands of Rwandan refugees who were hiding in extremely dense, inaccessible jungle.

The use of foreign militaries explicitly for humanitarian purposes in internal conflict is new to the post–Cold War era. It is extremely controversial on a number of fronts, not the least of which is the issue of sovereignty. In addition, within the deploying countries, the national foreign policy and appropriate use of domestic military come under criticism. Furthermore, many argue adamantly that the use of military units in support of humanitarian intercession and peace renewal is a contradiction in action (Dewey 1993). The use of armed force, they believe, simply reinforces the notion that coercion is necessary as a means to settle disputes.

The newness of identity conflicts strains the still-developing methodology of intercession. As discussed earlier, complex emergencies, by definition, require a multifaceted response, which in turn necessitates close coordination. Unfortunately, most of these mechanisms for humanitarian intercession operate with relative independence, each one developing in its own capacity amidst a rapidly changing global scenario. While the long-held recognition of coordination's vital role supports greater collaboration, the interplay among the various components is still notably limited. For example, recent strides made in human rights monitoring, new information about the impact of relief aid on the development process, and changes in humanitarian law have yet to be fully disseminated and incorporated into planning by the other sectors.

Beyond such inadequate sharing and cooperation, there are large gaps in our collective understanding of complex emergencies that have yet to be filled. Psychological, anthropological, military, political, environmental, and geographic input, for instance, are insufficient. Serious academic research in disciplines other than international relations and international law has only relatively recently focused on humanitarian intercession. Consequently, the bulk of available resources comes from organizational material and ad hoc publications, which are often lacking in comprehensive data or substantive analysis.

Media

The media have had a profound influence on intercession debates. Sophistication in technology now makes it possible for the press to reach remote places suffering from violence, to capture the images in engaging and poignant pictures, films and interviews, and to broadcast them around the globe in a matter of minutes. Radio is a standard means of communication even in the most remote regions, and television is increasingly common. Referred to as "the CNN factor," for the Cable News Network's role in publicizing the Gulf War, the press significantly raises the level of awareness of an otherwise removed and uninvolved audience. Though ostensibly a nonpolitical entity in most countries, it directly influences public opinion, frequently generating collective pressure for immediate response, particularly in donor states. As Arnison reflects, "Public outcry seems to be the only unifying theme bringing attention, albeit late, to these crises [i.e., Iraq, Somalia, Bosnia]" (1993:40).

As a result of the media's influence, John Naisbitt sees potential for a "new global code of conduct to protect rights, spread by reach of communication technology, ensuring community adherence to standards" (1994:25). The press up to this point has not achieved this potential. Despite their enormous capacity to spread information, the media have severe limitations vis-à-vis complex emergencies. First, reporters commonly lack understanding of the nature of complex emergencies and the specific context of the country in question. Combined with the sensationalist nature of journalism, this ignorance often leads to dangerous inaccuracies in the media's depiction of a crisis. The result can be a biased or erroneous public perception of the situation. Second, the depiction of suffering, usually of third world peoples, and the ensuing cry for foreign assistance, can be demeaning. Moreover, such images can increase the perception of Southern countries as incessantly in need and incapable of self-reliance. Third, public pressure takes time to build and does not always result in significant action, as seen in the first few years of conflict in the former Yugoslavia. Last, since the stories' sensationalism requires graphic images depicting human suffering, the media are typically not interested in the predisaster phase of deteriorating conditions. Early warning of an impending crisis, therefore, is out of the mainstream public's reach until the situation becomes serious enough to offer drama. This was clearly the case in Kosovo for most of the 1990s as the Albanian population struggled to address economic and social inequity through nonviolent resistance, but garnered little international attention. When, in early 1998, they resorted to violent means, they suddenly gained the eyes and ears of the international press and, subsequently, foreign diplomats. Despite their limitations, the media nonetheless offer a powerful motivating tool for provoking a range of responses to complex emergencies, as all who witnessed the events in Somalia, Rwanda, Bosnia, and Zaire through media channels can attest.

Preventing Complex Emergencies

The increased number of complex emergencies over the past decade and the limited resources with which to respond should lead us to look toward prevention. If successful interference in the development of a crisis precludes the need for further action, a proliferation of complex emergencies might be averted by the broad use of preventive measures. In the broad conceptual framework employing an expanded intercession time span, prevention occupies the first three phases of the framework—prevention, early warning, and early reaction. The discussion of intercession, therefore, logically must include anticipating or interrupting the progression of complex emergencies. A remarkable effort to address these issues came in 1994 when the Carnegie Corporation of New York established the Carnegie Commission on Preventing Deadly Conflict. Its task was to study the causes of violent conflict and to identify requirements and a process of implementation of a system necessary to prevent them. The final report of the commission, *Preventing Deadly Conflict*, was published in 1997 and suggests a multitude of ways in which the international community can avert the progression of armed violence. It includes such categories as economic measures, use of civil society, UN actions, security options, and judicial measures. This systematic review of such a colossal and important subject—perhaps only possible in the post–Cold War period—deserves special acknowledgment.

One of the areas the commission reviews and which has emerged in recent years as a new subject of academic and institutional focus is early warning. Barbara Harff (1993) of the University of Maryland, for instance, is researching models of the causes and dynamics of violent conflict, particularly centering on intense communal conflict and gross human rights violations. Various other studies and efforts are examining common phenomena, significant indicators, and the process of development in identity conflicts in order to ascertain advance signals. Another example is the UN's Humanitarian Early Warning System, which considers various factors in determining probability and potential for humanitarian crises.

Policymakers began to explore the options for prevention during the upsurge in complex emergencies. Boutros-Ghali developed the concept of "preventive diplomacy" in his *An Agenda for Peace* (1992a). The U.S. government contracted Creative Associates to develop a manual entitled *Preventing and Mitigating Violent Conflicts: A Revised Guide for Practitioners* (1997), which presents activities specifically designed to forestall complex emergencies in the Horn of Africa. The UN created a Framework for Coordination within which the operational UN agencies collaborate on early detection and action in regions of increasing concern. An evaluation of this model showed that while combining the expertise and resources of political, peacekeeping, and humanitarian agencies improved interdepartmental communication, it did not necessarily result in preventive actions. The process is currently being enhanced in an effort to find new ways to institutionalize preventive actions within the UN structure (D'Angelo 1997).

Other tools for prevention might include the use of conflict management sessions and training in areas of tension. In an effort to thwart the development of hostilities, conflict management specialists might present problem-solving workshops or skills development sessions to leaders of contentious parties. Theoretically, by addressing the root causes of the problem and developing skills with which to handle contention early on, the conflicting sides may be able to reduce the potential for a violent outbreak.

Human rights education campaigns similarly propose to introduce greater respect for international law and human dignity as a means to dissuade the public from violence. Proponents of such efforts maintain that a public understanding of fundamental human rights and the laws intended to uphold them provide a baseline for addressing human rights issues through legal means rather than through violence. They might offer training sessions to government officials and members of opposition groups, introduce basic human rights programs into the formal education system, and present programs for public consumption via the media. In a broader sense, development of all the aspects of civil society ultimately provides a voice to express discontent, and therefore an avenue for peaceful change.

International accompaniment is another tool that focuses on prevention of individual human rights abuse. Foreign persons physically accompany targeted or threatened individuals either in all of their daily activities or only on those occasions when their security is threatened. Successfully employed in Central America during the 1980s, accompaniment attempts to provide an element of safety as well as visibility to the situation. This is an area of growing international interest; a coalition of like-minded groups is developing a "peace teams" alternative to UN peacekeeping forces.

Lastly, development activities are thought to have a preventive component. The relief to development continuum, a much-discussed topic in recent years, implies a connection between emergency response and its long-term implications on the progress of the country. In reality, this seems to be more of a cycle. In a postcrisis situation, recovery and development efforts repairing physical, political, and social structures can be directed specifically toward deflecting hostility, encouraging joint decision-making, developing mutual appreciation and intergroup understanding, addressing issues of contention through nonviolent means, and encouraging the growth of civil society organizations. Thus, in the progression of the cycle, targeted development and civil society-building activities can contribute to the prevention of future crises.

Conceptually, therefore, prevention is the natural and ultimate solution. Careful monitoring, constant information exchange, and appropriate diplomatic, political, or other intercessions conducted continuously or at the first sign of trouble could arrest the development of a crisis. In reality, however, the international capacity has not yet arrived. Prevention philosophy presupposes accurate and early information, the political will to intercede, funding, and appropriate methods. None of these is sufficiently developed to a point where preventive action can reliably and effectively thwart complex emergencies. In fact, the interest in prevention mechanisms appears to have stalled somewhat, and less attention and resources are currently being allocated toward addressing the constraints. One could offer several explanations.

First, the information required to foretell and therefore avoid a crisis is inadequate. Although international organizations working in the field routinely collect copious data, it is often restricted to intraorganizational use. Moreover, prevention advocates have not yet agreed upon the content of the information necessary for disaster early warning. Therefore, even public field data lacks an established format as well as a method of distribution to potential forecasters. The concept of a centrally administered, standardized information collection and distribution system attracts substantial opposition on the legitimate grounds of expense, sovereignty issues, and the potential misuse of intelligence. Several Internet-based data-sharing systems such as the UN Relief Web and UNHCR Reflink, however, are helping to overcome some of these objections. Though not specifically early-warning tools, their usage could entail field-level information-sharing leading to early recognition of potential trouble spots.

Second, the international diplomatic community is unlikely to agree to pre-arranged standards for automatic intercession at an early stage of conflict development. Unpredictable factors such as the current national interest in the country in question, availability of funds, priority of individual conflicts relative to others, and media attention prevent general political will from being preestablished. Third, because the trend over the last decade has been toward applying international resources to emergencies rather than development or prevention, there is little funding available with which to research or conduct preventive action. Fundamentally, many observers argue that the global perspective falls far short of the ten- to fifty-year minimum for investment in preventive actions that can preclude the development of complex emergencies.

That said, many in the international community hope that prevention will provide the answer, as the multitude of complex emergencies continues to inundate the world with requests for assistance. To expand our time frame of intercession, we must deepen our understanding of the problems confronting us. Hence, the next chapter explores the nature of conflict itself as the roots of today's complex emergencies. In examining the underlying character of armed violence, perhaps we can come to a better understanding of the basis for today's conflicts.

CHAPTER TWO THE NATURE OF CONFLICTS AND COMPLEX EMERGENCIES

Since, in any war, the reasons that cause troops to fight constitute the most decisive factor of all, the time has now come to take our leave of strategy, looking into the human soul instead.

—Martin van Creveld (1991:161)

Violent conflict has always been at the center of human existence and a fundamental, if not pivotal, aspect of its evolution (van Creveld 1991). Human beings have been preoccupied with physical might and the threat of force throughout time, from clashes over mates, territory, or food to global positioning for nuclear war. Indeed, a brief review shows that written history is largely a history of warfare. Most states as we know them came into existence through violent struggle, conquest, or wars of independence (Keegan 1993).

A large part of military history literature concerns the various cultural and official roles that combat has played in diverse societies. Soldiers, armies, battle, and death in defense of one's loyalties have held distinct places of honor and have had different meanings, depending in part on the values of society and the ethics of the fighting force. The Chinese, for example, who may have had the first philosophy of war, exhorted moderation and the preservation of culture over the mandates of internal revolution or foreign conquest (Keegan 1993). Historians thus corroborate that violent conflict has played a vital part in the dynamics of human culture, politics, strategic development, and personal interaction.

At the same time, nonviolent conflict also plays a vital role in healthy societies (Fahey 1993). Discord generates new thought, breeds fresh ideas, and is the origin of innovation. Without elements of conflict, individuals, communities, and governments would have less impetus to progress toward positive social change. Nonviolent struggle has historically given voice to the disenfranchised to articulate their condition and work toward creative changes in domestic policies (Fahey 1993).

Equally apparent, however, is the fact that when conflict degenerates into the use of extreme physical force and provokes civil disorder, it begins to destroy the social fabric of society. Human rights abuse and violent disruption not only polarize elements of society, closing the door to creative problem-solving, but create massive humanitarian problems. If violent conflict is at the root of complex emergencies, then an examination of its essence is critical to addressing today's crises. Attempting to discern what causes individuals and groups resort to violence and to destroy their own habitat and entreat others to participate is a crucial aspect of responding to the ensuing humanitarian disaster. Only by understanding the foundation of, and factors affecting, contemporary conflict, can we adequately bring about its resolution. I suggested in chapter 1 that the conventional concept of war no longer applies in today's internal conflicts. Earlier in the century, rules governed the conduct of combat, but modern violence does not adhere to the same standards. It is therefore critical that we know it more intimately and attempt to explain its characteristics. In this chapter, I explore the foundation of modern armed violence in greater depth and show how it leads to complex emergencies. The first section describes the evolution of armed violence in the twentieth century and offers a new construct for the essential traits of today's conflicts. Next, I propose various conditions that foster such outbreaks of violence and consider factors involved in bringing them to an end. Finally, I analyze the complex emergency and its repercussions on all aspects of society.

Changes in the Nature of Combat

Over the course of modern history, the type of violent conflict and the methods by which it is carried out have undergone significant transformation. The twentieth century has been marked by three distinct evolutions in the character of major armed conflict. *Trinitarian war*—combat dictated by the state, conducted by its military, and waged on behalf of its people—presided over international military relations until midcentury, followed by *insurgent movements* until the end of the 1980s. At the end of the Cold War, these gave way to *identity conflicts*, which have dominated the rest of the century. Though by no means absolute, these phases seem to describe a historical trend in violence and its relation to the broader framework of social interaction and global affairs. Using these three general categories to explore conflict's evolution in recent history, we might better understand the factors that have contributed to contemporary violence, and thus gain insight into its effects on the world.

Trinitarian War

We began this century with the reign of the Clausewitzian universe, where "politics is the womb in which war develops." This model, presented by Carl von Clausewitz (1780–1831) in his celebrated book *On War*, bears the name "trinitarian war" from its foundation in the interrelationship between the three elements of government, army, and citizens. Clausewitz maintained that war is an extension of national interest as decided by the state and carried out by the military against opposing armies. By this definition, war is wholly rational and dispassionate, simply "an act of force to compel our enemy to do our will" (1976:75). The trinitarian model prevailed over the first half of the century, as exemplified by both World Wars. This form of combat was conducted by professional infantry on battlefields, for the most part, or in a more technologically removed mode by artillery and aerial units against enemy military targets. Military planning and field maneuvers were designed in strict consultation between political authorities and force commanders and carried out by combat soldiers (van Creveld 1991).

Despite Clausewitz's championing of the trilogy where armies, as a continuation of state will, fought on behalf of the people, the latter, as van Creveld suggests, was never an equal participant. Public input was unsought and unwanted, and citizens were all but excluded from the process entirely. To segregate the people from the mechanism of war, the state often isolated soldiers in special areas. It also kept arms away from the common citizen and maintained legal distinctions between war and domestic crimes for the same offense (van Creveld 1991:40).

Accordingly, during this phase of history, civilians as a rule did not take part in battle, though they were increasingly used as tactical targets for military gain and were consequently forced to flee their homes in search of safety. In World War I, for example, occupying forces on the Western front looted and burned cities and took civilian hostages, and strategic air raids terrorized civilian populations (Ahlström 1991). Still, civilian casualties were small in comparison to military casualties: noncombatants accounted for 14 percent of the deaths, while soldiers suffered 86 percent. In World War II these ratios reversed and civilians accounted for 67 percent and soldiers 33 percent (Beer 1981:37). Both wars caused massive human migrations.

It appears that two factors contributed directly to the demise of the trinitarian model of warfare. First, the advent of nuclear weapons in 1945 radically transformed the trinitarian notion that war is rational and seriously reduced its potential as a realistic extension of politics (Keegan 1993:391). Second, toward the middle of the century the colonial era gradually came to a close, forcing the issue of independence and focusing attention on internal power struggles. As a result, a new mode of violent conflict emerged, one that could be generically termed "insurgent movements." (Van Creveld [1991] labels this and all succeeding types of conflict "nontrinitarian war.") This was to be the first of two evolutions in combat after the demise of the trinitarian era.

Insurgent Movements

The second phase of conflict in this century consisted of independence movements, guerrilla warfare, political rebellions, socialist revolutions, national liberation struggles, counterinsurgency campaigns, and separatist and irredentist crusades. In contrast to trinitarian wars, these conflicts were generally fought within the confines of national borders, not against other countries. Nor did they appear to be the direct manifestation of state political policy or necessarily fully engage the government army. Examples include the Philippine Muslims' fight against the Catholic majority between 1946 and 1954, Algeria's struggle for independence from France, the Ibo separatist movement in Biafra in 1967, the Lebanese civil war in 1975–76, the Nicaraguan Sandinista revolution in the 1970s, and Guatemala's and El Salvador's guerrilla wars in the 1980s.

Insurgent movements were based on group conviction generated from mutual experience and massive appeal to a rational solution. Rooted in an ideology promising tangible outcomes, they required a certain amount of understanding of the rallying principles, strong convictions, and a will to subordinate personal agendas to the larger objective. They were characterized by grassroots inculcation, propaganda campaigns, crusades of ideological education, political agitation, social persuasion, and isolated acts of violence and intimidation. The semieducated and charismatic individuals who usually organized these movements attempted to erode the social status quo and win public support, demanding specific retributions.

Ironically, the part of Clausewitz's triad most isolated from trinitarian war, the people, was the most important in these conflicts. Insurrectionist movements depended heavily on the generation of massive public support among common citizens who were members of a particular group. Combatants were those with conviction, not necessarily those with professional fighting skills. However, because dedication to the cause often included covert military training, thousands of young recruits became semiskilled with conventional weapons. This resulted in a proliferation of arms-bearing youth and, as van Creveld notes, blurred the age-old distinction between soldier and civilian (1991:20).

Historically, each side of an insurgent movement was likely to receive military, financial, or technical support from a superpower. During the Cold War, the globe's division between the two camps often made it notoriously easy for faction and government leaders to seek and acquire copious quantities of money, training, and weapons. As a result, the period between 1950 and 1990 was characterized by a culture of violence permeating many parts of the third world, backed by world powers playing out their political agendas and aggravated by inordinate amounts of Soviet- or American-supplied conventional weapons.

Insurgent movements frequently seemed to gain gradual momentum and then maintain a level of constant but low-level activity over a long period of time. Thus the term *low-intensity conflict*, or LIC, emerged. According to van Creveld, of the approximately 160 armed conflicts between 1945 and 1991, three-quarters of them were of low intensity, never escalating to all-out civil war (1991:20). The lack of escalation may have been partly a function of inadequate human or technical resources to sustain an intense fight over a long period of time, or it may have been the result of a political strategy to erode the resolve of the opposition. Furthermore, each superpower supporting the opposing parties may have intentionally prevented the escalation in order to avoid domestic controversy and an expensive arms race. (After the United States' experience in Vietnam, for example, policymakers were notably sensitive to the public's uneasiness about third world involvement. In the following years, the U.S. government repeatedly dealt with harsh public criticism of its low-intensity involvement with insurgent movements, such as those in Angola, Afghanistan, Nicaragua, Ethiopia/Somalia, and El Salvador [Keegan 1993].)

The end of the insurgent period corresponded with the close of the bipolar era as the communist empire crumbled. International observers watched as the relatively sudden decrease in financial and military support for many third world countries left many ongoing struggles in the lurch, with neither material nor philosophical support. Some conflicts—those in Ethiopia, Cambodia, and Chad, for example—declined or halted rather quickly. Others, such as in Afghanistan and Sudan, continue relatively unabated, though the nature of the fighting and even some of the alliances and ideologies have changed.

Identity Conflicts

My experience in several post–Cold War battlefields around the globe reveals that a third pattern of violent conflict has emerged. This form involves not merely political dimensions but the full spectrum of societal interaction.

Rooted in individual identification with a group, these armed struggles can be called "identity conflicts." (The word *war*, it seems, entirely befits the trinitarian model, implying calculated interaction with another force of relatively equal strength. Insurrectionist *movements*, for their part, were generally just that: consolidated efforts to achieve a specific end. In contrast, genocide and massacres of unarmed civilians require a more emphatic term to describe the intensity of the engagement and the personal hostility that the combatants must possess. Thus the term *conflict* seems appropriate.) Recent examples include Sierra Leone, Somalia, Tajikistan, Rwanda, the former Yugoslavia, Liberia, Georgia, Algeria, and Chechnya, each of which began its present battle in the early 1990s.

It is important to note that identity conflict is not exclusively a post–Cold War affair, but it has set the trend for violence in the 1990s. At the same time, it shares attributes with insurgency movements. The latter's internal, grassroots nature and intimate involvement of the common citizen, for example, are also inherent in contemporary conflict. On closer scrutiny, however, identity conflict appears as a distinct form of armed violence by virtue of several unique characteristics. First, identity conflicts entail widespread citizen involvement. No longer confined to battlefields, isolated targets, or contested territory, the violence now flows visibly into houses, communities, schools, religious grounds, and communal property. No area is sacred and all land and structures are potential battlegrounds. Most combatants appear to be essentially untrained ordinary citizens of all ages and social status.

As in insurgent movements, combatants fight with low-technology weapons—in fact, usually arms left over from the Cold War era or, as in the case of Rwanda's conflict in 1994, crude agricultural tools (Carnegie 1997). Most fighters in insurgent movements, however, though recruited from the citizenry, generally had a modicum of training and indoctrination and belonged to an organized faction before partaking fully in the struggle. Their common discipline and orientation allowed for concerted tactical maneuvers. In identity conflicts, in contrast, the average level of training initially is significantly lower, as many combatants are simply normal civilians motivated by a common passion and personal survival. Their level of organization, however, is less, making them prone to disorder and unbridled action. In Tajikistan, for instance, whole communes were embroiled in the fighting, involving farmers, brigade leaders, and business owners. Other than membership in mostly very young political parties and the creation of a new national guard, there was minimal preorganized structure (Brown 1992). In protracted conflicts, both organization and training appear to improve over time.

Correspondingly, the victims are also common citizens. As many as 90 percent of all casualties in such conflicts are civilians. Since much of the fighting takes place in the community across identity lines, not against tactical targets, it involves business associates, neighbors, medical professionals, and educators, as well as relatives of mixed blood. This intimate nature of today's armed violence cuts through all relationships and structures of society. At the same time, identity conflicts produce massive numbers of refugees, equally representative of all aspects and tiers of society. Their movement exacerbates the intense disorder typical of identity conflict. International observers, including Gil Loescher, professor of international relations at the University of Notre Dame, contend that refugees affect local, regional, and international stability to an extent not known in the recent past (1993:12).

A second characteristic of identity conflict is extreme polarization of the population. From the previous era's discernible commitment to an intellectual agenda, the seat of violence appears to have migrated to a more internal and visceral arena. This arena is found in the most fundamental characterization of self, seemingly bypassing most ideological and even moral considerations, to the single most basic element of intrinsic uniqueness—whether it be language, culture, geographic affiliation, religion, ethnicity, nationality, tribal, or some other form of deep-rooted identification. At the risk of oversimplifying for the sake of illustration, one could classify the conflicts in the former Yugoslavia and Burundi as those primarily based on ethnic heritage, while Afghanistan's and Tajikistan's struggles exemplify geographic allegiance, and religion plays a fundamental role in the violence in Sudan and Nagorno-Karabakh. Most conflicts entail a mix of contentious issues, such as in Sri Lanka, where language, religion, class, and geography all serve as identity divisions.

It is this most basic point of personal distinction in the individual that generates the polarization of the population between those of differing characteristics (identities). Mark Duffield, professor at the University of Birmingham, uses the term "New Racism" to describe the breakdown between individuals of differing identities:

> What people feel about their culture and identity is paramount. According to contemporary racism, if people sense their way of life is threatened, it arouses deep-seated fear and hostility. . . . It does not matter whether these fears are real or imaginary: for them to be genuinely held is sufficient to threaten the national fabric. (Duffield 1996:175–76)

In and of themselves, these distinctions do not create conflict, as evident in the many years of relatively peaceful coexistence—including intermarrying—

between Serb, Croat, and Muslim Bosnians, between Russian and ethnic Chechens, between Tajik Kulyabi and Garmi, and between Armenians and Azeris. When the identity distinction is either threatened or used as a basis to threaten other identity groups, however, it becomes a rallying force, creating the will to fight.

Identity is first and foremost a function of the individual, not of the group, although it has critical social implications. Unlike the collective agreement and interdependence of the trinitarian and insurgent periods, as discussed in the works of such military historians as Clausewitz, Keegan, and van Creveld, the underlying foundation for modern conflict finds companionship and motivation in others with similar feelings, but remains a personal element. Its mutuality, however, becomes the shared pivot point in the execution of collective violence inspired by a sense of group self and its distinction with respect to others. Samuel Huntington, professor of the science of government at Harvard University, similarly suggests that the world is experiencing an identity crisis in which a shift is occurring away from a more united power structure and towards multipolarism and multi-"civilization." This neo-isolationism can lead to a "clash of civilizations." The new unifying element, he claims, is kinship-based ties between cultural kin (1993). This is portrayed in an inverted pyramid where the least important but most plentiful elements of society sit at the top, and the single, most fundamental, lies at the bottom. In a fictional society, for instance, class, local dialect, religious denomination, skin color, and place of residence may all have some bearing on individual identity, but in this case, tribal affiliation might be the foremost identifying factor.

The widespread identity conflict that erupted in Somalia in 1990 exemplified this distillation of complex consanguinity. Somali culture is structured on a genealogical-based clan system where clan loyalty is at the root of personal survival. According to Somali scholar Milas Seifulaziz:

> This [leads] to a clear hierarchy of loyalties and interests. In a society based on blood relationships, the extended family defends its interests where necessary, against other members of the sub-clan, while the elders of the sub-clan try to negotiate any disputes because of the need for the sub-clan to stand together against other sub-clans to defend its common interests and those of its component families. Sub-clans in turn, may fight among themselves, but present a common front against other clans to defend the clan interests. (Seifulaziz 1992:3)

When widespread interclan fighting escalated in Somalia in 1992, I watched as clan alliance often broke apart when subclans fought among themselves, ultimately disintegrating into the most fundamental unit of attachment, that of the extended family.

A third property of identity conflict is its roots in human emotion—often translated as repressed animosity. The targets in today's violent struggles do not appear to be selected with calculating strategy for a political end, as they were in insurgent movements and trinitarian wars. Nor is the fighting motivated *directly* by profound loyalty or an allegiance to the group itself; it is not the identification itself that seems to drive the killing. Rather, the victims appear to be the subject of social opposition and separatism, driven by individual acrimony. Liberia's civil strife, for example, built up over years of intensive animosity between tribes, erupted into fierce ethnic fighting in 1989 that resulted in tribal members consuming the body parts of their enemy (Shiner 1996).

Because the driving force of these conflicts is heightened mutual animosity—in short, feeling—rather than cognitive understanding and ideology, factions in identity conflicts do not always appear to have clear, coherent, or universal objectives. In fact, some of the chaotic nature of identity conflicts most likely stems from this lack of collective vision and organization. Combatants are civilians driven by their own personal sense of justice, making it difficult to harness their energy into a well-disciplined and organized fighting force.

This is not to say that strategy and leadership do not exist in identity conflict. On the contrary, it is often the leadership that instigates much of the fervor that propels the fighting. As the world saw in Rwanda, Burundi, and the former Yugoslavia, midlevel authorities made calculated public appeals to stir the repressed feelings of resentment into violent action. At the same time in Chechnya, Somalia, Sierra Leone, and Georgia, the leadership has played an apparent role in maintaining the sense of otherness for the purpose of continuing the battle. In fact it is often this new leadership structure, with its accompanying parallel economies, that often prolongs complex emergencies. This role of leadership, however, can be easily misconstrued as purely a play for political power. Indeed, the seductive allure of power plays an integral part of the appeal to fight and usually manifests itself in an overarching purpose. In today's armed violence, however, it does not seem to be the lure of power that most propels the fight, but the emotional drive rooted in identity alienation.

Because such fervor demands tremendous individual energy, high-intensity identity conflicts tend to be either short-lived or characterized by intermittent bouts, followed by recuperative lulls. This pattern is corroborated by the number of conflicts in this decade that have emerged and subsequently fallen off the list of major armed conflicts (SIPRI 1996). Similarly, the identity conflicts in Somalia, Rwanda, and Burundi are ripe for eruptions into new, intense rounds of violence. This obviously contrasts with the low-intensity conflict of many insurgent movements and the long-range strategy inherent in trinitarian wars.

A fourth unique trait of identity conflict is the resultant implosion of civilized life. Though all conflict can contain fierce fighting and inhuman brutality, today's bitter hostilities lay ruin to the most fundamental structures that make up community. As we have seen, both trinitarian war and insurgent movements united individuals around common, tangible goals. This left the foundation of the broader society relatively intact, even in defeat. In contrast, identity conflict appears to destroy the social framework, bursting it apart from the inside due to its ubiquitous nature and the extreme polarization of the population.

Given that identity conflicts are fought at the community level and among former associates of all kinds, every citizen is a potential victim and a potential combatant. Sacredness, then, becomes a casualty of violence along with respect and ritual. John Keegan observes how modern conflict has reverted to other "primitive" examples of combat, matching its ferocity and ruthlessness. "Primitives," as he notes, however, are able to limit the nature and effects of their actions through exemption of certain members of society from the fight, through timing, place, and season of attacks, and through ritual. The latter defines the nature of combat and requires that once the ritual has been performed, both sides have recourse to conciliation, arbitration, and peacemaking (Keegan 1993). In contrast, I've watched as the ever-present threat of violence erodes community cohesion to a point of virtual nonexistence and a culture of fear prevails, often scattering the membership around the region.

Furthermore, the intensity of the animosity across identity lines, and the ruthlessness with which it is often expressed, seem to separate the integrated aspects of mixed cultures. Because trinitarian wars were calculating and abstract, being driven by state decision-makers, they were largely dispassionate and strategic. Similarly, insurgent movements were grounded in a principle and specific objectives. Today's conflicts, in contrast, are rooted in the individual motivation to fight, a personal history, passion, and a primal internal force. This kind of fundamental animosity among neighbors and associates cannot help but sever relationships and destroy the fabric of society. The image of roving groups of machine-gun-toting youths in pickup trucks in the streets of Mogadishu suggests the unbound brutality that destroys any semblance of integration and amity. The accompanying picture of streets teeming with people carrying belongings and trying to escape their fellow citizens illustrates the unmistakable intensity of the fear.

A consequence of identity conflict, accordingly, is social collapse. The once-strong moral and social order that glued mixed societies together in a common culture seems to disintegrate. Without some semblance of social relationship, most societies cease to function effectively. As we have seen in Iraq, contemporary armed violence leaves scars that do not heal quickly. Moreover, solace and support from one's neighbor or community is not readily found under such pervasive alienation and disunion.

Ironically, despite this evolution in the nature of conflict over the century, much of the world has continued to operate under the trinitarian model. During the insurgent period, for example, the bipolar politics essentially assumed this paradigm by dividing the world geographically between allies and enemies. In spite of the model's inconsistency with the real world, the superpower agendas aimed to destroy their foe and defend their friends, whether communist or capitalist, in a trinitarian mode of self-protection (Keegan 1993). This outdated worldview, wherein "leaders of nation-states amass economic and military power to pursue objectively defined interests in zero-sum contests of material power against other nation-states" (Saunders 1996b:421), has guided most Western political and military policy-making into the post–Cold War period, as evidenced in our assumptions about the former Yugoslavia.

In trinitarian war, peace accords marked the end of hostilities, generally resulting from the triumph of one side, as in both World Wars. Upon defeat, the losers removed their forces and subjugated themselves to the victors in agreed-upon procedures. This was the final phase of the conflict, leaving only the oversight of the agreement, often by an occupying force, to complete the operation. The dispossessed, then, retreated to the confines of their own territory and nursed their wounds among themselves. Today's scene in the former Yugoslavia shows the persistence of this pattern of reasoning. The United States sent 20,000 military troops to Bosnia and Herzegovina to help enforce the Dayton peace accord. It did so under the supposition that, as in trinitarian war, the agreement requires oversight by military force until the transition to peace is complete. The United States similarly committed to a trinitarian time frame, initially sending its troops for no longer than a year. This suggests that policymakers expected a post–World War II model of steady, rapid recovery. Though time will tell, I suspect that a marched progression to a sustained peace in the former Yugoslavia is questionable.

Under the identity conflict model, where it is the passion of the people, not state will, that incites violence, this kind of state-dictated peace ultimately does little to preserve tranquillity. According to Duffield, "Issues of power are secondary in questions of family, custom and the psychological underpinnings of identity" (1996:178). More turbid lines of control and conquest have replaced the clear victory and adherence to traditional surrender protocol of the trinitarian era. These override notions of conventional ceasefires and call for new approaches to transition to peace. (This transformation from an environment of hostility to one of peaceful coexistence under contemporary conditions will be explored further in chapter 6.)

The trinitarian war model may endure partly because it supports self-defense against outside aggression, which remains the raison d'être for most national military forces. The suggestion is not that the threat of interstate war is obsolete in the post–Cold War era. In fact, the potential for international violence has become more complex with nuclear proliferation, chemical and biological warfare capacities, and the growth in state-associated terrorist groups. It is this ever-present, however small, risk to nationhood that legitimizes the maintenance of some configuration of a defensive military posture. Nevertheless, as we have seen, the reality of the contemporary international environment does not support the probability of significant interstate combat. As Harold Saunders explains, "Our increasing experience of the complex interdependence of today's world causes us to think beyond a system focused mainly on the nation-state" (1996b:421).

Another reason for the endurance of the trinitarian model is that the notion of responding principally and repeatedly to internal foreign conflicts has not been wholly accepted by the Western troops themselves. The sentiment and expectations of the armed forces, built up over nearly a century of preparation for outside aggression, are understandably resistant to change. Political and military policymakers, moreover, lack an equivalent, actuality-based model to fit the current global scenario, which itself retards any move away from the comfortable trinitarian paradigm. All this said, as the post–Cold War era evolves we may now be seeing the birth of a new doctrine. One sign is the U.S. military's significant professionalization in its new role as humanitarian protectors in complex emergencies. Another sign of changing times is the U.S. government's current reconsideration of its age-old doctrine stating it must be prepared to fight two wars simultaneously. Undoubtedly, unforeseen events will propel us to continue to adjust our philosophy as we roll into the twenty-first century.

In sum, I argue that the world has seen three shifts in the character of conflicts fought on its surface since the beginning of the century. Where conflict was once ideological and international, the predominant armed violence is now identity-based and intranational; once conducted on battlefields with trained soldiers, or remotely with high-technology weapon systems, conflict is now fought in communities by local citizens using basic weaponry in intimate combat. In this form of combat, community members regardless of age, sex, or status become immersed in the battle with neighbors, business partners, and long-term associates.

The type of conflict that has dominated the 1990s is born of divisions in society and thrives on their expansion. It is loosely analogous to the growth of a prolific, noxious weed. Increased segregation and worsening cross-identity relations are the soil that germinates misunderstanding and disconnection. The seeds of the animosity are sown when negative aspects of society are attributed to other identity groups. Yet it is the individual sentiment learned from experience and the personalization of the animosity that fertilizes the seeds and makes them grow. Personal differentiation is cultivated by its mutuality and nurtured by leadership encouragement and justification in tangible terms. The animosity then blooms into full-fledged violence, sending its seeds throughout the area to multiply and spread, thwarting benevolent growth in the process. Some of these seeds, then, carry to other parts of the country and outside its borders via human migration, further strewing malevolence around the region. The result, as scholar and conflict resolution expert Hizkias Assefa describes, is "community disruption, cultural alienation, disconnectedness, wide-spread misery and degradation, especially of the least fortunate" (1993:39).

Conditions That Foster Identity Conflict

It is difficult to conceive of conditions and factors that are so abhorrent as to breed the extreme brutality found in such identity conflicts as Rwanda. Despite an extensive search for the biological, psychological, or social rationale that induces aggressive behavior, no one has yet proven that collective violence is inherent or a given of human nature (van Creveld 1991). Nevertheless, it is vital that we continue to examine the factors that may bring about such action, particularly in light of the extreme nature of modern conflict.

Earlier theorists discussed the conditions for the outbreak of violence in terms of such variables as the risk-taking propensity of leaders, expected utility of war, capabilities, and alliances (Dougherty and Pfaltzgraff 1981; Knorr and Rosenau 1969; Voutira and Brown 1995). Though such variables are still relevant, today's relatively unrehearsed violence, based more on personal than political vendettas, involves less of this type of rational preparation. Identity conflict seems to stem more from a nonrational, nonlinear, emotionally driven impulse. Although planning and careful calculation no doubt are integral to identity conflicts, the grassroots force behind the violence is seemingly spontaneous. Personal motives and issues of power appear to combine to form a complicated internal struggle that even the combatants themselves cannot necessarily decipher. It would be a grave error, therefore, to mistake the conditions of past wars for those that prevail today.

Scholars have proposed many motives for war. Three of these appear applicable to identity conflict: denial of rights, economic disparity, and elite manipulation. (These can also be applied to, and may even derive from, the insurgent movement period.) Two more motives, historical vendettas and growth in social chaos, are more contemporary phenomena observable in identity conflict. Consideration of the circumstances of modern conflict, however, makes it clear that none of these explanations by itself is adequately comprehensive or sufficient, and that further research is essential to understanding the basis for today's violence and the means to address it.

Fundamental Denial of Rights

Rights are something that ostensibly apply to all individuals but, nevertheless, are more difficult to acquire for some than others. Political scientist Ted Robert Gurr maintains there are four dimensions of grievances that spark conflict: political autonomy, political rights, economic rights, and social and cultural rights (Gurr 1993). In an extension of his view, these grievances may take the form of politics of exclusion, restrictions on ethnic or religious expression, laws limiting cultural or linguistic practice, denial of political legitimacy, or possibly artificial geographic boundaries imposed during the imperialist era and maintained as a method of control.

Indeed, one could find evidence of denial of rights in many identity conflicts. Unfair treatment based on ethnicity, religion, culture, race, or other elements of personal identification often help cultivate the passions necessary to drive modern conflicts. However, where insurgent movements of the past may have been built around such claims to individual and group rights, in today's conflicts these claims seem to serve more to increase the sense of otherness and enhance animosity toward those outside the identity group. In contrast to Gurr's supposition, moreover, the denial of such rights may not be a necessary ingredient of identity conflict. While grievances of various types may be an underlying factor, they are not the determining motivation.

Economic Disparity

Many scholars contend that competition for resources increases as the division between rich and poor grows. Accordingly, in areas and periods of abject poverty, competition among the poor contributes to greater tension between groups and may develop into scapegoating and violence (Cuny 1991; Harff 1993).

Certainly, adverse economic conditions and contention over jobs, land, money, and assets can contribute to the development of identity conflicts. Here again, however, the cause and effect may be indirect. In the insurgent era, economic disparity characteristically aroused revolutionary fervor in the underclass, starting movements under the banner of greater economic opportunity (Gurr 1970). In contemporary armed violence, poor economic conditions merely serve to stoke the embers of enmity and retribution growing in individuals; they do not constitute a necessary foundation for identity conflicts. Even in 1985, Donald Horowitz, in his book *Ethnic Groups in Conflict*, suggested that the relationship between economic rivalry and ethnic conflict is not only difficult to establish but that some aspects of economic antagonism are actually impeded by ethnic pluralism. Though not entirely absent among the poor, economic friction is more a reality at the upper levels than the lower levels of a developing society (Horowitz 1985).

Elite Manipulation

One long-held theory suggests that the acts of mass violence actually stem from provocation on the part of the social elite (Harff 1993). In this view, the privileged few incite collective action against a perceived antagonist for their own purposes. Essential for success, presumably, is the ability of the leaders to convince the population that the movement will have broad popular benefit and is not simply a maneuver in their pursuit of personal power. During the insurgent period, when ideology was paramount to the struggle, creating the will to fight entailed the development of a strong just cause (Gurr 1970). Cuba in the 1950s is a prime example: a small guerrilla group, largely from the urban middle class and led by Fidel Castro, gradually gained greater and greater support from the peasantry and eventually took power and installed redistributive economic policies favoring the poor (Zolberg, Suhrke, and Aguayo 1989:185).

Public manipulation by powerful individuals also appears to be a significant factor in identity conflicts. In Bosnia and Rwanda, for instance, instigators used radio, newspaper, and other forms of public information to stir up long-held ethnic frustrations and hostilities. Over a period of time, the agitation grew into an obsession with taking up arms (Ransdell 1994). Under the identity conflict model, it appears that the extreme elements were led by those driven by a specific view of the country's relationships among ethnic groups.

Close observation reveals that in this respect, as in others, the process today differs from that of previous forms of conflict. The real motive behind the manipulation appears to stem from the contention itself, though sustained and encouraged by the leaders' personal concern with their own accumulation of power. Whereas in insurgent movements the drive for ascendancy may have been accompanied by a sincere belief in an ideology (Gurr 1970), in identity conflicts elites seem to use shared animosity to incite popular uprising. In both cases, the initial motivation may be overwhelmed by the lure of power. In insurgent movements, elites, driven by the vision of political change, agitated civilians to take action. In identity conflicts, leaders expressly attempt to control social interaction by dictating appropriate inter-identity behavior. In both forms of conflict, the allure of power—whether political or social—may become an end in itself.

The elites in identity conflicts do not necessarily come from the upper reaches of society or from national political circles. Instead, they are often middle-level citizens who have a personal agenda, charisma, and a strong will that support their leadership role. Laurent Kabila, leader of the 1997 armed takeover of Zaire, for example, despite some earlier insurgent activity, had been essentially a common citizen for thirty years prior to the October uprising in South Kivu. According to former special envoy Robert Oakley, Somali warlord Mohammed Farah Aidid was simply a shrewd clan leader with a knack for organization (McNeil 1996).

Moreover, the role of elites in insurgent movements was both to garner support for the struggle and to continue educating, supplying the intellectual foundation, championing the cause, and planning the political strategy. African liberation theologists Kwame Nkrumah, Patrice Lumumba, and Amilcar Cabral, for instance, offered both charismatic and intellectual leadership in Africa's liberation theology, creating and leading an educated following toward a political and ideological goal. Elites in identity conflicts, in contrast, seem to simply attempt to harness the enormous energy engendered by their provocation of identity fervor. Once the conflict reaches a certain scale, their efforts are devoted to steering the unbound hostilities as much as possible, trying to direct the course of events.

Long-held Historical Vendettas

I derive this explanation for armed violence directly from my experience with contemporary conflicts, where differences in identity that marked social, political, and even economic interaction for decades become the focus of intense animosity. Since the end of the Cold War, old disputes that have lain essentially dormant over the course of the last generation now appear to be awakening with a literal vengeance. As a result, societies that have lived in relative peaceful coexistence suddenly find that prejudices born even centuries earlier and carried forth in muted tones through the generations now have renewed vigor. Many identity conflicts today, such as in the former Yugoslavia, Liberia, Tajikistan, Rwanda, Burundi, Sudan, Ethiopia, Georgia, Nigeria, Azerbaijan, and Armenia, are rooted in earlier disputes.

Although this is clearly one of the conditions of contemporary armed violence, it is equally apparent that the presence of historical intergroup rivalry is not necessarily a predictor of conflict. Kyrgyzstan, for instance, though surrounded by other new states afflicted with contention and possessed of the same ingredients for ethnic turmoil, appears to be succeeding in maintaining a peacefully diverse society. It may be the presence of other ingredients that cause some identity-diverse cultures to succumb to armed conflict, while other equally varied societies live in accommodating fellowship.

Growth in General Social Chaos

A final theory of the motive for violence is perhaps the most conjectural as well as expansive. It is the notion that, on the whole, today's rapidly changing societal dynamics may simply be too great for—and consequently overwhelm— social systems of the past. The consequence can be social chaos.

In all but the most remote cultures, access to information through the media, computer links, advertising, personal interaction, and written communication has skyrocketed. The post–Cold War global dynamic has opened up economic markets and significantly decreased previous international restrictions on communication and cultural exchange. Urban residents in particular are exposed to a greater variety of material goods, fashions, music, ideologies, religions, politics, and technologies. They face more choices in lifestyle, dress, occupation, leisure activity, food, and living location than ever before. At the same time, the exponential increase in global population puts greater pressure on land, infrastructures, natural resources, cities, and social structures.

These changes can wear thin the social fabric that has traditionally provided strong guidance—sometimes to the point of severe restriction—from government authority, community unity, ideological allegiance, tribal and regional loyalty, and solid family ties. As a result, many young people from rural backgrounds are more likely to seek jobs in the city than to continue the family pastoral or agricultural way of life. They become torn between traditional cultural values and lifestyles, and an alien but seductive new way of life.

Throughout the world, the sheer pace of these changes and exposure to new information is dizzying. Without the direction of traditional structures, the changes create resistance, confusion, dislocation, and anxiety, and may lead to a sense of insecurity. At that point, it seems, individuals turn to their most basic attachment, that of their identity group. Far from a conscious decision, the mutual contraction into the familiar is simply a human reaction to the perceived threat of the unknown. As individuals gradually coalesce under the banner of their identity group, greater social divisions develop. This protectionism based on self-preservation can spawn scapegoating and inter-identity violence, as different identity groups cast accusations of blame for social problems at each other. Eventually, such mutual animosity can progress to unrest and violence.

The processes of national growth, according to political scientists Nazli Choucri and Robert North, are likely to lead to expansion, competition, rivalry, conflict, and violence (Dougherty and Pfaltzgraff 1981). Today, this is perhaps most evident in the transitional governments of former communist countries where the change is more abrupt and therefore disruptive. For these states, the transformation into free-market, democratic societies, many after nearly seventy-five years of communism, has been convoluted and unnerving. The experience of economic disruption and deteriorating conditions spurs disenchantment, while the exposure to new products, social and political structures, and models for interaction contributes to greater disillusionment. Under such conditions, newly consolidated identity groups have become more assertive and governments more repressive in an effort to quell the tension (Mills 1995). The resultant scapegoating coincides with increasing xenophobia, contributing to even greater identity divisions and proclivity to intergroup violence.

In Tajikistan, for instance, the rapid disintegration of the USSR brought a wealth of new life to the once-isolated communities. Seemingly overnight the population was introduced to different cultures that presented entirely new models for social interaction, exotic products, and unfamiliar political dynamics. In my own observation of this process, it appeared that the exposure to new ideas and lifestyles introduced questions of identity and ethnic roots, examination of religious beliefs, exploration of other philosophies, and the lure of material goods, creating pulls in different directions.

The conditions that foster identity conflict are by no means absolute or distinct. Clearly, more than one may be in place at the same time, such as when leaders use historical vendettas to stir up identity animosity. Moreover, a plethora of other forces may in fact influence the generation or reduction of enmity, as in imperative intergroup cooperation for mutual survival, geographic conditions such as topography and climate (which limit or promote access to certain areas), or the injection of regional support from sympathetic groups. Finally, this discussion is merely a preliminary survey of leading circumstances that may cultivate identity conflict; further scrutiny is clearly in order. By studying the conditions that lend themselves to armed violence, we may be better able to predict its development. Such an inquiry logically leads to a discussion of the eradication of conflict.

The Elimination and Preclusion of Conflict

The world's short experience with identity conflict offers little in the way of research on or illustrations of the termination or prevention of such violence. Some considerations, however, can be adopted from past forms of strife and others deduced from knowledge of the fundamental traits of identity conflict. I offer four factors that particularly seem to affect the continuation of armed violence: the capacity to tolerate diversity, eradication of the conditions for conflict, change in the circumstances of conflict, and the level of suffering and exhaustion.

Tolerance for Diversity

This explanation suggests that the prevention and ending of hostilities in identity conflict fundamentally emanates out of the personal will to tolerate otherness. It is the reduction in animus that sustains a prolonged peace. In this view, therefore, a lasting ceasefire, by definition, must be initiated by the antagonists themselves. This may develop through the visualization of a leader, back-channel negotiations, or a strategic collapse, says Helena Meyer-Knapp, author of *Cease Fire!* (forthcoming). Before such steps are taken, however, she contends that the negotiators must believe in the prospects for repatriation, prisoner release, and reparation. More fundamentally, because the motivation behind these conflicts lies within the individual, it follows that there must be sincere widespread desire on the parts of participants to coexist peacefully; the will to end hostilities cannot rest solely with the leadership.

Suspension of the violence, once achieved, is precarious. At once, the suffering and exhaustion that formed the incentive for ceasefire subside, and the lingering horrors of combat eventually give way to the demands of rehabilitation. At the same time, the means for renewed combat remain indefinitely in the form of massive weapons. (Even the huge disarmament campaign that the international forces conducted where I worked in Somalia seemed to do little to diminish the number of weapons in the area.) Moreover, the original enmity presumably lies just below the surface, requiring only minimal stimulation to reemerge into action. (Chapter 6 will explore the process of developing conditions of tolerance, including remorse, grievance, remuneration, equality, and justice.)

Eradication of Conditions for Conflict

One might presume that eradication of the roots of identity conflict would preclude its development. As we saw in the previous section, however, most conditions contribute to violent outbreak only so far as they generate mutual animosity toward others; it is the enmity itself that stirs the will to fight. Nevertheless, amelioration of economic disparity and furthering individual rights *may* contribute to the prevention or decline in hostilities simply by reducing the stimulation of hostile feelings. Similarly, limiting the influence of incendiary leaders would logically have a strong effect, especially over the development, but also over the continuation, of identity conflicts. Once inflamed, however, and particularly after sustained violence, hostile sentiments may not disappear readily, even in the absence of urging from leaders.

The presence of historical vendettas is undoubtedly not easily remedied. Still, even years of bad blood need not develop into outright aggression. One can observe that without stimulation, many long-held grievances continue to lie dormant or even subside. Restructuring constitutional rights or allowing greater minority participation can potentially also reduce individual animosity. Restoring educational opportunity for the Albanian population in Kosovo, for example, could well have reduced the tensions in the region long enough to avert the violent uprising that began in May 1998. However, once the age-old contention is reactivated with a new round of violence, the emotional fervor seems likely to linger, adding chapters to the historical dispute.

Even more remote is the hope of affecting the rate and form of social evolution. The complexities of the modern world are the result of innumerable influences, and far beyond the scope of prevention. However, society's tools for handling change, including social institutions, public support systems, informational guidance, and intergroup communication, may help reduce the level of confusion and promote intergroup tolerance. Precautionary measures might entail development of civil society components to address social change issues, increasing integration of identity groups throughout society, encouraging open dialogue on a wide variety of issues, or developing grievance forums for discussion of divisive problems. Simple amelioration of circumstances that foster identity violence, however, does not necessarily preclude or eliminate conflict.

Change in the Circumstances of Conflict

At times in the past, a significant change in the particulars of a conflict has contributed to the end of violence. For example, a clear military victory abruptly
ending the violence naturally affects the relationship between the opposing
groups. The clear-cut triumph in Rwanda, for instance, reversed the balance of
power and, at least temporarily, halted major aggression. Similarly, high-level
negotiated settlements have led to long-lasting ceasefires, whether they are
peace agreements addressing issues of borders, constitutional rights, or the
division of power, or simply a cessation in hostilities (Creative Associates 1997).
This looked to be the case in Mozambique in 1992, when peace accords suspended the major fighting (USCR 1995). Elections, too, can shift the focus from
armed violence to orderly political contention, as seen in the electoral victory of
Violeta Chamorro in Nicaragua and the subsequent end to the Contra rebellion.
Further, one side may simply grant concessions to the opposition, allowing
greater plurality or giving up increments of power. Should the state of affairs
change abruptly, displaced populations may begin to return, transforming the
social dynamics. (This will be discussed in greater detail in chapter 5.)

Such changes in the state of affairs, however, do not seem to adequately
address the dynamics of identity conflicts. While settlements over ideological or
political issues may have appealed directly to the source of contention in earlier
eras, it appears that they do little to appease the enmity that drives contemporary armed violence. Both military victory and political verbal agreement, I
believe, ignore the deep-seated roots of contention. As a result, the seeds of hostility remain and are likely to reemerge in the near future, as exemplified in the
resumption of violence in Rwanda, Angola, and Zaire/Congo in 1997 and
1998.

Suffering and Exhaustion

The primary ingredient leading to a ceasefire, according to Meyer-Knapp, is the
level of agony endured by the civilian population. Not only must the parties have
reached their endurance limit of war's torment, but they must be willing to break
the taboo of silence and let their anguish and weariness be known (Meyer-
Knapp, forthcoming). As in previous types of conflict, the level of suffering
appears to be an important determinant in identity conflicts as well. In the past,
however, suffering took the form of human and material loss, destitution, displacement, misery of daily life, and basic combat-weariness from exposure to
constant violence. Although these elements undoubtedly exist in today's conflicts as well, another and perhaps greater source of distress comes from sheer

emotional exhaustion. Identity conflict may come to an end when personal fatigue and indifference overcome the fervor that motivates the violence. This is not to say, however, that the enmity will not rise again after a short respite.

A Close Look at Complex Emergencies

Complex emergencies can be considered a negative outgrowth of whole bodies politic in that they involve nearly all aspects of society, including significant military, anthropological, sociological, geographic, civil, environmental, human rights, and economic elements. Fundamentally, however, they result from the convergence of political and humanitarian crises, and as such may be thought of as fallout from identity conflicts.

The complex emergency is an international problem receiving some of the highest intellectual, public, and political attention and consuming significant outlays of global resources. As is evident in the focus such emergencies receive at worldwide conferences, diplomatic meetings, international forums, and the media, their effect on international relationships, regional development, and individuals alike has made them an overwhelming priority on the international agenda. Although, technically, complex emergencies could and did exist during the previous conflict eras (e.g., the Sudan crisis, 1955–1972; Biafra, 1967–1970; Uganda, 1981–1985; and Ethiopia, 1984–1992), the surge in interest corresponds to the increase in identity conflict since the end of the Cold War. The rise in identity conflict, in turn, coincides with the plethora of complex emergencies in the early part of the decade.

These concerns are fed by global satellite imagery, which illustrates how the repercussions from complex emergencies reverberate throughout society, influencing all aspects of regional, national, and communal life and directly affecting future development. The resulting problems have recently become the focus of many academics, policymakers, and practitioners, who have contributed several volumes of new material on the subject. This embryonic literature is scattered throughout the disciplines of political science, psychology, sociology, international relations, environmental studies, conflict studies, and human rights.

Political Ramifications

The concern of some in the international community lies in the overall chaos that permeates the region in a complex emergency. An identity conflict evolves into a complex emergency when political upheaval and continual violence lead to famine, casualties, deprivation of access to resources, destruction of land and infrastructure, and mass migration. Carried far enough, as in Somalia, this process may cause the existing system of government to collapse, which eliminates any possibility of state-directed humanitarian protection or assistance. Mass migrations across international boundaries further disrupt any sense of control and create subsequent regional threats to national stability. Other political casualties can include due process of law, pluralism in government and decision-making, civilian police protection, civil liberties, parliamentary procedures, human rights preservation, and, ultimately, civil society itself (Creative Associates 1997; Kumar et al. 1996; Nordlander 1993; USCR 1995).

Economic and Food Security Concerns

Armed violence frequently destroys food production capacity, resources, and the national economic base, which is another focus of international attention. National markets, local trade, business, agriculture, and manufacturing all fall prey to disruption in commerce, ruined physical structures, diversion to fighting units, loss of human resources, and inundation of foreign goods. International exchange is often a first casualty, sometimes due to sanctions and often through disruption in production and foreign commerce. National revenues consequently plummet (Creative Associates 1997; de Waal 1993; Frohardt 1994).

Even if domestic capital remains largely intact, the government now diverts huge sums away from normal expenditures (including public assistance) in order to support the conflict. In countries dependent on imported goods, food supplies may be severely restricted. As a result of the economic decline, many people suffer critical loss of income, making access to available foodstuffs difficult. Experts in the humanitarian community, therefore, are concerned with the resulting decrease in agricultural production, limited transportation, and decline in imported goods, which can create famine-like conditions and induce hoarding. If humanitarian assistance is available, it often becomes the new economic base and even subsumes the old value structure, replacing once-cherished goods with relief supplies (Anderson 1996a, 1996b; Cuny 1991; Maynard 1994).

According to scholar Alex de Waal (1993), there are three reasons why conflict creates famine. First, fighting units consume large amounts of food and destroy the agricultural and production base. Armed fighters often requisition food to supply their own needs—both from civilian populations and from food aid shipments. In 1986, for instance, as much as 88 percent of the food aid intended for Somali refugees never reached its destination; much of it was redirected toward the army and local militias (de Waal 1993:33). The stereotypical looting and pillaging known of soldiers and combatants also plays a part in inducing famines. The damaged fields from indiscriminant movements of fighting units and the scourge of land mines contribute to the ruin of agriculture and livestock. In addition, the large number of young men volunteering or forced to fight depletes the population of agricultural hands, causing a decrease in production.

Second, as noted earlier, famine is often an instrument of battle. De Waal describes the tactics as sieges, in which armed units systematically prevent food from reaching civilians, and counterinsurgency campaigns in which they destroy the means of food production, manipulate trade, and control population movements, including forced relocation. Third, the ruling political and economic structure of the country, which feeds the militias, may systematically strip the assets of the population. Zaire's military during the Mobutu era, as an example, routinely plundered civilians in lieu of payment they never received from the ruling kleptocracy.

Humanitarian Consequences

The humanitarian concerns develop in complex emergencies when physical life is threatened. Though not universally defined as such, humanitarianism, in the strictest sense, addresses issues of human survival, such as malnourishment, homelessness, physical injury, or sickness. Conventional relief generally falls into the categories of shelter, water, food, medical care, and sanitation. While physical suffering has always been a component of disasters, the emergence of complex emergencies with identity conflicts has brought other humanitarian concerns to the agenda. These include nonphysical aspects, such as psychological care, social welfare, conflict management, and human rights, as well as indirect physical effects such as the degradation of the environment as a result of massive population movements, chemical contamination, and land mines. Such issues have direct bearing on the broader context of human welfare. These are relatively new additions to the humanitarian equation, and much less is known and written about their long-term effect or appropriate intercessions (Maynard 1997).

Literature addressing the physical aspects of complex emergencies, however, is abundant. It is well-recognized, for instance, that the burning of homes not only begets problems of shelter but spawns migration, creating refugee and IDP situations. Similarly, practitioners have witnessed how disruption in the water supply through deliberate or indirect sabotage imperils daily existence. When canals, pipes, pumps, and wells are destroyed or contaminated, secondary, often inferior or insufficient sources are used, inviting disease and death. In addition, famines may result from slaughtered livestock, destroyed crops, impaired irrigation, scarcity of farming tools, disruption in livestock migration routes, dearth of labor, negligible harvest, food hoarding, escalating food prices, migrant populations, lack of adequate transportation to distribute crops, or damaged road systems (Creative Associates 1997; Cuny 1991). Most of these factors were present in Sudan in 1998 at the onset of a new cycle of disastrous famine.

Health Implications

Violent conflict not only causes injuries requiring immediate treatment but can destroy health centers and hospitals, kill or force health workers to flee, disrupt vaccination campaigns, and ruin water and sanitation systems. Humanitarian workers know that disease spreads more rapidly in the close quarters of overcrowded homes housing displaced relatives, and in IDP and refugee camps. The massive cholera epidemic in the newly established refugee camps in Zaire in 1994 provided graphic evidence of this. Insufficient and imbalanced nutrition accompanied by inadequate water intake and quality, and inferior shelter from the weather lowers resistance to disease. The incidence of sexually transmitted disease, including HIV, also frequently rises, given the high probability of rape and unprotected sex (Jean 1995; Kumar et al. 1996).

Consequences on Vulnerable Populations

The humanitarian community is increasingly aware that certain sectors of the population are at greater risk than others. Combat is a man's domain, in the sense that men are still predominantly both the targets and the combatants. Consequently, the greatest percentage of casualties is male. In contrast, women and children make up 80 percent of all displaced populations (Loescher 1993). Children are patently more vulnerable in complex emergencies than are adults, but also have special concerns as family dependents. One of the repercussions of violent attack and mass migration is separation of family members, which results in numerous unaccompanied children whose parents have been killed, injured, taken prisoner, or somehow lost in the confusion (Kumar et al. 1996). Women, moreover, have their own needs as the objects of rape during battle, or as sudden heads of households upon the death of the male members of the family. In addition, the elderly are at risk when extended families disintegrate and they, like children sometimes, are incapable of caring for themselves (Deng 1993; Kumar et al. 1996; Sollis 1994; U.S. Mission 1995).

Psychosocial Repercussions

Beyond these physical matters, psychological trauma often affects a larger percentage of the population, as violence becomes more intimate. Children and
women are especially vulnerable, as both the object and witness of attack. "War
also impacts child development, distorting attitudes towards other members of
society as well as moral and ethical value," writes scholar Peter Sollis (1994:15).
Internecine violence, moreover, demolishes the normal patterns of daily life,
creating greater confusion, distrust, and apprehension about future prospects.
The more seriously traumatized are often unable to provide for themselves or
others and may become marginalized, requiring continual, long-term care
(Kumar et al. 1996; Maynard 1997).

The widespread upheaval that virtually destroys social cohesion also
damages the conventional support structures that may aid psychosocial
recovery. Intense violence can impair traditional welfare safety nets for dis-
advantaged or dependent individuals, suspend formal education, and
severely disrupt public health programs, as practitioners, academics, and policymakers alike now recognize. These institutions, along with the family
unit, comprise much of the psychological and social support in a typical society. In the pervasiveness of identity conflicts, however, both institutional and
familial sources of succor may be rendered incapable of providing adequate
assistance. At the same time, conflict remains an undercurrent in the society
and undermines recovery efforts. In such situations where the indigenous
ability to handle conflict has deteriorated, complex emergencies are notoriously prolonged (Creative Associates 1997; Kumar et al. 1996; Rupesinghe
1991).

Human Rights Issues

Human rights issues also come to the fore in identity conflicts as a result of
vengeance being played out on all sides, with no regard for law or morality.
Abuse may occur at the highest as well as the lowest levels of society, and may
be committed by individuals, factions, government, or military personnel.
Such abuses may be used as an intimidation tactic against an identity group or
as a method of eliminating specific individuals. Increasingly, it is also a tactic
used by displaced populations, themselves, to prevent return or intimidate the
resident authorities and civilians (Kumar et al. 1996; Mills 1995; Roberts
1993).

Human rights violations are most likely to occur closest to the area of combat, where disorder and animosity are the greatest. With the exception of safe

havens, zones of tranquillity and other safe areas, international protection against abuse is minimal for those inside the country, including IDPs, returnees, and common citizens, in contrast to refugees who remain outside the border and are under the guardianship of the UN High Commissioner for Refugees (Cuny 1991; Deng 1993; UNHCR 1993a). (The well-known case of the safe haven in Srebenica, Bosnia, wherein scores of people were abused and massacred is a tragic reversal of this concept of protection.)

Environmental Repercussions

Lastly, the impact of complex emergencies on the environment is yet another, though distant, consideration on the periphery of relief circles. Although visible to any observer, serious ecological repercussions from extreme violence are just beginning to receive formal recognition from the international community. Humanitarian practitioners have frequently witnessed the destruction or pollution of water sources, burned acreage, and contamination resulting from the demolition of warehouses, factories, and transportation equipment containing chemical products. In addition, displaced populations overuse water supplies, denude trees for shelter and firewood, trample fragile areas from overcrowding, poison the water table and vegetation due to the poor quality or absence of sanitation facilities, deplete edible plant varieties, and contribute to garbage pollution.

These various factors form part of a more refined understanding of the nature and consequence of complex emergencies, as evidenced in the growing literature on these subjects. The elevated awareness also corresponds to new approaches in the international response to complex emergencies. (These will be discussed in depth in chapter 7.)

Severity Factors and the Example of Rwanda

I propose that the severity of human suffering in a complex emergency is affected largely by four factors. The first is the length of incubation prior to the onset of a humanitarian crisis. Ostensibly, the longer the incubation time, the greater the decline in the economy, public health, physical infrastructure such as water, sanitation and heating systems, and the like. This may be partly attributable to a shift in fiscal expenditures from social programs to military buildup. The second factor is the number and extent of compounding ingredients such as drought, floods, political elections, or a dramatic drop in commodity exports. Some contributing factors may themselves produce a humanitarian emergency, while others can serve to complicate the root problems and draw attention away from efforts to solve them, thus increasing the risk of human suffering.

A third consideration is the degree of upheaval during the emergency, such as the scale of political disintegration or population displacement. Ultimately, severe disorder can hide serious human rights violations, complicate efforts to ameliorate the situation, and cause new humanitarian dilemmas such as children abandoned during successive population movements. Finally, the speed, appropriateness, and adequacy of the humanitarian response is a fourth determinant of the severity of human suffering. Immediate and suitable assistance can stem the humanitarian deterioration by providing food, water, sanitation, shelter, and medical and social care to those in need.

A brief examination of the complex emergency in Rwanda illustrates the impact of some of these factors. This synopsis and analysis is derived from my own experience as a member of OFDA's Disaster Assistance Response Team during the 1994 crisis and my research conducted under Study 4 of the Joint Evaluation of Emergency Assistance to Rwanda (Kumar et al. 1996). It also comes from many journal articles, newspaper reports, relief agency literature, books, interviews, and discussions that have emerged from the crisis.

Brief Overview

The genocide that devastated Rwanda between April and July 1994 erupted suddenly out of what appeared to be exemplary development conditions unfettered by major obstacles (save for a modest drought in the Southwest). Behind the scenes, however, for the preceding three years, leaders had been agitating the public, military and paramilitary contingents were developing combat methodology, a radio station had broadcast hate messages to incite interethnic violence, and tension between the two ethnic groups was clearly growing. This ethnic rivalry had surfaced thirty years earlier as a result of a power struggle that culminated in long-term refugees, perpetual animosity, and occasional severe fighting.

When violence did erupt on April 6, 1994, massacres spread throughout the capital city within hours and eventually overran the country. Whole communities moved around the countryside in mass migrations, the largest in human history. The extreme nature of the fighting and the speed with which it spread created tremendous chaos and disorientation. The fighting was marked by the use of machetes as the primary—though inefficient—weapon and the sheer number of people compelled to participate by those inciting the violence. The ultimate climax in the crisis came as an unprecedented million people streamed across the Zaire border, most within a 24-hour period.

The response of other nations was slow and inappropriate. Regional and international reaction was virtually nonexistent during the fighting, in which 800,000 people were massacred. Despite many diplomatic missions and development personnel in the country before the outbreak, few early-warning bells had sounded with any force. (The coming of a major uprising was apparent to some who were watching the developments from outside. To many living inside the country, however, the very fact of the massacres came as a surprise. In fact, Rwanda had recently been internationally displayed as a model of development and a success for peacemaking. Though hindsight has illuminated many warning signals, virtually no one claims to have predicted the extent and level of fighting that eventually took place.) The UN peacekeeping forces stationed in the country were drawn down from 2,500 to a meager 270 during the violence, leaving them virtually helpless. ICRC and the NGO Médecins Sans Frontières maintained a small crew throughout the siege. Not until France, under a UN resolution, attempted to contain some of the fighting in sections of the country did the international community react. In July, as hoards of people fled into Zaire, the victors (also the primary victims of the massacres) declared a ceasefire. At this point, international aid poured into the new refugee camps and gradually into Rwanda itself.

The assistance that emerged was largely conventional relief aid targeted primarily toward, in descending order, refugees, IDPs, returnees, and the resident population. Although the crisis clearly involved human rights violations, attention to these concerns was much delayed. Similarly, psychosocial assistance was an afterthought, despite the obvious destruction of the social fabric and resulting trauma. Furthermore, the dearth of attention paid to the resident citizens and non-mobile victims of the conflict left huge portions of the population languishing.

Analysis

In the case of Rwanda, the severity of the disaster was extreme, despite the lack of compounding factors. The more than three years of incubation had provided certain leaders time to inflame ethnic rivalry, create an emotional appeal for concerted action, garner professional and popular support, develop capacity, and plan combat tactics. When chaos did break out, the speed and nature of the fighting and the scale of participation in it exacerbated the mayhem. The overwhelming size of the human migration was the final component of unprecedented disorder. Finally, the lack of immediate international response simply compounded the problems. The delay of specific types of aid to address the conflict elements helped sustain the level of acrimony, reducing the potential for repatriation and reparation.

The Rwanda example, despite its exceptional barbarism and extreme repercussions, provides some insight into the evolution of identity conflict into a complex emergency. Clearly, the nature of complex emergencies affects all levels and aspects of society. One of the obvious consequences, illustrated in graphic form in the Rwanda case, is the number and nature of mass migrations. The following chapter looks at the conditions of conflict and complex emergencies that spawn displacement, and the social change that occurs among the uprooted, which eventually affects other aspects of society.

CHAPTER THREE FORCED MIGRATION: A CONSEQUENCE OF CONFLICT

The scale and complexity of today's humanitarian crises are a reflection of the instability of the period in which we live. The collapse of the old order has given rise to a more volatile world in which new refugee movements are likely to continue to occur. At the same time, the nature of the refugee problem has undergone fundamental changes which call urgently for new approaches.

—Sadako Ogata, UN High Commissioner for Refugees (UNHCR 1993b:iii)

F orced migration has been a common consequence of violence since the beginning of human history. When security is sufficiently threatened by war, military coups, insurrection, religious persecution, human rights abuses, political despotism, or "ethnic cleansing," people flee their homes in search of safety.[1] Although the major causes of flight have varied over time, one element of forced migration has remained the same: desperate and homeless people who are in danger of persecution, starvation, or disease.

Over the years, the impact of forced displacement on international relations and on the health of society has attracted interest from psychologists, sociologists, political scientists, economists, social policy analysts, and ecologists. In the past decade, scholars have begun to look more closely at the repercussions of displacement on host countries and communities (Chambers 1993) and at social changes that occur within the refugee camp setting (Cuny, Stein, and Reed 1992). More recently, environmentalists have been studying the effects of camps on the local ecology. Today, the implications of myriad requests for asylum in Northern countries is drawing extensive review (Hathaway 1996).

Like other issues, the end of the Cold War has changed the nature of population displacement and has dramatically increased its scale. Identity conflict and complex emergencies have contributed to such problems as internal displacement, protracted refugee situations, psychosocial trauma, legal culpability of refugees for crimes related to the conflict, and the increased use of camps for political and military purposes. Many scholars are calling for a renewed look at population migration in light of these current conditions (Chambers 1993; Cohen 1994; Hathaway 1996; Loescher 1993).

These issues are clearly of vital importance. We have seen how forced migration can not only seriously disrupt social stability but can jeopardize security in the region, particularly given the large number of displaced populations[2] worldwide. Therefore, this chapter first examines the phenomenon of displacement, including the different types, the motivation for and stages of migration, and life in asylum. Then it explores the repercussions of displacement on the region, the home country, the community, and the individual, and the particular impact of internally displaced persons on recovering societies.

The Profile of Today's Migrants

As Gil Loescher, author of *Beyond Charity: International Cooperation and the Global Refugee Crisis* (1993), points out, in the post–Cold War era, new conditions and scenarios brought about by rapidly changing global dynamics have affected the nature of forced migration. With the diminishing importance of geographic frontiers, for example, crossing a border no longer necessarily signifies safety. And despite international law guaranteeing refugee rights, asylum for those fearing persecution is increasingly being denied. One example of this occurred in the spring of 1996, when Ghana repeatedly refused a boat of Liberians fleeing civil war. Contemporary circumstances, moreover, undermine the traditional concept of forced migration by calling into question the defining characteristics of refugees, internally displaced persons, and others in personal danger.

Refugees

The definition of "refugee" itself is the subject of intense debate, as distinctions between types of people leaving home have begun blur. The 1951 Convention Relating to the Status of Refugees distinguishes a refugee as any person with "a well-founded fear of being persecuted [in his/her country of origin] for reasons of race, religion, nationality, membership of a particular social group or political opinion" (UN General Assembly 1951).[3] According to international law, then, refugees are persons outside their states of origin, whose former positive relationship with their government has collapsed, leaving them without protection or assistance.

Conditions of refugeeism were, of course, extremely different in 1951, when the statute was formed and the UN High Commissioner for Refugees (UNHCR) conceived. Today, migration results not only from persecution but also from conditions such as poverty, famine, disease, massive human rights abuse, ecological disaster, civil strife, fear of retaliation, and political or religious conviction (Loescher 1993; Newland 1993). Many of these new migrants do not fit neatly under the Convention definition, which specifies a fear of persecution but does not specify those conditions. The waters become even more turbid in the fact that economic and political motivations for migration are frequently intertwined. Since the reason for seeking asylum in both cases is a threat to life and freedom, there may be little distinction today between a person seeking freedom from starvation and another freedom from violence.

Economic migrants—that is, those compelled to move in search of work— now comprise a large percentage of the total number of people seeking asylum and are at times difficult to distinguish from those fleeing persecution (Cleveland 1993; Loescher 1993). They may be victims of diminished agricultural capacity, foreign business takeovers, changes in cultural norms, declining economy due to political or social turmoil, urban growth, political restructuring affecting employment and production, or simply increasing population pressures. Environmental refugees are also visibly growing in numbers. They are forced to leave their homes due to deteriorating ecological conditions from pollution, overuse of resources, contaminated or lost resources, overpopulation, or physical hazards causing loss of income and/or ill-health.

Consequently, the debate rages in international circles over the definition of "refugee" and over the appropriate application of the founding refugee statutes to today's conditions (Hathaway 1996). UNHCR, for one, in deference to its mandate, still gives priority to those who fall under the original definition of refugee. It provides qualifying refugees with basic security and material aid while in asylum, as well as assistance in voluntary repatriation or resettlement.[4] Ironically, these refugees often become a privileged minority who, because of their particular condition, gain access to sparse resources, legal protection, and possible admission into a country ahead of numerous prospective applicants.

Lately, however, UNHCR has extended assistance and protection beyond those who meet the formal definition of refugee—to nearly twelve million people in 1996, including IDPs, resident populations, "others of concern,"[5] and, most recently, those considered stateless (UNHCR 1996:12; UNHCR 1997). In Bosnia, for example, UNHCR played the lead role in providing humanitarian assistance to the besieged residents of Sarajevo; in Tajikistan it established resident operations in adverse areas; and in Sri Lanka it offered aid to displaced persons via Open Relief Centers. Nevertheless, many observers are calling for formal adjustments in the UNHCR or another UN agency mandate, or the creation of a new agency to cover the assistance and protection needs of migrants falling outside the conventional definition of refugee. Most significantly, perhaps, this would include the status of internally displaced persons (Cohen 1994; Cohen 1996; Deng 1993; Girardet 1993; UNHCR 1993a; UNHCR 1997).

Legal definitions notwithstanding, this book explores conditions relating to all persons who have fled their homes as a result of identity conflict and complex emergency, regardless of their motivation.

Internally Displaced Persons

The case of internally displaced persons is both parallel to and distinct from that of refugees. Although technically only a border crossing separates the two situations, the international community is becoming more aware of several important differences that distinguish IDPs from other victims of conflict. First, in today's world of internecine violence, IDPs vastly outnumber refugees by more than two to one, and the disparity grows with each new identity conflict and ensuing complex emergency. One reason for this changing dynamic may be that the increasing refusal of asylum has simply kept many inside the bounds of their own country. Second, the animosity inherent in such strife is often focused on IDPs who may have difficulty finding sanctuary and are therefore more vulnerable to abuse. They may be targets of human rights violations by opposing groups or the government itself, which may view them as the source of social disruption (Cohen 1993; Cohen 1996; Deng 1993).

Third, because IDPs still live under the jurisdiction of governments that may be directly or indirectly a cause of their flight, not only can they not expect domestic protection, but international law and institutional agreements do not cover their situation. In fact, many human rights provisions can be suspended when the state deems its security is threatened (Cohen 1996; UNHCR 1993b). UNHCR concedes, "In an internal conflict, the protection needs of displaced people are likely to be at least if not more serious than their assistance needs" (UNHCR 1993a:18).

Finally, my experience in various emergencies has been that humanitarian assistance to internally displaced populations is often inadequate, slow, and highly contentious. One reason for this is that IDPs most often flee to relatives living in other parts of the country, retreat to garrison towns, or eventually move to the capital city; only rarely do they stay in established camps. They are therefore difficult to locate and hard to distinguish from the local population.

Mogadishu, for example, was teeming with IDPs, some of whom had been drawn by the arrival of the international military force in the capital. Except for those obviously still en route with personal belongings at their side, they blended in with the city residents. IDPs in urban areas usually form small independent enclaves in shanty towns on the edge of the city and learn the life of the urban slum dweller. Another explanation is that the government, whose responsibility it is to care for its displaced citizens, may either have collapsed or assumed IDPs are opposition members and refuse to help them. In fact, authorities may adamantly oppose any assistance, charging IDPs with subversive action (Cohen 1996; Cuny 1991; Deng 1993). As a result, the government may also object to and interdict international assistance. Serb authorities often prevented humanitarian aid destined for Albanian Kosovars, for instance, from reaching the communities in need.

Yet another reason for insufficient aid to internally displaced populations is that even if the government does have the will to help, it may be unable to act due to a dearth of resources. Impoverished countries may already have inadequate funds for social assistance. A change in perceived priorities during civil strife often shifts any remaining funds to support wartime activities. In the case of Rwanda, the government that took control after the conflict was devoid of any funds for operational expenses, let alone social assistance. Though to the donor community it indicated a strong interested in helping both IDPs and returnees, the government was plagued with an empty coffer (depleted by the departing leaders), little international financial aid, and a strong external security threat that demanded expenditures for military maintenance.

Furthermore, since they technically fall within the domestic jurisdiction and therefore lack an international protectorate, IDPs are traditionally among the lowest priority for international donors (Deng 1993). ICRC is one of the only international agencies mandated to provide aid and protection to victims of violence within their own country. However, given large numbers of IDPs, the difficulty in locating them, and possible restrictions imposed by the authorities, ICRC may be overwhelmed while aid from other relief agencies may be negligible. Their sheer numbers and the inadequacy of assistance lead many experts to consider IDPs the greatest single group at risk in the world today.[6] The International Organization for Migration, for example, found that IDPs in Angola in 1995 experienced worse conditions than returning refugees; in Rwanda in 1994, the DHA reported that the nutritional status of the general population far surpassed that of the internally displaced (Cohen 1996:24).

Despite the lack of institutional support for IDPs, their circumstances and numbers have begun to draw significant concern. In recent years, the UN General Assembly and the Secretary-General have periodically asked UNHCR to formally expand its conventional mandate in certain circumstances and provide care for other displaced populations, such as IDPs, most notably in Iraq, Liberia, the former Yugoslavia, Somalia (UNHCR 1993a), and recently in Kosovo. (Only 5.4 million IDPs, however, were listed as "of concern" to UNHCR in 1995 [Cohen 1996:26].) In 1992 the UN Commission on Human Rights requested that the Secretary-General appoint a representative to specifically study the concerns and conditions of IDPs. The resultant appointee, Francis Deng, subsequently enlarged the meager information base and championed the IDP dilemma, contributing to a growing awareness of the problem. (Nevertheless, effective action has been hobbled by concerns for sovereignty as well as debate over appropriate international jurisdiction among the various UN agencies, or indeed the creation of a separate agency to house these matters [Cohen 1994; Girardet 1993; UNHCR 1993a; UNHCR 1997]. Under Deng's recommendation for the current UN reform measures, the IDP Task Force will be disbanded, folding IDP issues into other emergency relief structures but still not solving the question of agency dominion.)

In addition to the new types of forced migrants, the number of people fleeing persecution increased significantly until the mid-1990s. In 1951, when the UN drafted the Convention Relating to the Status of Refugees and created UNHCR, there were approximately one million people under its care around the world, all of them refugees. By the end of 1997, there were approximately 22.7 million protected by UNHCR, including refugees, some internally displaced persons, returnees, and others (UNHCR 1997).[7] Interestingly, for the twenty-year period prior to the mid-1970s, refugee figures worldwide remained relatively unchanged at about two to three million (Hakovirta 1986:147). At that point, however, the count began to rise exponentially and reached approximately twelve million a decade later.

The dramatic changes in the global refugee situation in the latter half of the 1970s increased not only the overall number of refugees but the scale of individual evacuations, their urgency, and their duration (Hakovirta 1986; U.S. Mission 1995). But it was the end of the Cold War that literally opened the spigot. A review of the various statistics shows that the shift from insurrection movements to identity conflicts corresponded to a 28 percent increase in displaced persons worldwide in the first five years of the post–Cold War era. The addition of new categories of populations in need in the mid-1980s accounted for much of the newly displaced. The numbers continued to rise for the next decade, reaching a total of almost 50 million uprooted people around the world by January 1995. That amounted to one out of every 115 persons in the world (UNHCR 1995). Then, in 1995, the number of displaced people began to decline. This can be attributed in part to the growth in refusal of asylum, as well as to several recent large repatriations, including those to Rwanda, Uganda, and Mozambique.

The massive movement of people has not occurred equally around the globe. Before the return of Rwandan refugees from Zaire and Tanzania, Africa accounted for seven out of the top ten countries of origin, amounting to 11 million uprooted people on the continent (Creative Associates 1997; UNHCR 1995). Second only to Afghanistan, Liberia alone had 778,000 refugees in 1997 (UNHCR 1997). The poorest of all continents, and the most politically tumultuous, Africa has the fewest resources with which to care for its displaced populations, yet still accounts for half of the top ten countries of asylum (USCR 1996:6). This creates a downward cycle, as identity conflict victims flood into neighboring countries for refuge, only to contribute to the host country's own instability. In 1996 Sudan, for example, was the world's eighth largest source of refugees, while simultaneously the place of asylum for refugees from Chad, Eritrea, and Ethiopia (UNHCR 1996:30; USCR 1996:6).

While Africa has been the source as well as the host to refugees and internally displaced persons for decades, the new republics from the former communist bloc are a relatively recent addition to the global forced migration scenario. Since the breakup of the old order, identity conflicts in Azerbaijan and Armenia, the former Yugoslavia, the Caucuses, Central Asia, and portions of Russia have spawned large numbers of forced migrants, creating new challenges to the international community. According to UNHCR (1996:33–39), in 1996 1.6 million refugees emanated from former Soviet states alone.

These dynamics create an entirely different international scenario than that of the 1980s, producing a multitude of security, humanitarian, and social dilemmas. Statistics and definitions, however, do not speak to the repercussions of mass displacement on families, villages, or geographic areas. The decision to leave home is part of a series of events that ultimately affects virtually all members of society directly or indirectly.

The Impetus to Flee: A Search for Security

Knowledge and policy about refugee and displaced person issues have improved significantly over the past decade, due largely to greater academic and field study of the issues. The work of Fred Cuny, former president of Intertect, a private relief and reconstruction firm, has been one of the more notable influences. As both a practitioner and a scholar, Cuny was a leading and influential thinker in the field of disasters and accompanying migration. In the early 1990s he participated in the International Study of Spontaneous Voluntary

Repatriation (ISSVR), which considered multiple refugee case studies in Central America, Africa, and Asia, resulting in *Repatriation Under Conflict in Central America* (Larkin, Cuny, and Stein 1991) and *Repatriation During Conflict in Africa and Asia* (Cuny, Stein, and Reed 1992). He also examined the issues of internal displacement in *Displaced Persons in Civil Conflict* (Cuny 1991) and with me in "Assessing Emergencies Involving Civilians Displaced by Conflict" (Intertect 1993). Cuny's work has significantly influenced the way international organizations address issues of forced displacement.

In *Displaced Persons in Civil Conflict*, Cuny outlined some of the fundamental motivations behind an individual refugee's migration. In his view, based on vast field experience, the primary reason for flight was security, followed by economics and then control over one's life. Despite their new profile and copious numbers, today's migrations seem to be induced by the same basic perceived threats to security and way of life as in the past. These are conventionally referred to in terms of push and pull factors.

Common *push factors* triggering exodus from a conflict zone include imminent fighting or human rights violations; food insecurity such as destruction of crops, collapsed agricultural networks, or food shortages; economic deterioration, including loss of assets, severe market volatility, or economic collapse. *Pull factors* include established assistance networks; the potential of finding sanctuary with relatives or other identity group members; the prospect of selling assets or gaining employment; and the possibility of relocating to an urban environment (Cuny 1991; Hakovirta 1986). In the modern experience of migration, the search for greater security and personal well-being might be modified by the depth of one's personal involvement in the dispute. By all accounts, the migrant's perception of the situation at both ends, which may or may not correspond to reality, is the critical factor.

Several social groups have historically tended to flee more than others (Cuny 1991; Intertect 1993). Early on in the conflict, those who live in the countryside, including rural laborers, farmers, and pastoralists are the most prone to leave. This is in part because their relative isolation creates greater exposure to attack, and partly because farms and herds are more vulnerable to disruption than many other economic enterprises. Obviously, those closest to the fighting and therefore most at risk are also inclined to flee, as are those specifically targeted in the conflict, such as members of specific religious, ethnic, tribal, or linguistic groups. In addition, extremely mobile sectors of the population like traditional nomads or migratory laborers usually leave the conflict area directly. I witnessed this repeatedly in the nomadic regions of Somalia, where vacating an area is a natural reaction to adverse conditions.

Cuny describes three types of displacement. One is crisis-induced, when fighting in or around the home region spawns a sudden exodus from the community. The intensity of today's identity conflicts creates large flows of crisis-induced migrants, as seen in April and May of 1994, when Rwandans first crossed the border into Tanzania in mass numbers. In contrast, community members may evacuate early, at an advance sign of trouble, in order to avoid violence or possible conscription. This second type, precautionary evacuation, affords families time to sell some of their assets and leave in an organized fashion. Many Bosnians fit into this category, particularly those I encountered in Macedonia in the early days of the conflict and in Kosovo in 1998. Finally, people flee for economic reasons, such as food and commodity shortages, dire financial problems as a result of a collapsed local or national economy, ruined agriculture or other means of income, or lack of business and trade (Cuny 1991). Much of the televised images of Somalis leaving their homes in search of food fit into this category.

The causes of migration affect the conditions under which it occurs and the choice of a destination. Crisis-induced migrants usually have few assets and flee to the closest perceived safe area; for those nearest the border, this may be a refugee camp. Precautionary and economic migrants generally carry more resources with them and thus tend to go farther away, possibly to a labor pole, the capital city, or in the case of the former Yugoslavia, to Europe. In such movements, migrants usually wait until the end of the harvest, the majority leaving two to three months later (Cuny 1991; Intertect 1993).

The season as well as the quality of the crop similarly affect farmers not under immediate duress. If the harvest is adequate to sustain the family for the next season, the farmer will likely stay at least long enough to determine the potential for the next cultivating period (Cuny 1991). Not uncommonly, the farmer will move the rest of the family to a safe zone and return home often and long enough to plant and work the fields, particularly if the place of asylum is nearby. In Rwanda there was noticeable field cultivation in areas that had been evacuated near refugee and IDP camps. Under today's circumstances, this type of long preplanning may not be as feasible as in the past. The typically rapid disintegration in social conditions is more likely to force an immediate evacuation, which allows little time for preparation.

Another finding of Cuny's is that the prospects for economic advantage traditionally affect the destination choice. IDPs searching for job opportunities will go where the economy is still functioning, which in most cases is in government-held territory (Cuny 1991). What I have found to be a more influential factor in identity conflicts, however, is group association. Uprooted populations choose destinations based on areas of like tribal, cultural, linguistic, or ethnic attributes, and particularly locations where relatives or associates reside. In contemporary conflicts, affinity to a group becomes paramount in virtually every decision. In Tajikistan, for example, the mixed ethnic and geographic community living in the capital quickly dispersed back to their respective regional bases when the conflict erupted (Maynard 1994).

Refugees may set out immediately to cross an international boundary—due to proximity, urgency, or personal threat—or may do so only after a series of migrations from sanctuary to sanctuary. In Rwanda, I watched whole communities roam the countryside, sometimes staying at IDP camps for weeks or months before many left the country. At the destination, strife may erupt in a microcosm of the bigger conflict or out of contention over resources and employment, particularly in areas occupied by several identity groups (Intertect 1993). Such conflict can provoke further migration to places of greater perceived safety. The infamous massacre at Kibeho IDP camp in southwestern Rwanda epitomized this. Hostility against the IDPs who had become entrenched in the area developed among local residents and military units and broke into a brutal battle. In today's conflicts, however, identity association usually more strictly defines destinations, minimizing the likelihood that mixed groups will occupy a contested area.

Stages of Migration

Cuny (1991) divides the process of displacement into five phases. He describes the preliminary phase as the period prior to departure, in which pressure builds from insecurity, diminished employment, increased competition for general resources, conscription, deterioration in the food supply, or decreased income with which to purchase food. Next is the evacuation or emergency phase, which includes the decision to leave, the process of evacuation, and the arrival in a place of relative safety. In addition to the general push factors mentioned earlier, according to Cuny, other considerations play a role in this phase. Loss of a family member due to violence, or imminent threat of physical danger or conscription, for example, can affect the decision to move.

Other community members' evacuation or the judgment of a community leader may also precipitate the decision. I observed this in both Somalia and Rwanda, where whole communities and subclans fled under the direction of a local leader. The destination, as mentioned above, is influenced by several factors, including the location of the nearest sanctuary, the distance to an international border, location of perceived income sources and employment, route access and safety, and, particularly in identity conflicts, location of relatives or other identity group members, as well as receptivity of identity groups in neighboring countries (Cuny 1991; Intertect 1993).

Field observation reveals that upon arrival at a destination site, most crisis-induced migrants are often traumatized, sick, or injured from the journey and are without many assets. For this reason, internally displaced persons will often gather around a health center, a relief post, or a watering hole, which may then develop into a camp. Most will immediately search for an income source. Some, particularly the earlier arrivals, may find work in nearby towns or on local farms, especially during the planting or harvest season (Cuny 1991).

According to Cuny, the emergency phase ends when there are no more new arrivals, health and nutrition rates have stabilized, and there is relative security, or when migration continues on from the initial place of sanctuary. The latter occurs if the area is invaded by conflict or overwhelmed with new arrivals. In that case, the job market soon becomes saturated and the wage scale severely depressed. Therefore, subsequent arrivals unable to find work, and those who can no longer survive on a reduced wage, may move on in search of adequate employment, or they may cross an international border and become refugees (Cuny 1991; Intertect 1993).

The third stage, then, is the secondary migration phase, when the displaced move out of their initial place of sanctuary in search of employment and better living conditions. Early in the migration pattern, secondary displacement may only take migrants as far as a spontaneous settlement near the sanctuary where farm or other work can be found. Logically, labor poles such as large industries or farming schemes become a major destination. But soon such job markets too may become saturated; when wages decrease, many eventually move on, often to the capital or other cities. It is at this point, it seems, that the volume of uprooted people flooding into urban areas becomes notable.

Thus the fourth phase, settlement, begins when the displaced reach a location where they can remain without overwhelming fear of physical insecurity, and without being forced to relocate again in search of income. For those who cross an international border, this is typically a UNHCR-managed camp, where refugees generally register, receive food and health assistance, and situate themselves in the camp setting. For those arriving at a refugee camp during this stage, the camp structure and procedures have already been defined, and they essentially integrate themselves into the surroundings.

IDPs may also stay in a camp, particularly if they have no nearby friends or relatives. However, in part because assistance is usually less forthcoming, security nebulous, and morbidity and mortality rates high, many ultimately move to an urban center, settling in squatter sections on the periphery of the city where they have family or identity group members (Cuny 1991). Those seeking refuge in the city are generally less likely to return home. Nevertheless, many IDPs and refugees alike attempt to reintegrate into their country and community of origin.

The final phase, then, is the return passage, which will be discussed in the next chapter.

Life in Asylum

Studies of refugeeism have found that, as a rule, living in exile substantially changes the attitudes and perceptions of displaced persons, whether they are inside or outside their home country (Deng 1993; Norwegian Refugee Council 1992). Their experience is marked by exposure to new influences, isolation, deprivation, and often a radically different environment. These experiences affect the skills, resources, and political views of a significant portion of the overall population.

Refugees

International aid specialists increasingly recognize that the experience of refugeeism is vastly different from that of internal displacement. The majority of those seeking sanctuary in a neighboring country stop initially in camps that spring up along the border. Almost immediately, however as Cuny (1991) notes, a portion of them will repatriate in the "refugee ricochet" process. This occurs when those swept up in the exodus abruptly return after determining the level of insecurity was not sufficient to warrant an evacuation, or that conditions in exile were not worth jeopardizing resources at home. Those who stay typically receive material assistance in the form of shelter, food, sanitation, water, medical care, and possibly education from UNHCR and partner NGOs. Under international law, moreover, UNHCR provides refugees with physical protection from outside aggression (UNHCR 1993b).

Despite the support from the international community, many experts acknowledge that refugee camp living is usually anything but healthy. Though physical needs are generally accommodated, the relatively languid environment of a camp usually offers little in the way of productive activities. Schools for children may or may not exist; when they do they are frequently inadequately supplied, especially initially. Nonetheless, the creation of an education system, many argue, offers productive occupation for both the teachers and children in the camp.

Other adults may search for work in the outlying areas. Those who are successful tend to be poorly paid, due to the size of the willing workforce. Some take up nefarious activities such as scams to pilfer relief supplies that may later be sold or bartered for services or other goods, refugee mafia circles, prostitution and drug rings, weapons trafficking, or intimidation of fellow refugees for material goods or services. In Afghanistan, this came to be known as the "Kalashnikov culture," in which drug trafficking, arms trading, smuggling, and other illegal activities contributed to a climate of violence and a general breakdown in social and civil order (Sorenson 1992). Still others simply become lethargic and while away time in inactivity.

The conflict that provokes their migration generally unites refugees under a mutual animosity against their aggressors, presumably members of other identity groups. In the crowded, apprehension-laden setting of a refugee camp, such as those along the Zaire border between 1994 and 1996, leaders garner support and consolidate means to battle the establishment at home. Using inculcation and indoctrination, displaced political, quasi-military, civic, or religious authorities are known to influence their captive audience into believing—legitimately or not—that they have been wronged, that their cause is just, and that they must fight for their rights, including that of return (Stein and Cuny 1991).

The camps, with their abundance of disillusioned, ostracized, and isolated young men, offer ready recruitment sources for malcontents (Zolberg, Suhrke, and Aguayo 1989). In Sri Lanka, rebel recruiters were enormously successful, particularly as the prospects for employment dimmed and economic reality began to take hold (Cuny and Cuny 1992). Many studies reveal how refugee warriors, in clear violation of international law, subsequently use the border camps as a safe haven from which to conduct cross-border raids and attacks on political leaders and opposition identity groups, thus harming the area's general stability. Clearly, the more refugees inspired by enmity who support the struggle, the greater advantage and leverage the leaders have against the reigning home establishment. The refugee leadership may use various forms of coercion, including threats, torture, and murder against those contemplating or attempting repatriation. The camps in Goma, Zaire, that held Rwandan refugees present a prime example. For many months, intimidation kept return at a near standstill, while bodies of those trying to, or suspected of, escape were found in and around the camps and rumors of rape and torture of the "disloyal" circulated the region (Kumar et al. 1996).

Access to, and accuracy of, information is another powerful influence over refugee action. Deliberate misinformation campaigns bias refugees' understanding of the situation in their country of origin. Such crusades affect their perception of the state of politics, the attitude of opposition identity groups, security, available assistance, legal procedures, military conditions in various home regions, the number and type of people living in their home communities, and their physical circumstances. Moreover, in an enclosed environment like that of a refugee camp, rumors of all sorts inevitably circulate (Harris 1994).

Most refugees lack adequate and reliable alternative sources of information about conditions at home. Radio and personal emissaries are among the few means at hand, and these may be altogether insufficient or unavailable. In some cases UNHCR or an NGO may establish a mail system from the camps to home communities, allowing cross-border communication in the form of letters from friends and relatives at home. Fundamentally, however, the refugees' isolation and distrust of information reduce their confidence in incoming news. (Some observers argue the opposite, that refugees are in fact privy to many indigenous news channels and reporting mechanisms, generally unavailable to the international community, yet surprisingly accurate. Unfortunately, little data has been collected to confirm the legitimacy and influence of such communication.)

The accuracy and availability of home community information is critical to the refugees' decision to repatriate. Families may not decide to repatriate until a member or trustworthy friend has visited the home and deemed the situation safe enough for return. Other refugees learn of conditions through these exchanges, which may be official programs sponsored by an NGO or UNHCR, such as that carried out among Tajik refugees in Afghanistan.

Some refugees may take advantage of the situation and travel back and forth across the frontier many times, possibly receiving assistance in both countries, conducting business, and perhaps playing the role of political go-between. This was conspicuously the case in northwestern Rwanda in 1994–95, where many way stations designed to assist repatriating refugees on their way home were frequented by the same faces many times over the course of several months. These travelers provide people on both sides of the border with information on conditions and the social disposition of various groups. In Guinea, Liberian refugees floating between their homeland and exile kept a small but almost constant trickle of information flowing between the otherwise remote refugee pockets and relatives at home.

Internally Displaced Persons

The IDP situation is vastly different from and in many ways invariably worse than that of refugees. Because they have not fled the country, IDPs have no international protection. Instead, they remain the responsibility of their government, which may be the source of their flight. Away from home, they usually lack access to resources or immediate employment. They are consequently more vulnerable to persecution, starvation, and disease (Cuny 1991; Deng 1993).

Beyond considerations associated with the conflict itself, the actions of IDPs are dependent upon the economic, cultural, social, and geographic makeup of the country. These elements become important factors in deciding whether IDPs migrate in clusters or as individual families, seek out personal connections or stay together with their identity group, leave the area entirely for a separate geographic region or flee to a cultural stronghold and, therefore, to perceived security. Generally, however, those leaving en masse will stop where they feel some semblance of safety. Such locations may become camps similar to those of refugees, and IDPs may find themselves only slightly less subject to intimidation while they must still face problems of reduced self-esteem and dependency (Intertect 1993).

Unlike refugees, however, IDPs require significant self-sufficiency. Without a governing international agency to draw attention to their plight, IDPs are a lesser priority for foreign assistance. Even when aid is available through ICRC, UNHCR, or NGOs, logistical problems often tend to obstruct or severely hinder distribution of relief supplies. Field analysis shows that IDPs, extremely conscious of continuous security threats, are likely to camp in remote, well-hidden areas that may be particularly inferior in terms of access to water, sanitation, and firewood, putting their health at risk.

The difficulty in locating and accessing these areas can cause what aid is available to be delayed. Assistance is generally more forthcoming once the groups have been located and either moved or the site rendered more accessible and developed into an official IDP camp. In Sudan, poor communication networks, insufficient data, and huge influxes into resource-poor regions resulted in delayed deliverance of food and medical supplies, culminating in extremely high mortality rates (Hogan 1992).

If a ruling government exists, however, it may adamantly oppose international aid for IDPs, under the justification that unbidden assistance is a threat to its sovereignty. Indeed, under international law it is the responsibility of the government to care for its own citizens. International assistance, therefore, may be negatively perceived as an intrusion into domestic affairs. Since many IDPs relocate to the more economically sound government-held regions of the country, international agencies must work through government channels to obtain access to the displaced populations. In Kosovo, for example, Serb authorities denied NGOs access to IDPs in part as a means of controlling the population. Those migrating to rebel-held territory are not only often faced with an extremely weak economy but are even less likely to receive international aid, since, typically, fewer agencies operate inside these zones (Cuny 1991; de Waal 1993).

IDPs living in camps are generally more likely than refugees to maintain contact with their home community, either through personal visits, written communication, movements back and forth, radio or television, interaction with other community members, or possibly by telephone. They may, in fact, begin to rebuild houses, rehabilitate businesses, and continue to cultivate crops through regular visits home while maintaining their registration in the camp. One of Rwanda's southwestern IDP camps, for example, was made up of a majority of people from within six kilometers of the camp. They openly continued to farm and repair their homes during the day, retreating to the safety of the camp at night. As a result of such movement, the fluctuation in IDP camp populations is often much greater than that of refugees. Moreover, as relief workers have noted, IDPs commonly have a better awareness of conditions at home and are likely to return sooner than refugees. Further reducing the likelihood of long-term entrenchment is the fact that conditions in IDP camps are usually inferior to those in refugee camps.

The circumstances surrounding internally displaced persons not living in camps are drastically different. These are usually families who have fled to friends and relatives in other, presumably safer, areas of the country. Living together in overcrowded conditions puts an extreme burden on the extended family. These IDPs, moreover, blend into the local community, making them virtually impossible to find, recognize, and verify. Assistance in these circumstances, therefore, is often unfeasible, except when it is addressed to the community as a whole. In Tajikistan many IDPs lived under these conditions. Some were reluctant to admit to being displaced for fear I would divulge their whereabouts to the authorities, while others hoped for assistance and therefore came forward. IDPs searching for employment to help in their own upkeep often meet with difficulty, given the generally poor economy and high unemployment. Frequently, they incur large debts to local residents, which serve to prevent them from returning home and make them vulnerable to manipulation by the surrounding community (Cuny 1990).

All else being equal, many IDPs, particularly young men, will choose to migrate to the capital city. Some may have considered such a move before the forced relocation, in the expectation of better opportunities for employment. The added residents contribute to the global pattern of urban growth. Once established in the city with at least some prospect for survival, the displaced may send for the rest of the family and generally do not return home. In Afghanistan, while regions of the countryside nearly emptied, the population of Kabul doubled during one period of the war (Sorenson 1992:280). Such urban migrants usually set up residence in shanty towns at the outskirts of the city. Although seriously marginalized initially, it is nearly impossible to distinguish the IDPs from other slum dwellers after six months (Intertect 1993). In this setting, they find relative anonymity and thus refuge from human rights attacks. The government, on the other hand, may become further aggravated with the IDPs for contributing to the country's urban growth and slum problems.

In the Aftermath of Migration: Facing the Consequences

As is evidenced in the forced migrations of recent years, displacement can have significant consequences on the region, state, locale, and individual. It can threaten international peace, border stability, economic, political, and social reconstruction, the national and community healing process, and even familial relations. Although the trauma of displacement is not a phenomenon specific to identity conflicts, it does carry with it serious new concerns.

Regional

Large numbers of refugees can constitute a threat to international peace, both physically and legally (Loescher 1993; Zolberg, Suhrke, and Aguayo 1989). Border violence increases both with the targeted raids from refugee camps and with the export of the primary issues of the conflict into border host communities. Moreover, the weapons trade, drug dealing, and other nefarious activities associated with refugee camps disrupt normal economic conduct and draw members of the host society into antisocial behavior (Zolberg, Suhrke, and Aguayo 1989). In Zaire, the government itself reportedly helped facilitate million-dollar deals with arms dealers in Britain, China, and South Africa for Rwandan refugees, while its secret police provided private cargo planes for the weapons transfers (Reed 1997:5).

Integral to regional deterioration is the well-documented economic burden a refugee establishment places on the surrounding host community. Beyond the fact that the sudden influx of abundant cheap labor lowers pay scales and diminishes indigenous opportunity for employment, local resources (such as firewood) may be overused or entirely consumed. The standard of living of the surrounding population may be significantly lower than that of refugees receiving aid from the international community (Chambers 1993). Consequently, as we have seen in many countries, contention may arise between the host nation and the refugee population. Entrenchment becomes a more serious obstacle the longer the camps remain in place. Establishing school systems and permanent structures can add to this aura of permanence. Some observers argue that as long as all their basic needs are met, refugees have little incentive to return home where they have to provide for themselves and services may be inferior.

However, the future of long-term international support is becoming increasingly doubtful. For several reasons, the international community is beginning to question the viability and appropriateness of sustaining large populations of refugees for long periods of time. The debate is occurring at a time when many conflicts appear intractable and periods of asylum indefinite. The continued requirements for humanitarian assistance worldwide amounts to a significant financial burden—currently amounting to billions of dollars annually. The approximately two million refugees resulting from Rwanda's 1994 civil war alone cost the international community a million dollars a day to support (Kumar et al. 1996:5). In addition, most donor countries are themselves experiencing greater domestic fiscal pressures and are consequently beginning to tighten their own belts.

Finally, and more controversially, some are beginning to question the moral obligation to assist all forced migrants regardless of circumstances. A border crossing does not presuppose innocence; in fact, it is increasingly used to hide legal responsibility and continue insurgent activities. For this reason, many in the international community believe refugee assistance may actually abet aggressive behavior. The Rwandan camps in Zaire are a recent example where sectors of the international community withdrew relief aid and others argued for only selective support (Jean 1995). The large numbers of people implicated in the Rwandan genocide who lived in these internationally managed camps, and the innumerable nefarious activities that took place there, flew in the face of international law and humanitarianism.

Therefore, fear of inadequate international assistance is beginning to cause regional trepidation about protracted refugee situations draining local resources. This may be contributing to the growing occurrence of refusal to grant asylum (Hathaway 1996; Ogata 1993). Some contend that selective closure of refugee camps would eliminate many of these problems, increase regional prosperity and security, and encourage repatriation. Two arguments, however, counter this notion. First and foremost, international protocol guarantees a safe haven and generally grants international assistance for as long as necessary. Depending on the circumstances, camp closure may be construed as a step toward forced repatriation and may therefore be in violation of international law.[8] Second, despite the reality of entrenchment and potential disincentive, there is little conclusive evidence to indicate that reduction or elimination in aid to refugees results in massive repatriation.

One question that arises, then, is whether massive voluntary repatriation is plausible. On the one hand, unwillingness to repatriate can become stronger the longer refugees remain in exile, in part due to reduced self-esteem, a hardened attitude toward the situation at home, lack of accurate information, deterioration

of skills due to lack of use, assumed loss of property at home, and simple iner-
tia. The refugee assistance system, therefore, may actually discourage repatriation, many contend. On the other hand, a "space" for repatriation may open up,
particularly if the situation in the host country deteriorates or conditions in the
homeland improve. Return IDP movement may indicate improvement in internal security or government outreach to the internally displaced populations.
Refugee populations carefully watch for and consider these indicators of better
conditions in their decision to repatriate. Significantly, most major repatriations
have occurred in conjunction with a notable change in home country conditions
(Norwegian Refugee Council 1992). Cambodia, for example, experienced substantial political change and national elections; Namibia went through a peace
process that dramatically transformed internal affairs; Nicaragua's elections
transferred power to the opposition; Mozambique underwent a national reconciliation process of sorts; and Guatemala similarly signed peace accords.

Home Country

Mass migrations clearly affect the state of domestic affairs as well. Large numbers of internally uprooted people attest to the home government's continued
inability to solve its national problems. Paradoxically, conditions in the country
of origin are unlikely to improve to any large extent as long as large numbers of
refugees along the border pose a menace to national security and rehabilitation,
and internal displacement drains resources and contributes to social instability.

The issue of security looms perhaps largest on the domestic screen. Border
raids from refugee warriors, insidious activities inducing social disruption, and
attacks on individual officials would give any government reason for apprehension. Similar activities may be planned and carried out by IDPs from within the
confines of the country, as reportedly occurred in the IDP camps in southwestern Rwanda. Until the majority of both populations have returned home, therefore, comprehensive rebuilding of the economy, social structure, political system, and civil society may be constantly undermined by the threat of insurgency, conspiracy campaigns, guerrilla warfare, public inculcation, social
infiltration, and economic sabotage. (Comprehensive repatriation, however,
does not guarantee stability either, as is evident in Rwanda since the massive
return of refugees in 1996.)

The absence of large sectors of the population can wreak havoc on the
economy as well. The usual concomitant decline in domestic production further deteriorates an economy already taxed by excessive spending on military
outlays. Even a government genuinely concerned with the welfare of its internally displaced persons may not have the means to provide support. At the

same time, monetary assistance from international lending institutions and bilateral aid depend at times on general amnesty or substantial reconciliation with refugee opposition groups and the return of displaced populations. The U.S. government's "Open City" program in Bosnia, for example, made aid contingent upon the return of displaced ethnic minorities. Genuine peacemaking efforts, however, may be long in coming and, as we have seen, superficial conciliatory actions to appease international donors are often short-lived.

The potentially grave political implications of forced migration are evident. Political pluralism, for instance, is a virtual impossibility without the physical presence of opposition members. Refugees, moreover, can intentionally undermine any movement toward free and fair elections through social intimidation, sabotage, or misinformation campaigns conducted from the safety of an external camp (Zolberg, Suhrke, and Aguayo 1989). Other issues under contention such as land rights, leadership positions, and legal accountability cannot be fully resolved while significant portions of the population remain displaced. In protracted displacement situations, one can imagine how these issues fester and become even more troublesome the longer populations remain absent. More profoundly, the process of national reconciliation cannot commence until adversaries begin to face each other. Before that time, each side presumably maintains a negative image of the other, which merely hardens over time and postpones a sense of justice and renewal until all sides come to terms with the events. (The process of overcoming these negative perceptions and intergroup healing is discussed further in chapter 6.)

Internal displacement alone presents a unique set of complex issues on virtually all aspects of national life. Foremost, perhaps, is the relationship between IDPs and their government. In conflicts involving government forces on one side, and the identity group(s) associated with the IDPs on another, officials may view those leaving their homes as subversives (Deng 1993). In the recent case of Zaire cum Democratic Republic of Congo, contention grew between the newly formed alliance of several ethnic groups that led the national rebellion and the tribes they displaced. Ensuing distrust, subtle manipulation, provocative malicious behavior and mistreatment, and outright aggression further undermine relationships. In Guatemala, for example, the army labeled those who had fled as guerrilla sympathizers and consequently threatened and abused displaced populations (Zinser 1991a).

Authorities may attempt to obstruct international relief activities for the displaced and resident populations. I have seen governments substantially undermine relief operations by denying visas, declaring certain organizations or individuals persona non grata, creating an inordinate amount of red tape, taxing incoming relief goods, confiscating equipment and supplies, arresting or otherwise hassling foreign relief workers, denying access to certain areas, or threatening international or local aid personnel with bodily harm. As Loescher points out in *Beyond Charity*, "In the 1990s, internal wars are fought not only by military means but by preventing international aid from reaching people living in conflict areas" (1993:77). This can ultimately affect not only IDPs but also besieged citizens and resident populations who are targeted by warring factions or simply become pawns in the geographic tug-of-war—precisely the case of Kosovo.

In addition, the government may develop aid programs for the internally displaced as a cover for pacification programs. Such tactics include removing the opposition's support base by resettling IDPs back into government-held regions in housing developments or "peace villages," forcing nonparticipants to join the government's side, or attempting to control IDP populations through location of relief distributions (Cuny 1990). Ethiopia's controversial "villagization" program appeared to numerous observers to be such a manipulative pacification scheme, forcing many citizens to seek refuge in northwestern Somalia (Zolberg, Suhrke, and Aguayo 1989).

Eventually, lack of adequate relief assistance becomes a national problem, regardless of the government's relationship to the displaced. Basic depletion of national reserves, destruction of the environment, and the increased looting that frequently results from the struggle for survival are generally associated with poor government control. Continued disorder and deteriorating humanitarian conditions, such as those observed in early 1996 in Liberia, undermine any semblance of progress toward a stable domestic situation.

Furthermore, protection of IDPs becomes a visible and highly charged issue on the international front. Donors, international monetary lenders, regional contingents, and refugees carefully watch for mistreatment of, or disregard for, IDPs as an indicator of government loyalties and intentions. Such conditions do not go entirely unnoticed. Watchdog and human rights organizations keep an observant eye on the lookout for signs of abuse, which reverberate throughout the world, sending negative messages about the home government or local authorities (Africa Rights 1994; Ahlström 1991; Cohen 1994; Deng 1993; Jean 1995; and Zolberg, Suhrke, and Aguayo 1989). Reports of abuse of both refugees and citizens in eastern Zaire/Congo between 1995 and 1997, for example, received much publicity (Human Rights Watch Africa 1997; Physicians for Human Rights 1997).

Finally, significant IDP relocation to the cities can have immense implications for national development, the economy, and social issues. The fact that most such migration is into the poorer outskirts of the cities contributes to the growth of urban slums and deteriorates overall living standards (Intertect

1993). Since provision of assistance is difficult and rare, new residents may turn to antisocial activities such as petty theft, drug dealing, or prostitution to survive.

The flood of IDPs to cities often brings with it a host of social problems such as low employment, diminished regard for cultural values, illiteracy, antisocial behavior, and decrease in the number of agriculturists (Intertect 1993). Moreover, IDPs carry with them a microcosm of the conflict, thereby transporting the potential for further violence (Deng 1993). In sum, domestic problems reverberating from massive displacement both outside and within national boundaries are ominous and potentially paralyzing.

Community

At the community level, social cohesion is permanently scarred by the violence, and the absence of large portions of the membership serves as a continual reminder of the rift that divides the population. Not until a significant percentage of people has returned can real healing begin. Moreover, those who remained at home often do not appreciate the personal anguish endured by those who fled, while displaced populations falsely perceive themselves as uniquely traumatized by events, failing to recognize the suffering sustained by the resident population (Intertect 1993).

Many difficult issues confront the home community as a result of the displacement. Though these will be explored in greater detail in chapter 5, they merit some discussion here as they relate to the return process. The community faces ongoing battles over property rights, for example, when land taken over by others becomes subject to dispute among the membership. Another dispute develops when community members loot the homes of displaced persons. In Tajikistan, for instance, local residents took apart vacant houses for the valuable wood framing the doors and windows. This forced returnees to either attempt to recuperate the material or find other sources.

Individual status within the community also changes as new patterns of social interaction and responsibility emerge in the absence of traditional leaders. In addition, the dearth of adequate manual labor may cause farms and other enterprises to go untended. The community, therefore, lives in constant anticipation of the impending return of its displaced members. A significant return has the potential to change the solidifying status quo in welcome and unwelcome ways.

In areas housing IDPs, other issues emerge. The ad hoc, slow, and insufficient nature of relief aid compounded by the difficulty in locating the internally displaced often puts a tremendous burden on the local population to provide assistance. As a result, coveted community food reserves may be spent on the newcomers, and health and medical facilities may be overwhelmed with demand. In the isolated Gorno-Badakhshan region of Tajikistan, for example, the additional population taxed the normal resources, and difficult road and air access impeded resupply (Maynard 1994).

Extended families and women fostering unaccompanied children, in particular, face special difficulties securing food, clothing, care, and housing. In complex emergencies, the number of female heads of households often increases, putting further stress on them and, by extension, on the community to provide assistance. In Rwanda, between one third and one half of all women in the hardest-hit areas were widows. At the same time, an estimated 21 percent of all households fostered unaccompanied children (Kumar et al. 1996:61, 66).

The presence of internally displaced populations may also lead to an upsurge in localized violence. The population pressure generated from secondary displacement, for example, frequently leads to employment and resource competition, potentially contributing to intergroup animosity and resentment by the host population (Intertect 1993). Factions that recruit and use IDPs to their advantage, or systematically try to disparage them, may intentionally or accidentally target the entire local population. Given a lack of adequate security protection, the host community may be at continual risk. Moreover, in city slums and labor poles and conceivably in host rural communities, the mixing of various identity groups can create a microcosm of the original conflict, replicating all the factors that can lead to localized violence (Cuny 1991). Thus, both the absence and the presence of displaced populations can contribute to instability at the community level.

Individuals

Displacement has a lasting effect on those individuals forced to flee. Languid refugee or IDP camp environments, for example, tend to decrease the level of self-reliance and grow what refugee scholar Harto Hakovirta describes as "DP apathy": the feelings of alienation and physical deprivation bred from dependence on free food and services common in camp settings (Hakovirta 1986:35). Livelihood skills and personal resources may also be casualties of displacement, and their loss may contribute to an overall sense of indifference. Moreover, the introduction, in some cases, and the rise, in others, of the antisocial behavior discussed above can change the dynamics of society. As a result of indolence on the one hand, and unprincipled conduct on the other, moral and personal ethics tend to decline, leading to reduced self-respect and resourcefulness. In Cambodia, for instance, boredom, indifference, and the lack of structured activities cultivated such practices as gambling, prostitution, illegal videos, and alcoholism, contributed to mental illness, and reduced refugees' abilities to make decisions (Rogge 1992).

Findings from the ISSVR study, however, emphasized another side of the refugee experience of asylum. They found that, given the frequently long duration in relative isolation, their difficult predicament, and the lack of contending influences in their closed environment, refugees were inclined to coalesce into politically organized communities and often supported activists' struggle for economic or social change. Those who disagreed with the political opinions and values expressed by leaders were more likely to separate from the rest and possibly repatriate (Larkin, Cuny, and Stein 1991).

The ISSVR study further observed that the experience of living in close quarters for extended periods of time with others tended to unify refugees' needs. The case studies indicated that the adversity in the camps engendered a willingness to subordinate certain individual rights for the greater needs of the community. Interestingly, upon repatriation, the refugees held on to this attitude, continuing to view unity as necessary for survival (Cuny, Stein, and Reed 1992).

As we have seen, then, the experience of uprootedness can have a profound and enduring influence on personal perceptions and attitudes. These powerful repercussions on the displaced persons as well as their community, country, and region lead to the quest for solutions. Given conditions of prolonged displacement, moreover, the potential for continued conflict and destruction of an integrated society demands serious attention. Though the complexity of the situation obviates simple answers, especially important is the possibility of widespread return home. The next chapter explores this possibility and its alternatives, the difficulties in achieving it, and the repercussions when it does occur.

CHAPTER FOUR **THE PROCESS OF RETURNING HOME**

Today, most voluntary repatriations occur during conflict, without a decisive political event such as national independence, without any change in the regime or the conditions that originally caused flight . . . frequently without an amnesty or a repatriation agreement or program, without the permission of the authorities in either the country of asylum or of origin, without international knowledge or assistance, and without an end to the conflict that caused the exodus.

—Barry Stein and Frederick Cuny (1991:2–3)

In the postconflict environment, the viability of remaining in exile for refugees and IDPs diminishes with time. By most measures, prolonged asylum is both undesirable and increasingly unsustainable. Camp establishments, by definition, are temporary structures meant to fulfill emergency needs when individual lives are threatened. Other settings, such as garrison towns and extended family residences also offer only temporary refuge; only urban migrants seem to acquire a semipermanent status. Thus, when the exodus abates and conditions in exile are no longer attractive, both the displaced populations and relief communities begin to search for the appropriate next step.

An obvious option is to return to the place of origin. In reality, however, the transition in the home country from persecution to peaceful coexistence is neither rapid, guaranteed, nor smooth. Returning home, therefore, is not necessarily the clear choice. Many choose instead to remain in place, others move to yet another asylum, and some do indeed repatriate. For those who do return, the reintegration process poses many difficulties. Research and field observation reveal that returnees face not only financial challenges and struggles to reestablish living quarters, occupations, and relationships but also the potential of targeted oppression (Stein 1991; Zinser 1991b). At the same time, the receiving communities confront increased contention, competition, and uncertainty.

These difficulties, however, can be ameliorated by experience of cooperative reconstruction, renewed friendship, and commitment to mutual aid. Still, the original issues of conflict invariably lurk beneath the surface, ready to undermine rehabilitation and development activities to the point of social disruption and renewed violence.

Understanding the motivations for and the process of return helps illuminate the issues facing both the returnees and the community to which they return. The return phase can thus become a deciding point in the greater picture of societal reintegration and rehabilitation. This chapter examines the options facing uprooted populations, the patterns of return, the returnees' decision-making processes, and issues involved in reintegration into the home community.

Alternatives to Displacement

Continued temporary exile is widely and understandably considered undesirable. With a few exceptions, the host countries and communities, the home government, the international community, and the uprooted people themselves all view displacement as disruptive and negative, "not only because of the cost and burden on host countries and the international community, as well as the waste of the refugees' lives, but also because in their second, third and fourth generation refugees can become a violent and destabilizing social element," write Stein and Cuny (1991:2).

Despite these problems, however, many refugees and IDPs do choose to remain in long-term temporary asylum. At some point, temporary asylum fades into semipermanence, muting the distinction between sanctuary and resettlement, particularly among IDPs. Some situations remain unresolved for years, as is the case of many Tibetans who fled to India in 1959. In recent decades, periods of refuge have extended into generations, exemplified by the celebrated case of nearly 350,000 Palestinians who have been living in asylum in Lebanon since 1948 (USCR 1996:120).

By virtue of their international status, refugee situations receive special consideration. Unfortunately, while the problem is compounded with each new refugee flow, the conventional answers are becoming less and less plausible. The three classic durable solutions for refugees—third-country resettlement, permanent residence in the country of first asylum, and voluntary repatriation—each presuppose the refugees' full synthesis into the society in which they ultimately settle. Recent history, however, shows that first and third countries of asylum are increasingly reluctant to assimilate refugees, and home countries are also often resistant to repatriation. Still, these alternatives remain the most considered options available.

Third-country Resettlement

Recent analysis from around the globe indicates that widespread third-country resettlement is perhaps the least viable option of the three, given the increase in worldwide xenophobia and a conceivable trend toward cultural segregation. The decreasing acceptance of immigrants appears to stem in part from domestic economic pressures, fear of social instability, and the disappearance of Cold War political and ideological motives to welcome refugees from socialist states in Western countries. In reality, however, permanent refugee asylum in industrialized nations has never been equitable or necessarily generous. In the United States, for example, between 1980 and 1988, refugee admittance dropped by two thirds while the world's refugee population nearly tripled in the decade preceding 1988. Of those admitted during that period, 93 percent were from ten countries, all but one of which were communist (Loescher 1993:102, 153).

In the last few years, European countries have also tightened control over immigration and shown less tolerance of third-world foreigners. Germany, for example, enacted a new asylum law in 1993 that reduced the number of asylum applications by 60 percent, indicating a shift away from its previous universal acceptance of asylum seekers (USCR 1995:142). Legal scholars such as James Hathaway charge that industrialized nations have developed ever more sophisticated methodologies "to prevent refugee flows from challenging their sovereign authority over immigration." "Governments increasingly deal with refugees on a harsh and unregulated basis," he claims, "because they see international refugee law's mechanism to reconcile state interest to refugee interest as an anachronism" (1996:16). Many countries rely on improved border-control technologies and other *non-entrée* mechanisms to prevent immigrants from entering the country. This avoids the international legal obligation to assist refugees and thwarts increasing claims of refugee status, according to Hathaway. Studies show, however, that despite these discouraging odds, many long-term refugees will remain in camps with the hope of eventually receiving refugee status in a Western state.

Residence in the Host Country

Permanent settlement in countries of first asylum is becoming less feasible as well. According to Loescher (1993), the more restrictive Western immigration policies have had a corresponding effect on the willingness of third world nations to grant exile. Host countries seem to be growing increasingly weary of the problems inherent in accommodating a large refugee population. In Guinea, serving as the long-term host for Liberian and Sierra Leonean refugees has threatened the fragile harmony among regions within its own territory. Offering refugees permanent status might further erode what internal cohesion exists.

Even when stability is not the issue, allocating large tracts of land to foreigners and providing them with housing and other amenities near citizens with lower living standards is politically controversial and injudicious. Moving refugees from a refugee camp to an independent, self-sufficient setting, moreover, is extremely costly. Donors are confronting the needs of the large numbers of refugees around the world, while simultaneously examining their own domestic resources more critically. They appear to be increasingly reluctant to expend the substantial sums needed for permanent resettlement of large populations.

There is abundant evidence that, despite the lack of an official process, many long-term refugees slowly assimilate into the life of the host country, finding employment and even becoming illicit landowners, though never obtaining citizenship, as in the case of many Afghan refugees in Pakistan (Sorenson 1992; USCR 1995). Children born to such refugees may never know their homeland and may feel greater affinity with the host culture than with their parents.'

These first two solutions may, therefore, be more attractive in theory than in practice. As of 1991, less than 1 percent of the world's refugees had resettled officially in first or third countries of asylum, according to the ISSVR study (Stein and Cuny 1991:2). Given current international conditions, it is likely that figure is even smaller today. That leaves the final option: voluntary repatriation.

Voluntary Repatriation

While returning to the place of origin is the optimal and common solution, it is also technically the most difficult to implement for two reasons. The first is the limited resources and attention span of the international community. Beyond the usual immediate expenditures for transportation home and a minimum of material aid, successful reintegration requires long-term physical reconstruction, political, economic, and social rehabilitation, rebuilding community networks, restoring sources of livelihood, and (re)establishing the rule of law. This demands a lengthy commitment, which does not come easily to most relief organizations. My experience has been that it is at this critical but anticlimactic juncture in the rehabilitation of war-ravaged populations that international aid provision traditionally diminishes, both in terms of security protection and assistance. Ironically, refugees remaining in camps in a comparatively low-risk environment on the other side of a border usually maintain the full complement of international assistance, including protection and material aid. It is when they attempt to rectify their situation by returning home that they face the greatest personal risk and lose their international advocacy. Though conditions in violence-torn communities have always warranted transition assistance, the abundance of such situations around the world has illuminated this gap in the relief-to-development continuum especially clearly. Because of the social disintegration that accompanies violent conflict, it is at this juncture that support in the form of reintegration and rehabilitation assistance is vital to developing long-lasting stability. Tajikistan offers an example of where such assistance was more forthcoming. NGOs and UNHCR provided relatively extensive on-site aid to returnees in the form of protection, housing reconstruction projects, quick impact projects (QIPs) aimed at immediate local economic gain, and other revitalization programs.

The second reason why repatriation is the most difficult durable solution comes from the refugees themselves. They may simply be unwilling to return home. Studies show that for reasons of politics, economics, intimidation, entrenchment, indolence, and/or security, many refugees prefer to remain in camps. According to the U.S. Committee for Refugees, of the 15.3 million refugees in the world in 1995, less than one million repatriated[1] "voluntarily" and at least 303,000 were expelled from their place of asylum (USCR 1996:4, 7).[2]

Whether reasonable or unsound, international law upholds the right of refugees to remain in asylum until such time as they choose to return (UN General Assembly 1951). Although forced repatriation by host countries or other authorities is strictly prohibited under international law, the interpretation of *refoulement*—forced repatriation—is fiercely debated. From a practical standpoint, the notion of "voluntary" return may be a misnomer since persuasion, encouragement, incentives, and pressure in one form or another have all been used to promote repatriation in the past. Research shows that even in refugee-induced returns, intense peer pressure, coercion, internal intimidation, or conflict in places of asylum can compel refugees to return against their better judgment or will (Cuny, Stein, and Reed 1992). The 1996 return of over 700,000 and 500,000 refugees from Zaire/Congo and Tanzania respectively to Rwanda, for example, raised many questions about its true voluntary nature. In any case, if the refugee population is not disposed to return, voluntary repatriation will not occur under the legal definition.

Although repatriation is considered the optimal solution to displacement, it has, ironically, received the least amount of scholarly inquiry. The bulk of the literature on the larger issue of population migration, moreover, has focused primarily on legal and institutional aspects, and the social implications have only recently begun to gain much intellectual attention. As a result, many of these issues—prolonged asylum, internal displacement, refugee warriors, intimidation factors, the role of rumors and indigenous communication networks, the reintegration process, and the social implications of displacement—remain largely misunderstood. This void leaves international organizations with few guidelines for aiding the transition toward viable, integrated community development.

Though the options facing internally displaced persons are the subject of even less solid academic research, I think certain deductions can be made simply from field observation. The majority of IDPs appear to have four basic choices in responding to their predicament of temporary asylum. First, with the exception of those in camps, they can remain permanently in their place of refuge. A prerequisite for abiding residency, however, is an adequate source of income, which is often difficult to secure under such circumstances. IDPs living in camps rarely have the option of such permanence. Historically, internal camps, by virtue of their assumed transient nature, perceived threat to domestic security, and inadequate resources, are generally disbanded rapidly. Thus, IDPs in camps must resort to the second, third, or fourth alternative.

The second option is to flee across an international border and become a refugee, thereby becoming eligible to receive protection and assistance and face the same choices outlined above. Third, displaced persons in one area can flee to another. Because this destination is often the capital city (as we have seen in chapter 3), it is usually a one-way excursion, and few return home permanently. Finally, IDPs, like refugees, can decide to return to their place of origin. Since they are closer to the source, as mentioned earlier, they often have better and more accurate information on the conditions in their home communities. This makes them better able to judge the appropriate timing and circumstances for return.

These simplified scenarios demonstrate certain observable patterns. Each situation of displacement obviously presents unique conditions and obstacles. A closer look at some of the more common aspects of the final option—return—helps illuminate some of the issues at stake.

Common Patterns of Return

In virtually every situation, the vast majority of forced migrants, whether long- or short-term, crisis-induced or precautionary, internally displaced or refugees, state emphatically that they wish to return home. Although huge portions, particularly of IDPs, remain uprooted for extended periods of time, a significant number do eventually make their way back home. According to Cuny's study of migration phases, those most prone to leave are city dwellers, such as professionals, teachers, business owners, and government officials (assuming they still hold an office). Also highly likely to return are migrants residing near the edge of the conflict, since their proximity allows them better information on community conditions and opportunities for a safe return. Similarly, agriculturists will return to farm their land and prevent others from taking it (Cuny 1991).

A major finding of the ISSVR study mentioned in chapter 3 is that most returns occur while the conflict is still in progress, not after peace has been established, as had been commonly thought (Stein and Cuny 1991; Stein and Cuny 1992). As a result, many returnees face formidable risks, especially since they can expect little international protection once they are in the home country. Continued conflicts in El Salvador, Sudan, and Cambodia, for example, did not deter repatriation. They did, however, make it impossible for some refugees to go all the way home, relegating them to displacement within their own country (Fagen and Eldridge 1991; Hogan 1992; Vieira de Mello 1993).

Return occurs in a wide range of contexts with different degrees of internal violence: from fundamental political change (including victory), at one extreme, on to basic political settlement, to a divided country with areas of relative calm, to ongoing, low-level, or sporadic violence, to an unmitigated conflict zone at the other extreme (Stein 1991). Presumably, the closer to the former, the greater the potential for major repatriation (Cuny and Cuny 1992). National elections or a change in state apparatus, for example, precipitated the eventual mass returns in South Africa, El Salvador, Cambodia, Mozambique, Ethiopia, and Nicaragua. Nevertheless, closer to the other end of the spectrum, many internally displaced persons and 200,000 Somali refugees returned home despite the dim prospects for long-term peace in Somalia (Sommer 1994b).

Another example of repatriation under conflict is the case of Afghanistan. Half of the refugees living in Pakistan repatriated following the Soviet withdrawal from Afghanistan, despite a lack of political structure. Continued violence forced many more to flee their homes, yet again they returned in large numbers, although there was still no political solution (Sorenson 1992). By the end of 1995, nearly three million Afghans were uprooted. During that same year of ruthless fighting, 347,000 repatriated from Iran and Pakistan, and more than 187,000 displaced persons returned to the capital only to find themselves, yet again, in the midst of violence (USCR 1996:94). Barry Stein suggests that one reason why refugees repatriate under grave danger is a general change in attitude. Their experience of being collective social outcasts, Stein offers, makes them more aggressive and willing to take risks and hence return to a conflict zone (Stein 1991).

While each culture, conflict, and asylum is ultimately unique, it is possible to make several generalizations about patterns of return. The ISSVR study found five distinct patterns that seem to fit the common experience of return. (I make assumptions about the parallels between the refugee situation and internal displacement, using my own experience as a guide where research on the latter is wanting.) Ricochet return is the first type of return, which begins almost immediately after the exodus. Ricochet repatriation, according to the ISSVR study, occurs in nearly every crisis-induced migration, when those who fled out of the panic and chaos of the moment, but did not feel particularly threatened or fell into disagreement with their fellow refugees, promptly return home. One exception to this pattern is the exodus of Sri Lankan refugees to India, which did not induce any immediate rebound (Cuny and Cuny 1992). Ricochet returnees may have crossed an international boundary or simply fled to the nearest sanctuary before they reversed their decision.

The second pattern is relocation-stimulated return, which occurs among those not immediately attached to a camp, but living independently along the border or in regions inside the home country. This takes place when host country officials attempt to relocate these refugees into camps or, similarly, when the home government tries to round up IDPs and place them in a designated zone. Facing relocation, many will decide to return home instead, according to the ISSVR study (Stein and Cuny 1991).

Community and alienation are the roots of the third pattern, which occurs as the "space" for return gradually increases. The ISSVR study indicates that this type of return may be triggered by a decrease in intensity of the conflict in the home territory, improvement in the political or economic situation, or a more porous border and easier internal access, allowing cross-border trade and emissary missions to scout the homeland for return potential (Stein and Cuny 1991). Experience shows that refugees will, when feasible, carefully watch the actions of IDPs. When they see internal movement, the more peripheral members of the refugee community, in particular, will begin to repatriate. In El Salvador, for instance, the return of 600,000 IDPs precipitated three years of refugee repatriation (Fagen 1993).

Since any attrition among the exiled population undermines the political and moral authority of the exile elite, refugee and IDP leaders and others who benefit from asylum may try to obstruct any return (Zolberg, Suhrke, and Aguayo 1989). They may use verbal intimidation, physical threats and actual abuse, misinformation campaigns and rumors, or planted evidence of the dire consequences of return. I have also seen refugee warriors go back to the homeland for the express purpose of carrying out threats against those who have returned, or use repatriation as a cover to instigate subversive activities inside the country of origin. Both of these occurred frequently during the two years Rwandan refugees were in eastern Zaire (Kumar et al. 1996).

The fourth mode of return is secondary relocation-stimulated repatriation, which occurs when the host government proposes to relocate the camps away from the border, or the home government once again attempts to collect the displaced and relocate them to specified areas. As in relocation-stimulated return, many refugees and IDPs may decide to return home rather than move elsewhere. Such measures often signal the beginning of the disintegration of strong refugee cohesion, opening the space for further repatriations (Stein and Cuny 1991).

Historically, these patterns of return have tended to be relatively quiet, often with the intention of concealing the process and previous absence both from camp and home authorities. Nevertheless, UNHCR, the International Organization for Migration (IOM), and NGOs may offer transportation and material packages consisting of bulk food, blankets, cooking and cleaning utensils, agricultural tools, and plastic sheeting. The aid is meant both to assist those who need it and to provide added incentive to return. According to Stein, however, the majority of returnees are not likely to take advantage of external aid, preferring to remain anonymous and avoid public exposure (Stein 1991). Their reluctance, especially initially, may be in part because such international assistance is usually accompanied by a processing procedure that involves identification and registration. Under such circumstances, the return migration may be perceived as more risky and traumatic than the exodus. Because most such returns occur without significant international assistance and under difficult conditions, many returnees arrive home in dire physical condition, according to Stein and Cuny (1992).

The ISSVR study's last category of repatriation is a major return, such as those that occurred in Namibia and Cambodia. These large-scale refugee repatriations are generally marked by the heavy involvement of UNHCR and other international agencies and may accompany a peace settlement of sorts. In addition to the assistance mentioned above, in a major return international agencies plan the repatriation operation, coordinate the logistics, and facilitate the initial resettlement. An exception was the massive "spontaneous" return of Rwandans from Zaire and Tanzania in October and November 1996, which was unplanned by international agencies, though aided to some extent. Though rare and on a smaller scale, recent international efforts have also assisted major returns of IDPs in Rwanda, Bosnia, and Iraq. Still, in both types of migration, actual transition assistance at home has generally proved to be short-lived, lasting only long enough for basic reconstruction (Kumar et al. 1996; Stein 1991).

International experience over many years has shown that in all patterns of return, the decision involves multiple factors and complex reasoning, which contribute to or inhibit the will to go home. Presumably, the stress inherent in making such a critical judgment puts a tremendous burden on the head of household, particularly when the decision contradicts the will of the refugee or IDP leaders.

Deciding to Go Home: Variables Affecting the Decision

Many elements influence the decision of refugees and IDPs to return. Considerations include the state of the home community (such as conditions of houses, water systems and the like), land ownership, degree of insecurity, length of time in displacement, income-generation opportunities in the home community, location of family and identity group members, and the judgment and influence of community leaders. Each migration home is unique. Generally speaking, however, the foremost concern is protection and security, followed by economic considerations, both of which are affected by the available information and the length of time in exile (Deng 1993; Stein 1991; Stein and Cuny 1991).

Security

Most experts agree that, particularly in the initial stages, safety takes precedence over material considerations (Ruiz 1993; Zinser 1991b; Zolberg, Suhrke, and Aguayo 1989). In this early phase, displaced persons move cautiously and stay within familiar territory. Because many are adverse to moving further into unknown environs, secondary relocation often results. For them, the option to assume preestablished social identities with understood rights and obligations offers greater stability and control over their lives than does remaining in precarious circumstances with undetermined consequences (Stein and Cuny 1992).

Experience also reveals that uprooted populations frequently fear registering in camps or applying for assistance upon return. They often believe that the list of beneficiaries will circulate among government forces or insurgent groups and associate them with a specific faction, possibly putting their lives in jeopardy. In Guatemala, returnees avoided official channels in order to reduce military control over their location and material assistance (Zinser 1991a). International agencies in Rwanda sometimes had difficulty locating those in need, for the very reason that they wished to remain anonymous rather than make themselves and their needs known.

Another concern of returnees, emphasized especially in Fred Cuny's work, is being recruited by insurgents to participate in the struggle. Many Sri Lankan refugees repatriated from India out of fear of conscription by the factions that controlled the camps. When they arrived home at one point, however, they became targets for terrorist attacks and were unprotected by the mandate of UNHCR (Cuny and Cuny 1992). Opposing ethnic groups in Sudan similarly raided IDP camps, ostensibly in an effort to increase ethnic tensions and the sense of insecurity (Zolberg, Suhrke, and Aguayo 1989). Conversely, experience shows that some may take advantage of a massive return to gain leverage in the fight and intentionally increase insecurity. Refugee warriors, for example, may repatriate with others in order to instigate subversive activities, thereby creating greater apprehension at home (Zolberg, Suhrke, and Aguayo 1989). Large numbers of such antagonists were said to have returned in the massive repatriation to Rwanda in the fall of 1996, causing serious security concerns.

Such fears of personally targeted violence and association with certain groups have often proven to be well-founded, particularly in the context of identity conflicts. In Cambodia, for instance, despite its public appeal for repatriation, the home government reportedly encouraged locals to view returnees with suspicion, though outwardly welcoming their arrival (Rogge 1992). In El Salvador, returnees protested what they characterized as a "campaign of systematic harassment by the military" (Fagen and Eldridge 1991:170).

Another security issue that has received a great deal of global attention is the threat of land mines. In Cambodia and Afghanistan, arguably the two most heavily mined countries in the world, refugees and IDPs alike fear to return home because of the indiscriminate and widespread mining. Out of populations of 8 million and 12 million, Cambodia and Afghanistan have 25,000 and 20,000–30,000 amputees respectively, as a result of land mine injuries (Jean 1995:105). In countries subjected to extensive violence, whole regions have often been rendered uninhabitable by mines, which requires enormous resources, energy, and time to clear.

In addition, in the decision to return, each refugee and IDP has considerations based on his or her involvement in the conflict. I witnessed the great power such concerns had on Rwandan refugees, large numbers of whom chose to flee further into eastern Zaire rather than repatriate when their camps were dispersed in the fall of 1996. For some, returning meant risking individual retaliation or arrest and legal persecution, whether merited or not. I spoke with one woman who lived in the Kibeho IDP camp, six kilometers from her home community, about her fear of returning. During the genocide she had killed a man at the threat of being killed herself. Though her desire to return was strong, her trepidation was obvious, not knowing whether she would find arrest or other possible reprisal awaiting her at home.

Culpability is not necessarily a simple issue. Different degrees of latitude may be appropriate for the various types of involvement. Those who committed crimes under threat of death, for example, might deserve a different judgment from those who aided the participants but did not commit crimes themselves, or from those who are related to or closely associated with known criminals. For this reason, the existence of an operating judicial system might either deter or encourage repatriation, depending on the level of individual culpability, among other factors. Publicized arrest procedures and established legal means of reclaiming property, for example, might promote the return of those who fear arbitrary arrest and disputes over land, while deterring the return of those heavily involved in the fighting and therefore legitimately at risk of imprisonment. Under such conditions of nebulous security, unknown intentions of adversaries, and unclear judicial policy, personal protection becomes the critical factor in the decision to return. Because most repatriations occur in small numbers and under conditions of conflict (Larkin, Cuny, and Stein 1991; Zinser 1991b), each family and individual must weigh the security risks at their destination location against the benefits of return.

Over the years, we have found that when the state of security and other determinants appear to permit relocation, IDPs, who are the best informed about local variables, will begin to return, and refugees—particularly those from the same area—will follow. Assuming these initial moves occur in relative calm and are reasonably well-received, others in exile will take it as an indication of relative local security and will join the movement (Zinser 1991b). The process of return thus builds on itself. The momentum often continues unless or until serious security violations reintroduce overwhelming anxiety. In Tajikistan, for example, almost half the exiled population had repatriated when cross-border fighting broke out and abruptly suspended the return migration (Maynard 1993).

Many factors influence the security of returnees, not the least of which is third-party protection. The existence of a substantial international presence has served to avert major human rights abuses in the past (Fagen and Eldridge 1991). The lack of such a consistent presence in many parts of Kosovo presumably had an encouraging effect on violations against Kosovars in the summer of 1998. At the same time, strong community ties and local identity-group presence contributes to a sense of guardianship, presumably adding to the attractiveness of the return option (Zinser 1991b).

Economic Considerations

The ISSVR study concludes that, after security, the next most important factor in the choice to return is personal material resources and economic welfare. Refugees and IDPs may repatriate for the express purpose of regaining proprietorship over income-generating sources (Zinser 1991a; Zinser 1991b). Field experience shows that reestablishing businesses, planting crops, or reclaiming professional occupations are high priorities in the minds of most uprooted persons. They seek semisustainable opportunities that will provide adequate subsistence for the entire family. Given the notoriously inadequate employment options in refugee situations and the intense competition for jobs in areas supporting internally displaced persons, the pull of potential return to previous occupations can be strong. For example, the lack of job opportunities in India equal to those they had left impelled many self-settled Sri Lankan refugees to repatriate (Cuny and Cuny 1992).

Several factors relating to material welfare play roles in the decision-making process. First, knowledge of conditions affecting displaced persons' former source of livelihood, whether a factory, store, government office, herd of animals, fishing boat, or parcel of land, influences their sense of potential for renewed employment. If their shop was located in a section of the city that has been razed, for instance, or their land has been occupied by others, the pull of potential income generation will be weak.

Second, new skills learned while in asylum offer possible fresh opportunities in the country of origin. Some trades, in particular, are better plied in certain areas than in others and may add to the probability of relocation within the home country. Newly trained electricians, for example, are likely to find more work in a city than in the countryside, while health workers may gravitate toward provincial hospitals. More insidious forms of income generation pull participants into particular, often sordid, corners of the home country (Rogge 1992). Drug trading, for instance, is more likely to take place near the borders, in and around financial centers, and near transportation hubs such as ports, airports, or trucking routes. Third, changes in the political and economic fronts at home may offer new opportunity for gain. Aspiring entrepreneurs may take advantage of the lack of competition and high demand for products. In the aftermath of significant destruction in a complex emergency and during the reconstruction phase, it is common to see enterprising individuals peddling building materials and repair services.

Some ambitious or well-placed individuals may also consider the opportunity for employment in a new government, should one have emerged from the turmoil. The potential for active participation in deciding national or local issues, as well as aspirations for personal power, may spur the return of aspiring politicians. In Guinea, I spoke with several young refugee men for whom this was a serious factor in their decision to return to Liberia. Many Ethiopians have returned with the promise of new opportunities with the new government. Conversely, those directly opposed to the new rulers have little political employment incentive to return and may even leave.

Finally, personal assets and resources influence a family's decision. Those who possess large amounts of material goods in exile, whether acquired while away or taken from the place of origin, are likely to consider the transportability, security, salability, and value of the commodities at the various locations (Intertect 1993). Those who left behind substantial resources while fleeing, particularly houses, are likely to consider returning sooner in hopes of recovering their possessions.

Displaced populations may also have economic disincentives to return, as is the case with many Afghan refugees living in Pakistan, according to John Sorenson, a contributor to the ISSVR study. Some work in trades, providing manual labor or transportation, while others are involved in drug and arms smuggling or profiteering from diverted relief aid. As a result, many refugees accrue much larger incomes than they would were they to return home. This is not the case for all Afghan refugees, and those who profit least from the economic opportunities are presumably more likely to repatriate (Sorenson 1992). Experience shows that large debts accrued while in exile further inhibit return until enough funds can be earned to both pay the amount due and cover the expense of relocating (Larkin, Cuny, and Stein 1991). This can be a formidable task, given the difficult employment environment in places of refuge.

Material Assistance

External assistance also influences the decision to return, although, according to the ISSVR study, it plays a much less significant role than is commonly thought (Zinser 1991b). UNHCR guidelines insist that four conditions must be fulfilled before it will support refugee repatriation: the conflict that spawned the flight must have diminished substantially; a tripartite agreement must be established among UNHCR, the host country, and the country of origin; the return must take place in safety and dignity; and the repatriation must be voluntary. These stipulations call for ideal conditions for repatriation, which, in reality, are rarely met. Were it to adhere strictly to these guidelines, UNHCR would be limited in its participation in the return process (Stein and Cuny 1991). In addition, the ISSVR study found that return is a purely self-regulating process, in which the returnees are in complete command as the decision-makers. The study contends that the timing and conditions under which repatriation occurs have surprisingly little to do with international efforts, but are based solely on the displaced population's perception of their situation in exile and the conditions at home (Stein and Cuny 1992:16–17).

The international community has traditionally used the terms *unorganized* or *spontaneous* in reference to refugee repatriations not directed, assisted, or managed by international agencies. These words imply an image of unplanned, haphazard, and perhaps unruly events. Such returns, however, are not necessarily disorganized or even unassisted. Research shows that refugees themselves may facilitate the process, or be aided by guerrilla forces or even host governments, as happened in the repatriation organized for Cambodian refugees by the Thai government in 1980.[3]

According to the ISSVR study, the vast majority of refugee repatriations and virtually all returns of internally displaced persons take place "spontaneously." Over 90 percent of the seven million refugees who repatriated between 1975 and 1991 returned without significant international aid and in a nonorganized fashion (Stein and Cuny 1992:25). In Guatemala, for example, the refugees themselves negotiated an agreement with their home government that assured their collective return to self-chosen areas and guaranteed government security, access to land, and exemption from conscription for three years (Guatemala Partners n.d.).

Information

Each return is predicated on incoming information. Especially in refugee camps, the decision to return may be complicated by a lack of adequate and accurate information on conditions at home or the larger political situation (Zinser 1991b). In Afghanistan, for example, refugees were ignorant about which *mujahedin* groups controlled their home regions and about the movement of government troops. In contrast, Mozambican refugees had detailed knowledge about their home areas, but they lacked information on political developments, including the protocol allowing safe return of refugees (Norwegian Refugee Council 1992).

Some international observers, as mentioned above, dispute this assessment and claim that refugees are connected to extensive verbal networks that provide accurate and efficient information about site-specific details. Aldolfo Zinser, a participant in the ISSVR study, claims that Guatemalans had particularly good communication across the border, in part because they were not totally isolated and were able to use local languages and ancient forms of communication to stay informed (Zinser 1991a). The experience of others, including myself, however, has been that, in general, refugees' isolation removes them from the source and makes it difficult for them to ascertain the accuracy of reports. Their vulnerability also makes them an easy target for manipulation from both sides of the border, as I've witnessed in various camp settings.

As we have seen, displaced populations may be exposed to intimidation in camps, disinformation campaigns, coercion, and peer and leadership pressure. In Cambodia, for example, a refugee study indicated that only a small percentage of the population had any direct or recent communication with relatives in the homeland. At the same time, the camps were inundated with political propaganda, reducing the probability of a realistic view of conditions at home (Rogge 1992). Each refugee situation is affected by different conditions, offering some more direct, reliable information than others. Most experts agree that internally displaced persons, by virtue of their proximity, have the advantage over refugees in this regard, having access to more avenues and direct lines of communication. This enables them to better determine the hazards and benefits of return and take advantage of a lull in the conflict to go home. In Sudan, for instance, IDPs exchanged information all along the migration route about current government relocation policies, drought-affected areas, economic conditions, labor markets, and the location of other displaced populations. Because of this communication network, they were able to determine the appropriate timing of their movements, the composition and size of the returning groups, transportation, stopover points and destination, as well as the security risks en route, and the conditions and prospects at the destination point (Hogan 1992).

Length of Time in Exile

The amount of time spent in exile also appears to have significant effect on the return decision-making process. First, as time passes, uprooted populations are more prone to take risks, particularly if conditions in the host country or place of asylum deteriorate (Stein and Cuny 1992:19). Prolonged asylum under difficult living conditions commonly leads refugees to request formal repatriation assistance from the host, home, and international communities.

Second, economic concerns and job opportunities appear to take on a higher priority the longer the time in exile. Extended periods of refuge afford greater time to acquire new skills, and displaced persons become anxious to begin profiting from them (Zinser 1991b:204). Because farmers and business owners, in particular, fear eventual loss of previously owned skills and enterprises, they may have greater resolve to return and salvage their trade. Lifestyle habituation, a third potential consequence of long-term exile, may also discourage the return home (Stein 1991). While in asylum, refugees become accustomed to certain standards of living, benefits and services. If these constitute an improvement over previous standards, they may be difficult to reach upon return to the homeland. Assistance provided to returnees by home government and relief and development agencies is generally insubstantial compared to that of refugee camps. Those long-absent from their rural roots, therefore, may understandably be reluctant to return to areas that offer few of the services to which they have become accustomed, such as utilities, education, and health care. In contrast to the poverty, illiteracy, and disease they experienced in Afghanistan before leaving, for example, many Afghans enjoy substantially higher living standards and basic services in Pakistan, in part as a result of the relatively lucrative employment opportunities (Sorenson 1992). Consequently, Afghan refugees—perhaps 15 percent of whom were born in the densely populated camps in Pakistan—are not inclined to repopulate remote rural areas to pursue agriculture, something to which the young people have hardly been exposed (Sorenson 1992). The large number of widowed and female heads of households may also have difficulty repatriating to an agricultural way of life, particularly if they are inexperienced or have lost their skills during the long absence.

The literature indicates that after long-term exile and the ensuing change in ability, attitude, and lifestyle, many refugees will choose to return not to their home of origin, but to the capital city. Those with newfound skills will attempt to compete with urban professionals, frequently adding to intergroup tension (Intertect 1993). Those without a legitimate vocation will likely remain at the outskirts of urban society, often continuing antisocial activities learned in camp, such as gambling, prostitution, drug dealing, and product smuggling. In Cambodia, the young, usually male, refugees who learned a trade while in the camps, or were involved in the camp's antisocial underworld and thus developed street smarts, were the most likely to return to urban areas, along with demobilized soldiers. In contrast, adult males with small families who were at least somewhat educated and were cognizant of the situation at home, yet not aligned with any political faction, were the most likely to return to their former agricultural lifestyle (Rogge 1992).

In another example, the long-term asylum of Guatemalan refugees in southern Mexico had notable repercussions on refugee attitudes that eventually served to facilitate their repatriation. While in exile for ten years, the refugees developed skills and training in organizing, health care, education, literacy, problem-solving, leadership, trades, human rights, and political awareness. The women in particular assumed larger roles in the community, increased their wage-earning capacity, and became literate. This social development spawned a self-assuredness that led to a unique repatriation process, planned and carried out by the refugees themselves (Guatemala Partners n.d.).

Facing Reintegration

Considering the debilitating effect of violence on individuals and society as a whole, the reintegration of diverse groups is understandably a fragile and tentative process. Because identity conflicts and extensive human rights abuses sever cooperation and divide societies, they create a difficult environment in which to reintegrate. To complicate matters further, those repatriating from exile in another country may find huge portions of the local population internally uprooted. Many repatriating refugees may join others from their identity group elsewhere in the country rather than return to their home community (Zinser 1991b), thus exacerbating social chaos throughout the homeland.

In this state of disarray and confusion, the home government, the resident population, and the returnees all confront huge challenges. While each group has its own particular issues to confront, collectively they face the task of national reconstruction. Among the more daunting uncertainties is their own readiness and willingness to reintegrate.

Attitude

The experience of asylum can radically alter the individual and the collective sense of identity. This experience, as we have seen, can dramatically affect the attitudes, standards, and customs of exiled populations. As outlined in the findings from the ISSVR study, group priorities tend to supersede individual needs, whether communities seek refuge together and remain largely intact in exile or form a new group upon arrival. In El Salvador, for instance, this sense of subordination to the greater good continued following repatriation, with the understanding that unity was a prerequisite for survival. This attitude helped returnees maintain a sense of community, enabling them to persevere in an endless war zone. It also, however, set them apart from those members who had remained, creating another division in the community (Fagen and Eldridge 1991).

At the same time, corrupting influences encountered in exile can introduce new forces, values, and ethics that contribute to a breakdown of traditional society and ultimately diminish the potential for reintegration. In Cambodia, for instance, the traditional role of parents and the accompanying respect they received diminished when survival became preeminent and children resorted to petty theft, which was subsequently rewarded for its contribution to the family's resources (Rogge 1992).

Psychological problems also frequently result from long periods of asylum and lethargy. This can add to the dysfunctionality of individuals, general distrust, and lowered community spirit (Maynard 1997). In the end, uprooted populations returning to their home communities may have fundamentally different values and attitudes than those who remained.

Reception

The extent of welcome given to returnees appears to depend on a number of factors. Although the return can help alleviate residents' political fears of external insurgent movements from refugee and IDP camps, it brings with it a host of other potentially volatile problems, not the least of which are the roots of the original conflict. The fact that only 30,000 of the 350,000 Bosnians who had returned by the end of 1997 had gone back to areas in which they are the minority speaks directly to the issue of fear of hostile reception.

The return phase, however, can also represent a potential window of opportunity for reestablishing community cooperation and overcoming separatism. I have witnessed occasions during the early period of reintegration when both returnees and resident citizens seem strongly predisposed toward better relations. I credit this to the fact that fundamental to the displaced populations' decisions to return home is the perception that life will be better at the place of origin than in the place of asylum. Hence, often at great risk, some opt to move their families and their remaining belongings back to their home community. Under these conditions, they presumably are willing also to risk confrontation with their antagonists and are thus anxious for peaceful relations. At the same time, depending on the state of the conflict, the resident population in the communities may be suffering from lack of human resources for agricultural production, social services, commerce, and reconstruction. They may also be war-weary and, therefore, similarly disposed to overcoming mutual animosities. (Chapter 5 explores the state and attitude of the home community in more detail.) Under these conditions, I have seen home communities reach out in acceptance and welcome to homecoming members. On several occasions in Tajikistan and Rwanda, for instance, community members helped rebuild the houses of returnees and offered other gestures of goodwill.

Where conditions are adverse, however, due to substantial illegal occupation of houses, subsumed land or looted property, or if the source of the conflict still rages within the core of the local community, the return of displaced populations can exacerbate the hostilities. The intensely complex checkerboard-like situation in Bosnia, in which houses of one ethnic group are occupied by another because theirs, in turn, are also occupied, makes return not only physically difficult but socially and politically dangerous. Historically, in fact, there have been few warm receptions from the home government or population for returning citizens. In the repatriation of more than a million Africans between 1988 and 1991, only Burundi, Namibia, and Zimbabwe were at peace and openly welcomed returnees (Stein 1991:23). Cambodia serves as another example in which the government gave public support to the repatriation of its citizens (Vieira de Mello 1993).

Upon close examination, it appears that part of the uneasy relationship between returnees and those who remained is that the former are frequently viewed as traitors to the homeland or suspected of opposition involvement. Community, government, or military officials may thus bear tremendous hostility toward returnees, particularly in areas where the fighting continues (Zinser 1991b). Indeed, studies show that during their time in asylum, the political view of refugees, in particular, may move closer to the insurgent group, and subsequent returnees may have hidden agendas of bringing in arms, gathering support, or inciting revolt (Kumar et al. 1996; Zolberg, Suhrke, and Aguayo 1989). In this case, home country officials are justifiably suspicious of returnees.

As a result, returnees fear accusation—whether accurate or not—of association with subversive elements and consequent rejection, persecution, or continual dispute. In the case of Guatemala, for example, the military considered all refugees to be allies of the guerrillas and thus reportedly detained, harassed, "disappeared," or even killed some of those who returned (USCR 1995:178–79). For the same reason, refugees feared that by returning they might put their home village and even their ethnic group and culture in jeopardy of military attacks. In contrast, El Salvador and Cambodia committed themselves to progressive reintegration of refugees into the economic, political, and social development process (Fagen 1993; Fagen and Eldridge 1991; Vieira de Mello 1993). These two cases, unfortunately, are anomalies. The general rule appears to be that the longer one stays away, the more difficult the absence is to justify in the eyes of the resident population, and the more suspicion and contention exist upon return.

Returning refugees, moreover, often assume that their plight during the period they were gone was far worse than that of those who remained. In actuality, however, refugees generally fare better than others with the assistance and protection they receive from international agencies (Zinser 1991b). It is possible to understand how conflict could develop when refugees believe that their internationally recognized status makes them deserving of special compensation, and they fail to see the needs of those who remained, possibly under far worse conditions.

Economic Conditions

Whether the return process contributes to a restoration of normalcy or leads to further destabilization appears to be in part determined by the economic conditions of the receiving community. In areas where basic needs and living standards are met, the return of displaced populations seems to represent a welcome and vital ingredient to pacification. In these situations, land and property disputes are likely to be minimal, and the community may even assist the returnees in reintegrating and resettling. The other extreme occurs under conditions of intense competition for resources and employment and massive infrastructure damage. Communities struggling with a floundering economy and damaged traditional methods of livelihood are understandably more prone to harbor intergroup hostility and resort to scapegoating. Unfortunately, most contemporary returns occur under circumstances closer to the latter extreme than to the former.

Assistance

The fact that most returnees go back to impoverished communities, suffering from destroyed homes, lands, and livelihoods, tends to predispose them to depend on material assistance. This is particularly true during the transition phase but may continue for long periods thereafter (Stein 1991). In the case of Kosovo, because of the 70 percent unemployment among Albanian Kosovars, many residents were dependent on material aid even before the 1998 outbreak of violence and massive displacement. Because the domestic economy and government finances, not to mention internal political will, are often meager in the postconflict period, the majority of initial aid usually comes from international sources.

Sri Lanka, however, serves as a notable exception. The Sri Lankan government established an elaborate assistance program that benefited all those affected by the war, declaring all citizens loyalists unless proven otherwise. The aid included payments for injuries, lost property, and loss of income, as well as grants, in-kind donations, and loans. The government, moreover, offered assistance to spontaneous returnees in the form of cash, food, and material contributions for housing repairs. Unlike in most civil conflicts, the aid program became a major pull factor in the return process (Cuny and Cuny 1992).

The usual international assistance provided to returnees, particularly in major repatriations, offers initial material support in the form of food, agricultural tools, and household items. In contrast to NGOs, which may have somewhat longer aid programs, this is where UNHCR's mandate for the care of migrant populations normally ended and the responsibility of the state began again, at least until recently (UNHCR 1993a). In current conflicts, however, the lack of a viable government, the continued disarray of political and social affairs, and a devastated economy have left many returnees without means to make the transition to self-sufficiency. Consequently, UNHCR on an ad hoc basis has offered programs designed to aid returnees during this stage, including help in rebuilding livelihoods, homes, and community structures. In Tajikistan, UNHCR operated inside the country, establishing not only small economic revitalization projects but also protection (Maynard 1994). In Bosnia, it is involved in income-generation and reintegration projects. However, UNHCR's mandate, as Barry Stein points out, still officially only extends a small step beyond resettlement, leaving a significant gap in international agency assistance during the transition period in most cases (Stein 1991:17). Consequently, postemergency aid tends to be rare, usually short-lived and minimal, seldom spanning the period to actual self-reliance. History shows, moreover, that the transition period may be extended by dependence built up through long-term asylum in camps. The recent upsurge in international interest in postconflict rehabilitation, however, may bring new external resources and research to this critical period in the recovery process.[4]

Practitioners and scholars alike have begun to document the occurrence of increased intergroup hostilities resulting inadvertently from well-intentioned international assistance designed to reestablish peaceful homelands (Anderson 1994; Prendergast 1995). (Chapter 7 will discuss this phenomenon in more detail.) Government authorities, suspicious of or hostile toward returnees, for example, may try to control or disrupt the deliveries. In so doing, they may divert the supplies or request return payment or favors for them. On the other hand, as was the case in El Salvador, they may insist on delivering the goods themselves, possibly for the purpose of ascertaining the identity of each returnee for potential future harassment, or intercepting the goods for their own purposes (Fagen 1993; Fagen and Eldridge 1991). The community thus may be faced not only with returning homeless and resourceless members but accompanying unwanted attention from militia or military units. Their presence may then reignite hidden animosity or create new contention based on current problems. Community members, in addition, may be more likely to resort to force with the experience of violence so near the surface.

Recent scrutiny shows, furthermore, that targeted relief aid can create inequities between the beneficiaries and other members, leading to tension or further violence (Anderson 1994, 1995b). I have observed in places like Tajikistan, that it can also focus unwanted attention on the beneficiaries, such as returnees or women, making them potential targets of manipulation, isolation, coercion, or persecution. More fundamentally, aid intended only for returnees simply ignores the needs of the community as a whole and the most vulnerable elements in particular, potentially causing further deterioration in its overall well-being. The Cambodia repatriation illustrated the repercussions of such selective aid practices: when returning refugees who had benefited from international assistance reintegrated together with internally displaced persons who did not receive many services, tensions rose out of the disparities and led to intergroup violence (Deng 1993:105–106).

Property Rights

Communities that attempt to reintegrate returning members confront not only the original issues that divided them and the now divergent social values but a host of new problems as well. Land and property rights tend to be among the more volatile issues. Frequently in conflicts, agricultural parcels are severely damaged, made useless by the planting of land mines or, alternatively, taken over by others. The process of restoring rightful ownership or compensating for unusable tracts can be extremely contentious, and legal proceedings may be biased or nonexistent.

A multidonor evaluation of the Rwanda crisis, for example, found that two sets of returnees often laid claim to the same property. One of these groups was from the 1994 evacuation, while the other was from the exodus thirty-five years earlier. Although the government upheld the agreement that abrogated the right to claim property abandoned before 1982, animosity has grown out of the dispute (Kumar et al. 1996:88). Furthermore, some members of Rwanda's military occupied homes and refused to relinquish them to the returnees upon presentation of the appropriate papers. In the absence of an operational judicial system, claims have largely gone unheard officially and have been resolved only on an ad hoc basis. In Guatemala, the land exchanged hands from one set of refugees to a different set of returnees, which created an extremely delicate situation and impeded refugee return (Fagen 1993).

Ultimately, resolution of land problems—and thus significant incentive or disincentive to return—rests with the government of the country of origin. It may leave the disputes to the contenders (or even exacerbate the situation by confiscating more property), or it may intervene in buy-back schemes, land reform legislation, enforcement of equitable and strict legal regulations, transference of public lands, and the like. The contentious land issues in Rwanda, for instance, led the government to seek new options in public lands, national parks, and rangeland.

The Issues of Conflict

The bulk of research shows that, although repatriation and return are not contingent on a peace settlement, a substantial change in the conflict can radically affect the process (Stein and Cuny 1992; Zinser 1991b). Conceivably, then, addressing the basic causes of the exodus can favorably affect the return and, more fundamentally, create a positive atmosphere in which to begin reconstruction and rehabilitation. In addition, ensuring the accountability of both resident individuals and returnees for crimes committed during the strife could have a substantial pacifying effect on the population as a whole by providing a sense of justice.

Establishing peaceful conditions is undoubtedly a long, ambiguous, and intricate process. Peace efforts conducted at the leadership level often tend to be focused on the most tangible issues. As such, third parties approach the problem with the goal of achieving an agreement that will end the fighting but may disregard the historical matters, psychological issues, long-held animosities, and other complex elements, which at the grassroots level become extremely important. In discussions with Kosovars, for example, I found that Albanians understood the absolute need to arrest the fighting, but saw an exigency in addressing existing inequities in Kosovar society before all fighting could cease.

The society's ability to address its own issues is most likely severely damaged by the fighting. Understandably, returnees and receiving communities alike may be initially paralyzed by fear, unable to help themselves or to make efforts toward integration or development. In the throes or aftermath of identity conflict, the justice system may be collapsed, too weak to function, or extremely corrupt and partial. Moreover, the local structure for conflict management, whether it be elders' councils, community committees, tribal authority, or a conflict resolution designate, has also often disintegrated, leaving few traditional alternatives. These structures may have been inequitable or inadequate even before the onset of violence.

Under such conditions, opportunists can exploit the confusion, reaping the material and personal benefits of a weakened social order. Unjustified public accusation of criminal wrongdoing may result in the arrest or expulsion of an individual, leaving his or her property for the taking, as occurred in Rwanda and Guatemala (Kumar et al. 1996; Zinser 1991a). Without a bona fide judicial system, accusations and penalties for assumed participation have been left up to local authorities or individual action. This appears to be precisely one of the fears that inhibit return.

I strongly believe that the reintegration process is a determining point in the future of intergroup relations and country stability as a whole. As we have seen, both returnees and resident populations face tremendous challenges in reestablishing social, political, economic, and cultural interaction. Unfortunately, very little research to date has studied these situations, leaving much room for speculation. Precisely for this reason and because of my estimation of its importance, the next chapter will turn to the other side of the equation and explore the experience of the home community embroiled in armed violence.

CHAPTER FIVE **COMMUNITIES IN CONFLICT**

Unhealed severe trauma from any source destroys the unnoticed substructure of democracy, the cognitive and social capacities that enable a group of people to freely construct a cohesive narrative of their own future.

—Jonathan Shay (1994:181)

Although the ruinous effect of war has been documented since ancient Greek times, the plebeian and widespread nature of contemporary conflict necessitates renewed examination of its effect on the individual and community. Ironically, although international attention focuses first on refugees and second on internally displaced persons, the majority of war victims never leave their homes for any length of time. As yet, survivors in their own communities have received minimal recognition as another category of victim in complex emergencies.

According to Médecins Sans Frontières, an international NGO, these survivors can be divided into three categories: those targeted as a "stake in the conflict," those threatened by being trapped in the conflict, and vulnerable populations weakened by disruption in food and health care provision (Jean 1995:129). Amid the animosity and adversity of a violence-ridden community setting, they each face the ruins of their lives alone. Beyond physical reconstruction, they carry the extra burden of having to support now-marginalized members with extremely limited resources. Eventually, when displaced neighbors return, they are forced to confront the issues of contention—both the original problems that led to the violence and the repercussions that ensued.

The fact that in the literature as well as the field the experience of resident survivors goes largely unexplored in international circles could be the result of several factors. It may be because grassroots identity conflicts are a relatively new and unfamiliar phenomena, because the common citizen in his or her home lacks visibility, or because, in contrast to refugees, resident victims of violence have no mandated caretaker. Therefore, the international eye has not yet been trained to look closely at the ground. Because the plight of the community has been relatively absent from our list of concerns, we know less about conditions pertaining to communities caught up in armed violence than we do about other aspects of complex emergencies.

Whereas the previous two chapters looked at uprooted populations, this one explores those who remained. Using literature on related issues such as psychological trauma and community development, case studies of specific incidents, personal experience, and anecdotal evidence, it offers a view of identity conflict and complex emergency from the inside. It attempts to speak not only to the tangible reality of this experience but the consequences within the community and the long-term issues confronting its members. Because today's armed violence so thoroughly permeates the grassroots, attempting to understand its impact on the community is critical to our larger perception of complex emergencies.

A Close Look at a War-Torn Community

Local populations ravaged by identity conflict often see little in the way of help and even less in the way of hope. Taking a walk through a fictional mixed-identity community reeling from recent extreme violence, we might find the following scene.

Physical devastation is everywhere. Large sections of the residential areas have been razed or indiscriminately destroyed by shelling and attacks. Acres of land are blackened and the few live animals to be seen are roaming at will. The community center, at the heart of the battlefield, shows severe damage. Many structures were simply the casualty of erratic shelling, while other businesses were specifically targeted and looted. Rubble and burned-out automobiles clog several streets. Some buildings are boarded up; some remain eerily open and empty, their windows broken. The normal trading, markets, and street life are barely visible; only small-scale commerce shows any evidence of life.

Many members of this community fled before or during the fighting; the survivors who remain are mostly women, children, the elderly, and the disabled. Some suffer from serious injuries. Lack of physicians, medical facilities, and supplies forces them to rely on second-rate care, if any, and some die as a consequence. What facilities may be operating are viewed with distrust, and even the most needy may not seek their services.

Individuals are shell-shocked by the violence, by personal loss, and by the breakdown in community integrity. Some are incapable, as a result, of caring for themselves. In the trying postconflict period, community members of like identity share resources and assist each other in daily survival, offering food, care, and manual labor. Women take in children who have lost their parents in the chaos. The destruction of homes has forced large numbers of people to live together in single dwellings. Furthermore, the loss of community leaders in the carnage and flight has compelled remaining members to take on leadership roles.

Some members who fled to nearby areas returned almost immediately. Similarly, many of those who crossed international boundaries came home in the refugee ricochet process. More return daily. The community is thus faced with newly arriving members, some of whom are homeless and destitute. Their presence increases the level of tension in the community, reigniting hidden animosity over the original problems and sparking new contention over responsibility, retribution, and atonement. Suspicion runs high about participation and allegiance in the struggle. Other contentious issues such as leadership, rehabilitation, and community process loom ahead as well.

In the aftermath of disruption, assistance for this typical community is extremely minimal, save for some food aid and plastic sheeting from the ICRC. Relief workers from an international health NGO visit intermittently, attempting to revitalize the local health care center. Under these conditions, community members are forced to rely on each other, an extremely difficult undertaking given the animosity between the identity groups.

The Pandemicity of Intimate Combat

This dismal walk through a violence-ravaged community makes evident the comprehensive effect of communal violence and the difficulty of reintegration and rehabilitation. Although each situation presents distinctive circumstances, identity conflict seems to pose two common challenges that stem from its unique characteristics.

Personal Involvement

First, the nature of intergroup fighting, as we saw in chapter 2, is extremely intimate, invasive, and largely unavoidable. Since identity conflicts are based on personal attributes, it is nearly impossible for individuals to escape being drawn into the battle. All members in society, depending on their religion, tribe, race, or birthplace, are involuntarily identified with one side of the conflict or another, for the most part regardless of personal beliefs. They may subsequently become targets for intimidation, abuse, forced movement, or extermination.

The inability to prevent such random attacks can spawn rampant fear and distrust. In many circumstances, the current of anxiety and suspicion may begin with mere social segregation and grow into isolated cases of verbal abuse and frequent threats. Eventually it can develop into acts of aggression, from scuffles to disappearances to physical destruction and armed violence.

The animosity feeding this progression can occur between contending towns or regions where communities are internally relatively homogeneous. In towns containing greater comingling, violence may erupt between communal members themselves. In either case, belligerents are presumably familiar with each other and may have once lived in harmony, conducted business together, and relied on each other for everyday needs.

Intermarriages may be common, particularly in integrated communities, producing children of dual heritage. Twenty percent of all marriages in Bosnia-Herzegovina, for example, were of mixed ethnic background (Gurr 1993). Relationships of every category may be at stake in identity conflict, even those between spouses, between neighbors sharing common living areas and child care, between friends, and between teachers and their students and doctors and their patients.

All social institutions become drawn into the conflict. The impartiality not only of civil government, the military, and any form of authority structure, but also of school systems, health facilities, civic welfare agencies, and all other institutions is now called into question. I recall an injured Rwandan man adamantly refusing to visit the hospital because he feared to submit himself to the care of an unknown physician.

When the act of violence occurs in an intimate setting where well-acquainted rivals meet in familiar territory, it does more than physical harm. House-to-house massacres can wipe out whole families or, alternatively, leave children, the elderly, and women to witness the brutality. Rape is a common and extremely invasive tactic. Often women are taken as hostages for sexual as well as military purposes. Human Rights Watch's description of the Abkhaz-Georgian identity conflict exemplifies the horrors of internal violence. "Troops on the ground terrorized the local population through house-to-house searches, and engaged in widespread looting and pillage, stripping civilians of property and food. We have received countless reports on both sides . . . that combatants raped and otherwise used sexual terror as an instrument of warfare" (Human Rights Watch 1995:3).

I have seen how the technical weaponry and offensive tactics used in today's identity conflicts can also have serious personal repercussions. Random attacks on villages, or sniper fire (such as occurred repeatedly in Sarajevo, for instance), have a terrifying effect on populations, as opposed to a broad offensive through the countryside, which is undoubtedly ominous but at least offers some warning. Similarly, whereas air raids, shelling, and even machine-gun fire are fast and effective in destroying large numbers of people rather indiscriminately, hand-to-hand combat demands explicit personal rancor and determination in order to kill.

Rwanda's genocide, in which the machete was the primary weapon, is the modern-day extreme of intimate violence. A few months after the massacres, a UN colleague spoke with one of the leaders who illustrated this point. He explained that because each murder required several blows, he and his fellow perpetrators eventually became exhausted. At that point, they hobbled the survivors by severing their Achilles tendons and went home to drink and sleep. The following morning, well-rested, the slayers returned to the houses to continue the carnage.

In a country that is 74 percent Christian, thousands of people fled to churches for safety. When their pursuers discovered their whereabouts, sometimes with the help of the pastor, and sometimes literally across his dead body, they locked the doors to prevent escape and systematically butchered the occupants. Those suspected of still breathing after the hand-slaying were shot; when no movement was detected, the attackers left. Another eventual colleague was among the more fortunate. Like several others, she survived by lying beneath the carnage for several hours pretending to be dead while she listened to the moans of her mother several meters away.

Another tactic used in Rwanda was the intimate involvement of vast portions of the population. Through manipulation, encouragement, incitement, or sheer pressure, the perpetrators forced ordinary citizens to participate in the massacres. This technique not only expedited the killing but created a base of support through popular involvement, polarizing the groups further. In merely one hundred days in Rwanda, possibly 800,000 people were killed and hundreds of thousands are suspected of participating (Ransdell 1994:68). That is nearly three times the killing rate of the Holocaust in World War II. These conditions exemplify the intrusion of the conflict into every inviolable aspect of life. The personal disruption and invasive effect of such intimate exposure to violence is vast, pervasive, and long-lasting.

Combat Tactics and Physical Destruction

The second common factor in identity conflict is the prevalent demolition of community buildings and infrastructure. Because of its grassroots nature, such widespread devastation tends to have a long-lasting effect on nearly all aspects of, and individuals in, society.

In the process of communal aggression, physical structures may be specifically targeted or simply stand in the way of reaching the human objectives. The aftermath leaves dilapidated houses, dead animals, polluted fishing waters, burned crops, broken telephone, gas, and electric lines, contaminated water systems, torn-up and obstructed roads, ruined community buildings, and burned and looted businesses, stores, and warehouses. In addition, institutions such as schools, hospitals, health centers, worship centers, and civic monuments may be ruined.

The type and extent of the damage depends partly on the tactics used. In Tajikistan, for instance, I saw how local aggressors had retrofitted bulldozers with homemade spikes, which they used to ram houses and break apart the mud-brick bond. In some cases, nonresident belligerents target the viability of a community by destroying just enough to render it incapable of survival. They may destroy roads leading into the area, burn agricultural land, cut off incoming water sources, electricity, and gas, or deprive whole communities of food supplies. At the same time, they may strike a town, or individuals within it, with periodic attacks. In the early 1990s, the whole world watched as Sarajevo suffered just such a siege. I witnessed Kosovo residents being subjected to each of these tactics in village after village in 1998.

Alternatively, antagonists may sweep through a community destroying, killing, and moving on, or they may occupy it for long periods of time. When the violence comes from within the community, the aggressors will likely use tactics of scapegoating and intimidation along with threats and assault. As Meyer-Knapp notes, "Dreadful human suffering and environmental destruction become the medium in which [the] contest for guardianship [over land] plays out" (forthcoming, 19).

The Fallout from Communal Warfare

Though all armed conflict is destructive, grassroots violence is unique in that it offers virtually no one immunity. Identity conflict lays waste to nearly all aspects of society, not only the physical infrastructure and the economy but also self-reliance, social services, social networks, leadership, and the psychological health of the population.

Self-Reliance

The physical damage discussed earlier not only impairs electrical lines, water and road systems, houses, crops, and herds, but destroys structures that housed commercial ventures and industry. Their loss can affect the proprietor, the con-sumer, the sharecropper, the landlord, and the employee, and can ultimately lead to economic degradation. Lack of production and trade means lack of resources, which in turn inflates local prices (Cuny 1983).

All commerce may shut down entirely during the heart of the fighting, leaving remaining citizens without necessary goods. Industrial production in Georgia, for example, fell by 80 percent and agricultural production by 60 per-cent between 1989 and 1994, largely as a result of identity conflict (Gluck 1995:11). Except in subsistence-farming communities where the land was basi-cally undamaged, this demise in output can result in a severe humanitarian emergency, such as occurred in Somalia in 1992 when as many as 240,000 people died from starvation and related illness (Sommer 1994a:120). Loss of human resources to death and migration can further limit the recuperative capacity of war-torn communities. In Tajikistan, the dearth of laborers severely hurt the production capability of the agricultural communes. Other areas that may have been physically untouched by the turmoil suffer from isolation and disruption in trade, which leads to commodity shortages and declining markets for their own products.

The threat of violence and an inadequate food supply typically incites hoarding, creating a superficial food deficit. The laws of supply and demand inflate prices, which soar out of reach of the average citizen, who at this point may not have sufficient purchasing power anyway. The combination of all these forces creates famine conditions, not from drought or crop damage so much—though they may be an additional factor—as from economic and labor disrup-tion (Deng and Minear 1992). The Ethiopian famine in 1984 is an example of how political instability and violence, compounded by an accompanying drought, eroded the capacity of the country to feed itself. We are witnessing this same cycle repeat itself in Sudan in 1998 and 1999.

Social Services

Social fallout from internal warfare is generally more difficult to assess and reverse at the community level than the physical and economic effects. Many of the essential services to the community, such as education, health, and welfare, may have disintegrated with the destruction of buildings, loss of personnel, lack of equipment and supplies, apprehension, and insecurity. Without education, children not only may become listless, they may turn to antisocial behavior both for entertainment and profit. And without intellectual influences to challenge war's ever-present dominion, they become subject to the dominant paradigms of violence, antagonism, fear, and mistrust.

With the reestablishment of stability, however, schools may recommence and continue to run on an irregular basis, provided teacher availability and a semblance of facilities, such as renovated school rooms. In Somalia, I helped organize "classrooms" which initially consisted only of a large tree, a teacher, students, and a smattering of paper, pencils, and books. Still, a multitude of problems may reduce attendance, such as insufficient clothing or shoes, mental health problems from exposure to extreme violence, physical wounds and disabilities, lack of transportation, unwillingness to integrate in the schoolroom, shortage of food, or distrust of faculty.

Conflict-induced disruption in the public health system—due to lack of adequate buildings, equipment, supplies, personnel, or, as in other social institutions, segregation based on distrust—also affects the community. In Rwanda, for example, an estimated 80 percent of the medical professionals either fled the country or were killed in the fighting, including many of the traditional healers (Kumar et al. 1996:50). Interruption of immunization campaigns is one of the more serious consequences of a fractured health system. This not only leaves many children susceptible to rapid-onset deadly diseases such as measles—which can kill 10 to 20 percent of the children infected (Jean 1995:159)—but the destruction of records and regularity of the program breaks down the community- and country-wide health coverage. Polio—a disease once thought nearly eradicated—reemerged in Kosovo in 1998 during the disruption in comprehensive immunization campaigns. In the absence of medical facilities and prevention programs such as prenatal care, nutrition, sexually transmitted disease and HIV intervention, family planning, and women's health care, the community faces higher public health risks in general.

State, community, or extended-family assistance for the vulnerable elements of society tend to be among the early casualties of armed conflict. The elderly, mentally ill, widowed, infirm, and orphaned, who once depended on such services, are often left to the mercy of local benefactors for their survival in a war-torn community. This occurred in Tajikistan when canteens and nursing home facilities were shut down during the violence and social assistance was drastically reduced. I spoke with many, mostly minority, elderly Russians without families, who had become homeless or homebound without means of support. Although ethnic Russians were not the primary antagonists in the civil war, they were considered partisan and therefore became a focus of hostility. Outreach to these marginalized individuals, therefore, was minimal (Maynard 1993). Moreover, extensive violence inevitably leaves a disproportionate number of community members disabled and without a safety net to aid their recovery or any means with which to support themselves. Amputees from land mine accidents who are unable to farm or ply a trade fall into this category (Chabasse 1995).

In some cases, the recovery from a collapsed social system may never be complete, leaving whole sectors of the population without literacy skills and suffering from high morbidity, mortality, and malnutrition rates (Deng and Minear 1992). Haiti's deplorable social conditions show the results of years of repression and violence. As of 1989, Haiti had 80 percent illiteracy, the highest infant mortality rate in the Western Hemisphere, and consumed the second lowest level of calories per capita in the world (Zolberg, Suhrke, and Aguayo 1989:193).

In addition, children who grow up in such chaos-ridden countries as Haiti, Nicaragua, or Palestine often have few influences beyond the culture of violence. Eventually, fighting becomes a way of life, weaving its way into the social fabric. In prolonged wars such as Lebanon's, militia factions may attempt to control certain areas by establishing their own social welfare systems (Hansen 1995). Under such circumstances, children learn to associate force with problem resolution, and the perpetuation of violence with community survival.

Social Networks

Another, more subtle casualty of communal conflict is the interrelationships and interaction among individuals. In a normal community social system, members rely heavily on each other for everything including products, labor, subsistence support, guidance, information, services, and security (Cuny 1983). When this structure breaks down, the divisiveness within society disrupts normal operations, potentially seriously damaging community viability. The effects are presumably all the more ruinous in communities that have had close intergroup ties, including mixed marriages, neighborhoods, business associations, church membership, and academic fellowship.

No longer might a shop, for example, be able to count on buying goods from farmers or producers from across identity lines. Because of the rampant distrust, only those from the same identity group might patronize the store, diminishing the income of the owner. In agricultural regions, as another example, farm labor is often shared between members of the community. When the full complement of community members is no longer available, crops may go to waste and fields may lie fallow for lack of planting. This was the case in Tajikistan, where there was sometimes inadequate help to tend to the family's own garden plot. This vital source of income, consequently, was unavailable (Maynard 1994).

Experience shows, moreover, that the initial divisions of conflict based on identity may subdivide into other cleavages, such as between those who remained and those who fled, or those receiving assistance and those not, thus further hindering community reintegration. In the aftermath of the most heated violence in Somalia's nomadic northern region, for instance, severe contention arose between clans with deep roots in the region and those who had migrated more recently to the area. Such inability to depend on normal support, assistance, and interaction seems to devastate community cohesion. Once trust is destroyed, returning the community to a level of deep faith and assurance requires serious effort, commitment, and time (Montville 1993).

Particularly in protracted conflicts, hostilities may have debilitated the more formal social networks and internal mechanisms to assist in the process of rehabilitation, such as elders' councils, community legal and quasi-legal procedures, review boards, and guidance committees. The system may now be tainted by a degree of distrust or bias, rendering it no longer capable of community guidance. This occurred in Burundi, where the traditional mediators lost official status and were overcome by the extent of intergroup animosity (Refugees International 1995).

Leadership

Fighting also frequently takes its toll on local leadership. Given their position in society, religious authorities, elders, political officials, union heads, civic leaders, and social administrators are often more at risk of physical attack than the average citizen. They are, therefore, highly likely to flee when conditions warrant.

These same people who once provided moral and directional guidance may be instigators of the conflict, and their fate may therefore depend on the outcome. The preplanned and well-executed massacres and evacuations in Rwanda, for instance, were reported to be the work of thousands of community religious and civic leaders who led their followers to kill as well as to leave by the hundreds (Ransdell 1994). In 1995, an estimated 10 to 15 percent of the refugees in camps, primarily those in Zaire, may have been such individuals, according to the multidonor evaluation of the Rwanda crisis (Kumar et al. 1996:98). At the same time, some of the first killed were political and community leaders who stood out as moderates in the eyes of the assailants (Ransdell 1994).

Whether by evacuation, death, or peer rejection, the end result is that communities lose their customary leadership. Decision-making capacity may be damaged, leaving remaining community members to devise new power structures, take on leadership roles, and become more involved in the process. Though necessary, this may be extremely difficult, particularly if leadership roles are chosen by specific members of the community, or dictated by hierarchy or inheritance. At the same time, certain individuals who have traditionally been excluded from decision-making, such as women, members of the lower class, and certain identity groups, are unlikely to get involved.

Psychological

Finally, war-torn communities may suffer from psychological damage as a result of exposure to extreme, intimate violence. Such mental trauma among civilians appears similar in some ways to that found in combat veterans, which was first seriously studied in the 1980s among U.S. veterans of the Vietnam War (Maynard 1997). Subsequent research conducted in Western countries examined matching symptoms in such groups as survivors of rape, incest, and physical abuse, and adolescent Vietnamese war survivors immigrating to the United States.

A small but growing literature explores the incidence of psychological trauma in civilian combat survivors, particularly as a result of identity conflict. The growing but still insufficient data, however, requires observers to assume some transferability of the findings from the larger literature on psychological trauma to the context of identity conflict. (In making this leap, I think it is important to consider not simply the dissimilarities between combat soldiers and civilians but also between Western and non-Western cultures. While it is easy to assume culture-blind responses to violence, Western understandings of trauma may not apply to other societies. Furthermore, in my view, the animosity inherent in identity conflict plays a substantial role in the psychological effect of violence.)

The research has shown that psychological trauma at the individual level stems from continual physical threat, such as prolonged exposure to low-grade violence, the persistent fear of land mines, intimidation, military infiltration, exposure to mistreatment either as the object or witness, or from basic insecurity. Jonathan Shay, in his study of combat soldiers, *Achilles in Vietnam: Combat Trauma and the Undoing of Character*, describes four clusters of traumatic war experiences that contribute to psychological trauma: exposure to fighting; exposure to abusive violence; physical deprivation; and loss of meaning and control (1994:123). Civilians living in combat zones have very similar experiences.

Physical danger can be a daily occurrence in combat zones. A study conducted in Lebanon in 1988 found that over 90 percent of the children sampled had been exposed to shelling or combat, 50 percent had witnessed violent acts such as physical injury, intimidation, or the death of a friend or close relative, and 26 percent had lost someone close to them. Sixty-eight percent, moreover, had been displaced, and 21 percent had been separated from their families (International Peace Research Association 1990). Rwanda's 1994 civil war produced remarkably similar figures (Kumar et al. 1996).

The symptoms of psychological trauma range from anxiety to depression, substance abuse, social withdrawal, hostility, estrangement, despair, isolation, meaninglessness, anticipation of betrayal, hypervigilance, destroyed capacity for social trust, and post-traumatic stress disorder at the far end of the spectrum (Shay 1994). Different individuals and cultures may manifest their own variations of these symptoms. My observations in Guinea, for example, were that many traumatized Liberian refugees were unduly confused, apparently depressed, and unable to engage in coherent conversation.

Women and children appear to be particularly susceptible to psychological trauma as combat moves onto the home front. In today's conflicts, women who survive the indiscriminate violence have often lived to witness attacks on family members or have been victims of abuse themselves. Rape, which thrives in violent conflicts, causes profound psychological injury. In Rwanda, where rape was widespread and often public, the multidonor evaluation found that mental trauma was a serious outcome. In addition, rape resulted in an estimated 5,000 pregnancies and an inordinate amount of sexually transmitted disease, possibly including HIV (Kumar et al. 1996, 66).[1]

The loss of family members is especially psychologically deleterious to those who depend heavily on a provider, such as women, children, the disabled, and the elderly. The multidonor study of Rwanda reports that between one third and one half of all women in the hardest-hit areas of the country were widowed in the genocide, according to government statistics, while 95,000 to 150,000 children were either orphaned or temporarily separated from their parents (Kumar et al. 1996:61–63). Despite their lack of resources or familial support, many women, including widows and single women, took in the unaccompanied children of relatives and neighbors.[2] Understandably, the evaluation concludes, "the *de facto* foster system . . . places extreme financial and psychological pressure on the care-givers," who led an already marginal existence (Kumar et al. 1996:64).

In a community ravaged by war, normal psychological support, in the form of extended family, friends, elders, and religious figures, usually deteriorates along with the community's social structures, such as schools, religious institutions, community organizations, and medical facilities (Maynard 1997). In a 1995 UNICEF training course on psychological trauma I attended, a survivor of Rwanda's genocide reported, "In a normal situation, one can get support and assistance from school, extended family, work, the state. All these are gone in war. There is nothing. You can't trust anyone. All is gone. There is no protection. The teachers, the mayors, even the family has killed." This loss of familiarity in routine and trust in leadership is likely exacerbated by estrangement following migration. Individual self-esteem plummets as a result of such disruption, compounded by the inability to provide for oneself from the loss of manpower, economic erosion, and ruined income sources. This process can have devastating psychological effects.

Since exposure to intimate violence is recognized as a primary cause of mental trauma, it can be assumed that psychological damage has become more pervasive as the number of identity conflicts has increased. Moreover, the sheer number of individuals exposed to violence potentially multiplies the personal nature of traumatic psychological injury. While single incidents may be disturbing, more numerous cases can understandably overwhelm a community plagued by physical and social chaos. In such circumstances, psychologically traumatized individuals may quickly become marginalized and burdensome to society. This was evident in Tajikistan's identity conflict, where many repatriating widows, devastated by the fighting and the loss of their families, were incapable of functioning rationally. They required complete care and could no longer contribute to productivity. Yet the communes, reeling from civil war, were unable to provide for them adequately (Maynard 1993).

The paranoia and distrust common among the mentally traumatized, moreover, may influence the community mindset at a time of extreme vulnerability. This distrust can lead to prolonged segregation and hostility, which decrease the odds for community rehabilitation and reintegration. At the same time, ruined social institutions and intergroup relations further the impression of disorder, exacerbating psychological vulnerability (Maynard 1997). As a result, the initial shock of identity conflict seems to have extremely deleterious and long-term ripple effects on the psychosocial health of communities subjected to violence, which disrupts the intricate network of society far beyond the immediate physical destruction.

The Challenges of Community Rehabilitation and Social Reconstruction

Under these conditions of economic, social, and psychological breakdown, the challenge of rebuilding a community can be daunting. Several factors tend to exacerbate the situation, such as problems of security, inadequate and inappropriate rehabilitation assistance, and diminished democratic participation. These issues deserve greater scrutiny.

Continued Security Issues

Severe, protracted disputes are not easily overlooked and naturally continue to produce suspicion, accusations, and demands for remuneration. They can lead to further scapegoating, incidents of individual reprisal, group fear tactics, political repression and, possibly, renewed armed conflict. As a result, security becomes a constant concern for community members (Stein 1991).

The more apprehensive families and individuals, I have observed, may be unwilling to venture outside of relatively safe areas, even for the purpose of production and commerce. Both in the northern nomadic region of Somalia, where I was living, and in many parts of southern Sudan, intergroup fighting cut off normal animal migration routes and made pastoralists reluctant to herd their cattle and camels in regions governed by opposing groups, for fear of losing their herds (Lowrey 1995). One can see how fear can pervade intergroup interaction and social relations, and diminish the ability of the community to heal.

Deteriorating living standards can increase this sense of insecurity. The demise in productivity and resulting reduction in income and employment can contribute to distrust and hostility and potentially lead to a continuation of the revenge cycle (Anderson 1994). Basic competition for resources often leads to overprotectiveness, defensive attitudes, and intergroup fighting (Cuny 1991). Returning members who fled during the violence, moreover, may inundate the struggling community.

In this climate, returnees may find themselves in an intensely hostile environment. In the worst-case scenario, they may be completely ostracized, targeted, or abandoned. The confluence of the divergent experiences and attitudes of returnees and those who remained may renew the original dispute. In Tajikistan, for instance, returning community members accused of participating in the fighting were sometimes killed, and their family members threatened, beaten, and raped during the earlier phases of repatriation (Anderson 1995a). Such conflict clearly exacerbates insecurity and creates a very difficult setting in which to attempt community reintegration.

Inappropriate or Inadequate Rehabilitation Assistance

Another potential factor in the rehabilitation equation is outside assistance. Under conditions of instability and destitution, relief aid can provide a critical boost to the recovery process. It also, however, can bring new difficulties to the community.

First, assistance from the state, national organizations, or international agencies generally does not benefit the whole community until the late stages of the reconstruction phase. At that point, the bulk of the assistance will likely be in the form of seeds and tools for agricultural rehabilitation, health center and school renovation, and possibly shelter reconstruction. Initially, however, aid is usually directed specifically toward returnees or special groups such as unaccompanied children. ICRC is the only international agency whose mandate it is to assist all resident victims in need; other organizations routinely give priority to the requirements of select subsets of residents, such as children, or populations other than local citizens. This pattern can create several problems. In cultures or circumstances where sharing resources is rare, the needy who are neglected may become the most marginalized members of their community (Prendergast 1995). In addition, those excluded from assistance may not tangibly benefit from any indirect economic boost that comes with aid. If they represent a large percentage of the population, they may, in fact, adversely affect the community economy (Cuny 1990). Furthermore, limited assistance can create significant tension between those who benefit and those who do not (Anderson 1994). In Tajikistan, for example, a housing reconstruction project focused attention on the ethnic group most affected by the destruction. Animosity developed over the perceived favoritism, leading to a potentially violent incident in which the offended demanded equal benefit (Anderson 1995a).

Another potential problem stemming from long-term assistance to displaced populations is its tendency to encourage dependence on outside sources and, thus, to discourage self-reliance, motivation, and self-esteem (Cuny 1990; Hakovirta 1986; Prendergast 1995). This dependence can have serious long-term repercussions on community rehabilitation, not the least of which is the diminished potential of individuals to reenter society as self-sufficient, productive members. Not only do long-term beneficiaries generally contribute less to the community's development, but, should the outside benefits decrease, their dependent attitude and loss of skills may cause them to become a burden to the rest of the population. I visited families in Kosovo who had received international assistance for six years, due to the oppressive job environment and consequential massive unemployment. One household of seven was hosting twenty-three displaced persons, many of whom had also received assistance before fleeing. The disruption in outside aid due to the outbreak of violence seriously threatened the ability of the household to sustain itself.

Diminished Democratic Participation

The damaged trust and intergroup reliance makes cross-conflict cooperation in helping the needy and rebuilding the community much more difficult. Inasmuch as individuals distrust others, fear for their safety, have a limited sense of the future, and tend to see the world in black and white, their ability to contribute to group decision-making and constructive future planning is negligible. As a result, both immediate and long-term needs may go unmet.

Real benefit from relief programs, in my experience, requires strong community participation. Humanitarian agencies generally need assistance in locating, counting, and supplying vulnerable members of the community, many of whom cannot make their own needs known. Since they are unfamiliar with local particularities, international organizations are less able to determine specific shortfalls, appropriate priorities of assistance, nearby resources, gender-specific requirements, and other issues pertinent to the locale. The earlier example in Tajikistan, where homebound elderly women were unable to meet their own needs, illustrates the necessity of community participation in locating the most vulnerable. A community that, because of a disintegrated decision-making process, cannot pro-actively engage in the relief strategy to meet its own requirements may suffer as a consequence. In addition, it may miss out on the substantial opportunities for developing community capacity through training, participation, and employment with international organizations.

Furthermore, the relief-to-development cycle finds its return to the disaster stage precisely in this kind of environment. In the throes of rehabilitation and reintegration, communities that cannot plan for the future, design reconstruction programs, and move forward into development because of an inability to make decisions, may find themselves back in the heart of turmoil. Conversely, where a community is able to develop a joint strategy for development, its clear need for reconstruction and the presence of international organizations offering potential funds and technical assistance give it a chance to progress beyond minimal repair. Such efforts can result in substantial development and improved local resources, structures, and standards.

While the challenges in reestablishing community cohesion are real, there is nevertheless equally real opportunity to renew community relations and begin the healing process. The loss of customary leadership and fractured social and civic institutions, for example, can potentially remove the normal reliance on authorities for community planning and provide space for other decision-making strategies to emerge. The willingness of the displaced to risk return, moreover, and the weariness of the resident community, may provide additional incentive for positive reintegration.

This brings us full circle, having discussed the conditions of the displaced and those of the community residents. We are thus poised to examine approaches to reintegration and eventual community renewal in the second part of the study. The next chapter will explore the conceptual process of recovery, looking at the nature of conflictual relationships and the necessary evolution in their healing.

PART TWO

TOWARD A HOLISTIC APPROACH TO ASSISTANCE

CHAPTER SIX **REBUILDING COMMUNITY COHESION**

Since wars begin in the minds of men, it is in the minds of men that the defenses of peace must be constructed.

—Constitution of the United Nations Educational, Scientific, and Cultural Organization

---

Global change has outpaced our ability to react to complex emergencies. While international agencies have learned significant lessons over the past eight years, natural disaster methodology has led the international response, even as we studied the unique ramifications of identity conflict. Physical and economic sectors still dominate the reconstruction efforts. Though critical, this approach often leaves the significant psychosocial needs to today's crises lacking attention and funds. Left unattended, gaping psychological and social wounds can fester and eventually cause a reversion to conflict, slowing the long-term healing. The challenge of international assistance, therefore, is to expand and address these broader needs. As identity conflict seeps down through all aspects of society, it ultimately pools at the lowest point: that of the community and its members. Consequently, rehabilitation efforts must address the inherent grassroots nature of today's emergencies.

This chapter attempts to build a conceptual framework for reintegrating communities torn apart by violence. It examines the concepts behind reconciliation and the complex processes of reestablishing relationships damaged by conflict and displacement. Finally, from a more theoretical perspective, it outlines a comprehensive approach toward rebuilding community cohesion and reconciliation.

Developing a Concept of Peace

The premise behind community reintegration stems from the notion that the ideal state of human society is harmony among its members (Voutira and Brown 1995). Indeed, nearly all parties to, and observers of, conflicts profess that "peace" is their objective. What peace represents, and how to attain a sustainable truce, however, are contentious questions. Violence—that is, physical harm to persons and property—lies at one end of a long spectrum, and deep mutual respect and intergroup collaboration are at the other. Understandings of "peace" might fall anywhere from the midpoint to the far end of full harmony.

At its place near the center of the spectrum, "peace" may simply mean the absence of overt violence. In *Peace and Reconciliation as a Paradigm*, Hizkias Assefa discusses various conceptions of harmony, in which he describes the absence of violence as a "negative peace." Manifested in enforcement and balance structures such as police forces, justice systems, and nuclear deterrence, its primary goal is the pursuit of stability and control of violence. Regardless of the resulting "law and order," writes Assefa, this form of peace can breed structural violence, defined as "social and personal violence arising from unjust, repressive, and oppressive national or international political and social structures" (1993:3). Negative peace can lead to abject poverty, malnutrition, homelessness, and servitude at the hands of the powerful and wealthy, which may ultimately be as devastating as more overt forms of violence, according to Assefa.

Further along the spectrum, peace may connote an atmosphere of serenity, free of dissension or discord. This definition ignores the realistic and beneficial roles conflict plays in any society. Most observers would concur that disagreement itself is an essential element in progress, rational decision-making, and building healthy relationships (Fahey 1993). Handling disputes, generating positive outcomes, and synthesizing the conflicting elements require effective means. At the far end of the spectrum, then, lies what might be the most constructive concept of peace, that of genuine, respectful relationships among people engaged in mutual contemplation and cooperation. In this form, conflict is not absent, but it does not descend to a level of mutual abuse, and structures exist to help transform disagreements into achievable solutions.

This notion of peace coincides with the larger concept of complex interdependence. Assefa describes it as "a philosophy . . . [that] provides a framework to discern, understand, analyze, and regulate all human relationships in order to create an integrated, holistic, and humane social order" (1993:5). To achieve this level of peace, fundamental relationships and root issues must be explored.[1] The notion of interactive relationship, rather than technical and impersonal contact or agreement, is at the root of a broader conceptual paradigm presented in this book, one that is designed to fit the conditions of today's identity conflicts. The deep-rooted nature of these conflicts, which pervade all aspects of society, necessitates expanding our concept of peacemaking beyond negotiated settlements between nation-states to include rebuilding a sense of trust, equality, and participation.

Contending Methodologies of Conflict Intercession

Certain basic assumptions underpin the notion of conflict intercession. The goal of intercession is to help restore order and balance in a society (Voutira and Brown 1995). Intercession does not always achieve this end, particularly in identity conflicts, for several reasons. First, the mechanisms may not be well developed, or they may not fit the specific conditions of the conflict and culture (Lederach 1992). Second, those conducting the intercession may be inappropriate, biased, or otherwise unfit (Moore 1993). Third, intercession itself may be construed as interference in domestic affairs and therefore be unwelcome to certain parties (Awoonor 1993). And fourth, intercession may be the wrong tactic altogether for the particular situation; there may be situations that require absolute noninterference. Though this option is rarely considered, I believe that it should be seen as an option in discussions of responses to identity conflict.

These shortcomings notwithstanding, intercession can be a valid response to intergroup conflict. Somewhere between art and science, the field of conflict management[2] has yet to develop precise theoretical and methodological categories. Two basic approaches appear to dominate the field, each of which contains finer variations and complements the other in the broader picture of whole bodies politic.

The Leadership Approach

The first might be called the "leadership approach," since it focuses on the upper levels of the decision-making structure. This approach primarily employs mediation and negotiation in an effort to reach an agreement on ending the cycle of violence. Other instruments of statecraft may also be used, such as economic sanctions and incentives, propaganda, and force as discussed in chapter 1 (Saunders 1996b). This is by and large a technical process, conducted around a table in which the various parties attempt to address the issues, symptoms, power balances, and costs of violent conflict through psychological maneuvers, establishing trust, and articulating claims (Scimecca 1993; Volkan, Julius, and Montville 1990; Voutira and Brown 1995).

These proceedings are critical to laying the foundation for substantive conclusions to the conflict; any ensuing agreement can establish a premise for peace and cement the basis for future cooperation. Such agreements are, however, as Harold Saunders claims, "like skeletons without ligaments, muscles, sinews, flesh, nerves or blood vessels" (Saunders 1996a:2). Many scholars agree that the roots of the conflict are left untouched by the leadership approach, along with the broader disruption in civil society and the political process. More important, in its technical approach it does not address the more complex subject of human relationships. Another, less formal process is necessary in order to go beyond government negotiation and into the network of human interaction.

The Relationship Approach

This more far-reaching method might be called the "relationship approach." Fundamental to it is the notion that the fuel of contention lies in the underlying human relations; these relations, therefore, are the focus of transformation. The "relationship approach" is a process more than an action; it addresses conflict as a function of deep-seated patterns rather than a technical problem; and it takes place in a domain outside the heart of government (Volkan, Julius, and Montville 1990).

Saunders describes the steps involved in this approach in a letter to Cyrus Vance:

> Citizens outside government during a civil conflict begin dialogue across the lines of conflict—a public peace process that paves the way for official talks and provides ideas when the official peace process stalls. They create organizations to help refugees return home. They create their own organizations to build relationships across the fault lines and to teach political practice to citizens outside government. They begin to generate connections between the coagulations of warring groups—the sinews of nascent cohesion in a society building peace. (Saunders 1996a)

The two approaches are complementary in that relationship-building can aid the leadership negotiation effort by motivating and supporting settlements, while the technical framework and absence of violence resulting from an agreement at the leadership level can increase security and lay the foundation for more substantive relationship development. In my experience, nowhere is this more evident than at the grassroots where identity conflict has attacked the heart of community interaction.

A Multidimensional Approach to Rebuilding Community

The intricacy of complex emergencies as well as the upheaval associated with identity conflict require an equally multifaceted intercession. The process of rebuilding must incorporate all elements of society, such as the economy, politics, and education, as well as culture, entertainment, technology, and the media (Volkan, Julius, and Montville 1990). The approach should center on human needs, addressing selfhood, security, and physical comfort, while specifically focusing on durable social reintegration rather than short-lived interaction (Gutlove et al. 1992). Intercession must attend, furthermore, to the psychological dimensions of healing for both the victims and the victimizers, without which the effect would be merely superficial (Montville, forthcoming).

Community rebuilding must include a vertical component, one that addresses the conflict between the community and the surrounding territory as well as between it and the rest of the country, and even the entire region. A study of 233 communal groups in conflict conducted by Ted Robert Gurr of the University of Maryland bears this out. Gurr's study (1993) found that where concerted efforts were made to accommodate and integrate dissenting minorities within the cultural and political system, conflict tended to abate. In the study, integration involved pluralism, devolution of power to ensure citizen participation, democratization, and protection of civil rights.

There appear to be three foci in the evolution of intergroup dynamics within the community itself: the leaders, the individual, and the community as a whole. Each of the three elements has various influences on the opinions, attitudes, and perceptions of the common citizen. At the same time, each is in itself influenced by experience and other entities.

The Leaders

Leadership-directed change may come about through the technical process of redirecting the community's development. The leaders may begin to reexamine relationships among members, develop plans and projects based on improving relations, and attempt to diminish barriers to cross-group interaction. For example, in an effort to place community cohesion over other priorities, leaders might suggest a road reconstruction project between sectors containing members of opposing groups, rather than new housing for local authorities.

Leaders with foresight will set longer time frames and extend objectives to encompass a gradual regrowth in community relations, including specific intermediary steps. They can use their role as administrators, moreover, to establish community policies that promote cordial relations and encourage cross-group interaction. As the members begin to coalesce and several successful reintegration projects come to pass, the leaders may come to view their participation as a powerful tool in conflict transformation.

The Individual

The daily communication among individual community members establishes patterns and expectations. Proactive efforts to bridge identity group gulfs may bear positive results in terms of community rebuilding. As a member of an identity group, each individual develops an attitude toward opposing groups, based to a large extent on the prevailing group sense. The growing collective animosity between the Abkhaz and the Georgians, for example, had a strong effect on the individual community members (Gluck 1995).

A rebirth in civil society may also have distinct ramifications on individuals. Those independently involved in some component of civil society, such as membership in a women's group or labor union, may feel a magnified effect through personal participation. Nevertheless, the sheer existence, let alone the growth, of NGOs, trade unions, professional associations, the media, and the like are apt to touch the lives of everyday citizens. Through their social and political advocacy and publicized opinions, these organizations can ultimately influence individual attitudes toward the issues of conflict.

The Community

The third focus is the community as a whole. The experience of deteriorating, improving, or stagnating conditions understandably significantly affects the general outlook for reintegration and rehabilitation. These conditions include the state of the economy and the status of the physical infrastructure, as well as the level of tension among members. The process of decision-making a community employs in reconstructing destroyed structures, for instance, will tend to influence the overall level of revitalization. A gathering of diverse members to set community goals and attempt to meet the needs of the society and its marginalized members, for example, will result in an overall sense of cooperation.

Likewise, group activities designed to involve the entire community in the process of rebuilding can have positive ramifications. A conspicuous illustration is joint reconstruction projects, whether of individual houses or community structures. A public ritual might officially give homage to a symbol of reunification, such as a ceremony to honor recent heroes, blessing of a new or surviving structure representing peace, or the dedication of an area for peacemaking. As in the first two foci, the process of reintegration and concerted efforts toward positive relationship-building can offer a powerful experience that, in itself, can affect the larger efforts.

In this approach to rebuilding community, it is vital to use a large conceptual framework to look beyond the immediate experience and smaller issues. A broad perspective offers the opportunity to go beyond the previous conditions and reach for higher objectives. As scholar Peter Sollis puts it, "Reconstruction should not mean a return to the status quo ante, with emphasis placed solely on the repair of damaged physical infrastructure and production capacity. Reconstruction is an opportunity to address those inequalities—political, social, economic and gender—that together were the root causes of the humanitarian emergency" (1994:11).

The process of rebuilding community also carries the potential for rechanneling the question of identity toward a positive end. By exploring new forms of political identity, wiping clean old, outdated ones, and searching for creative avenues for cooperation, the restructuring can conceivably contribute to a more stable nation-state with internal cohesion and a solid structural framework upon which decisions can be made and problems resolved. This holistic approach must be composed of achievable steps. The next section offers a five-phase process for healing community wounds.

Five Phases of Community Healing

I propose a sequence of five steps for rebuilding community cohesion: (1) establishing safety, (2) communalization and bereavement, (3) rebuilding trust and the capacity to trust, (4) reestablishing personal and social morality, and (5) reintegration and restoration of democratic discourse. There are three important considerations. First, the healing process requires time. Given the profundity of the wounds left by identity conflict, an adequate—often lengthy—recuperation period is critical.

Second, the process must be based on the principle of participation. The more members involved in each phase, the greater the opportunity for healing. Ideally, participation would include members from each identity group, both sexes, a variety of ages, representative occupations, and all levels of social status and class. This process draws on the principle of whole bodies politic and the need to address every aspect of society.

Finally, each phase builds on the others. While there may be a high degree of overlap, each step nevertheless requires a firm foundation in the previous phase. As the fundamentals of one are achieved, even before full completion, the next phase may begin. Elements of subsequent phases may be launched throughout the process, but careful consideration should be given to not skipping any phase.

Establishing Safety

Critical to any healing is removing the danger and replacing it with a foundation of security. In communities tormented by repeated violence, as we have already seen, safety is the most compelling motive for action. Unstable conditions tend to be exacerbated by the return of community members who fled during earlier bouts of fighting; land disputes, threats, retribution, and intimidation are common. Individuals may be frightened by other individuals or gangs, identity groups as a whole may be afraid of large-scale retribution or attacks based on association, and the community at large may be threatened by other regions, the military, or government persecution. Healing under these conditions can be extremely difficult. Therefore, freedom of movement within the community, absence of personal or group threats or attacks, property security, and access to community resources are necessary first steps on the path to recovery. The principle of safety must apply to all members of the community, regardless of status.

Part of the process of establishing safety is coming to a sustainable ceasefire. Peace agreements at the upper level of authority do not necessarily end the fighting at the community level. Leaders may be too weak to be able to implement any settlement and the national structure may be so frayed or nonexistent that inadequate support exists to follow through on the details. Moreover, the dispersion of the population may simply make any agreement substantively irrelevant.

Real ceasefire, by definition, must occur at all levels, not merely the top. Each group in society must participate in order to sustain a ceasefire. The process of obtaining a comprehensive ceasefire is time-consuming, but it is a necessary step in the achievement of a sustainable peace. The tendency to accelerate the transition can cut short the essential psychological massaging, realizations, acknowledgments, and group interaction that lead to complete ceasefire.

Certain conditions can encourage the voluntary end of hostilities. According to Helena Meyer-Knapp (forthcoming), an expert on ceasefires, suffering is the key ingredient. When a population as a whole has endured more anguish than it can bear, continued fighting is no longer viable. Each culture, it would seem, has its own tolerance for misery, allowing certain armed conflicts to persist for decades, as in Afghanistan, where fighting has continued for more than twenty years. As I have suggested throughout this book, although all levels of society endure horrific pain as a result of violent conflict, the grassroots nature of identity conflict translates into pervasive suffering at the community level. It is therefore likely that it is here that the first demands for an end to the violence emerge.

A further condition for a sustainable ceasefire, according to Meyer-Knapp, is that those party to the conflict lead the quest for an end to the violence. She suggests that it may be an ordinary civilian who sees the opportunity for leadership in a peaceful society and initiates and drives the effort. The implication is that outsiders have difficulty establishing a motivation for ending the fighting; a ceasefire in an internal conflict must be internally generated for it to be taken seriously and therefore hold. The Chechen-Russian ceasefire of August 1996 may satisfy that condition. In contrast, the Bosnian ceasefire, which was externally facilitated, may meet its demise.

Finally, Meyer-Knapp maintains that a lasting ceasefire depends on the three "Rs": repatriation, release of prisoners, and reparation. I have experienced for myself, in places like Tajikistan, Afghanistan, and Rwanda, how lingering reminders of the unfinished business of conflict, such as refugees living just outside the borders, missing persons, and a destroyed physical infrastructure, serve as a continual reminder of the root issues themselves. Restoring life as much as possible to its preconflict state—or an improved state, particularly under previously oppressive conditions—may help build a sense of a potential common future.

In countries experiencing recent conflict, all aspects of society appear to be extremely fragile. There have been, in the places where I have worked, few if any domestic development programs, little legitimate government control, and even less trust in any ensuing national plans. In this context, the local level grows in importance, as individuals depend on their communities for direction. At the same time, however, conditions in the community such as large numbers of IDPs, recent returnees, little infrastructure, a foundering economy, few jobs, and possible land mines tend to add to the sense of instability.

Yet another factor is the ramifications that grow from the militarization of society. The abundance of weaponry makes eradicating the threat of violence much more difficult, even if a disarmament agreement is reached. Weapons may be cached or simply removed from the immediate area for access at a later date. Demobilization is an equally complex process, given the difficulty in distinguishing civilians from fighters. The division between police, military, and irregular forces is often faint. The use of force, moreover, corresponds to the ability to obtain resources. In an economically impoverished country, hence, demobilization often translates to diminished income generation for the former soldier. Furthermore, individuals in war-torn societies, particularly those involved in protracted conflicts, have often grown so used to fighting that many know little else. Resources and options for other occupations may be limited, and even basic skills such as literacy may be rare (Stafford 1993).

Under these conditions, the danger that the violence will reignite is real. Joseph Montville, a leading expert in conflict management, speaks of a "wounded group self" which, much like a wounded animal, is dangerously poised to defend itself and extremely vulnerable to attack. He describes three characteristics of victimization in this state: the victim experiences traumatic loss, including security and/or faith in the future; the precipitating violence cannot be justified legally or morally; and there is a constant fear of repeated attack (Montville 1995). The establishment of safety is thus critical to mollifying the fear that paralyzes intergroup interaction and to beginning to heal the wounded group self.

While physical security is essential for individual and community rehabilitation, it does not, by itself, exhaust the concept of safety. Economic security and some semblance of livelihood, for example, are also vital to establishing a sense of security and beginning the healing process. Realization of certain freedoms, such as movement around the community and country, communication with whomever one pleases, and expression of opinions are also important aspects of security. Restrictions on these freedoms, such as government monitoring of conversations, denial of access to certain areas or visiting rights, or the inability to contribute to planning and long-term objectives, in contrast, increase the sense of fear and exposure. Furthermore, safety must include a sense of future, both for the individual and the community, and for the next generation. A limited time frame tends to instill a sense of impending doom that perpetuates an impression of insecurity.

Communalization and Bereavement

Perhaps most critical to the rehabilitation process and a sustainable peace is a reconsideration of the violent offenses. Communalization—the act of sharing traumatic experiences, perceptions, resulting emotions, and responses with other people in a safe environment—together with a period of mourning over the losses, are essential beginnings of the healing process. Communalization, in addition, establishes a public record of historical events, an acknowledgment of circumstances and occurrences crucial for (re)establishing national identity. This extremely important phase, however, is often neglected both in an effort to avoid painful recent events and in the rush to move on.

Sociology, psychology, and conflict studies literature are replete with the idea that processing traumatic experiences and violations is essential to healing. Psychologists have found, for example, that retelling stories of loss and injury is critical to the recovery of combat veterans, as well as victims of domestic violence who suffer from post-traumatic stress disorder (Shay 1994). Communalization and mourning help restore, as Montville terms it, "self-consciousness" in the wounded group self which has been destroyed by rage, disrespect, and insult (1995:166). The process is important for all levels, including the individual, the identity group, the community, and the nation, wherever the tendons of selfhood have been severed. In Bosnia, the Project on Genocide, Psychiatry, and Witnessing is attempting to help Bosnians reconstruct a sense of shared history, under the assumption that having a historical memory is critical to establishing a pluralistic society. According to Stevan Weine, codirector of the project, "Individual survivors must learn how to reconcile the hatreds they feel with their vision of living together. . . . They need to learn how to reconcile their desire for justice or even vengeance with their desire to live in a multi-ethnic democratic society" (Weine 1996:31).

Beginning the journey of communalization can be a difficult step, given the intensity of the animosity and grievances in identity conflict. Individuals involved in violent conflict frequently adamantly avoid revisiting the disturbing experience and resulting emotions. An honest recounting of painful violations, however, can begin to relieve the pain attached to the injustice; grieving over losses eventually subdues the suffering. Both victims and perpetrators benefit from this process, and the community as a whole begins to establish a collective memory based on combined input. Scholar Lucette Valensi examined the consequences of failure to engage in this process in the context of the French military involvement in Algeria between 1954 and 1962. She argues that the Algerian wounds will never heal completely until their side of the story is told, while at the same time, "the Algerian conflict . . . is an unhealed scar in the political consciousness of France" (Watson Institute 1997:14).

In this phase of healing, the essential element is storytelling in an atmosphere of compassion, encouragement, and support. Communalization may transpire in an identity-mixed environment or under segregated conditions; it may occur within a group setting, in an organized public fashion, or individually. The contexts may be a women's organization, a nationwide truth commission, a health clinic, an official workshop, or informal gatherings of friends and family. The Project on Genocide, Psychiatry, and Witnessing used mental health workers as "witnessing professionals." The witnessing approach offers individuals a listener for their story and then seeks appropriate ways to share their story with others (Weine 1996). Under very specific conditions, a judicial process may contribute to communalization. Montville (forthcoming) describes an exercise of "taking a history" in which each party expresses fears, rage, anxiety, and perceptions of the opposing party in a historical review of events. Both grieving and communalization can require substantial periods of time. Partly for this reason, this step is often omitted in the rehabilitation process.

If fully realized, the process of communalization and bereavement will lead to acknowledgments of wrongdoing and forgiveness. At this point, according to Montville, parties to the conflict describe explicitly the acts of violence committed against the other and take moral responsibility for the resulting traumatic losses. This begins the process of true reconciliation. Restitution, if possible, finalizes this phase by symbolically or otherwise offering contrition to the victim in a gesture of true remorse. Though such an outcome is optimal, significant healing can occur simply by beginning the process of communalization and bereavement; submitting to this phase is essential to the overall rehabilitation of the population.

Rebuilding Trust and the Capacity to Trust

The next phase in rebuilding community cohesion and reintegration is reestablishing mutual confidence among individuals across identity lines and redeveloping reliance on one another. After identity conflict so mercilessly tears the fabric of society, faith in others is fundamentally shaken and suspicion prevails. In the absence of any modicum of mutual confidence, however, the community will likely remain unable to function effectively. As we have seen in chapter 5, trust is essential to community transactions of all kinds—in economic cooperation, trade, mutual assistance, reconstruction, care for dependents, decision-making, and future development.

The endeavor to rebuild trust requires penetrating people's sense of being (Volkan, Julius, and Montville 1990). It includes reestablishing a relationship based on fundamental knowledge of the other, considering his or her cultural values, fears, hopes, perceptions, wounds, and historical experience (Saunders 1990). This clearly goes beyond the purely political dealings of state affairs. As interdependence begins to rebuild, however, government authorities, opposition parties, and faction leaders become increasingly interested in the relationship quotient.

Mending relationships, then, is a major function of restoring confidence. In conflicts in which the violations were extremely deep and essentially one-sided, as in genocide, this step can be exceptionally long and intricate. At the community level, the process is complicated by a history of intimate interaction and shared culture, creating a unique experience of communal relationship (Montville, forthcoming). At the individual level, the implications of each personal contact with other members of the community raise the personal stakes of interaction. This can directly affect the will of individuals and the community at large to improve relationships, recognizing the potential long-term benefits of positive relations as well as the ramifications of disastrous ones.

According to several scholars on the subject, building relationships occurs through a series of processes. Saunders, a pioneer in the concept of relationships, suggests that it is "a cumulative and generative process of continuous interaction at many levels that can gradually change perceptions and create opportunities for solutions that did not seem to exist before" (Saunders 1990:18). This kind of interaction presents opportunities to facilitate constructive communication and discover new information, which may counter prevailing stereotypes.

The challenge, nevertheless, is substantial. In cases of extreme animosity, such as those found in identity conflict, Montville maintains that the opposing groups tend to be exceptionally fixed in their perceptions. They are, therefore, unlikely to consider positive change even possible, often viewing adversarial characteristics as genetic givens (Montville 1993). The process may require an extended period of time and indulgence from all those involved. Research on psychological reaction to encounters with antagonistic individuals suggests that short-term or one-time exposures often reinforce negative stereotypes, while consistent interaction over time provides multiple opportunities for new experiences and therefore reversal of previous perceptions (OTI 1995). The potential for stereotype reversal is ostensibly higher in cases where the outbreak of violence has been fairly recent and the deterioration in relationships relatively rapid. In these situations, the process involves reconnecting old unions and redeveloping past mutuality (Montville 1993).

Montville (1993) also discusses how communication becomes critical in rebuilding relationships and establishing trust. The length and consistency of engagement and the resulting perceptions ultimately affect the evolution of the relationship. Each party's perception of the other's credibility influences its decision to use intellect and discussion, or to resort once more to physical force. "As two [groups] recognize the interdependence of their interests through interaction, the quality of their interaction may change, and they may find more ways to communicate, to change perceptions of each other's motives, and eventually to work together on problems that affect them both," writes Saunders (1990:19).

Montville (1993) notes that some degree of management of the interaction is important. Virtually all societies appear to have intrinsic systems of behavior regulation for various conditions. Primitive societies, according to John Keegan, limited the negative repercussions and increased the potential for positive outcomes of combat through the use of tacit constraints. These included tools regulating combat; restricting certain members of society from attack, such as the elderly, women, and children; carefully selecting the place and time of combat; adhering to a season for conflict; and performing rituals that defined the nature of combat as well as the recourse to conciliation, arbitration, and peacemaking (Keegan 1993).

In the more formal framework of a community decision-making process, or within the structure of civil society, interaction can be regulated by means of standards of practice and mutually agreed-upon rules. Generally, in the early stages of meeting, groups seem to establish agreements for self-management and positions of fallback, such as acceptable representation, appropriate means of communication, and an equitable decision-making system. According to Montville (1993), in the less organized setting of everyday individual interaction, regulation may frequently be a product of ritual or custom emanating from shared culture. Regulation may occur, for example, by recognizing areas of appropriate cross-group contact, such as business, maintaining respect for certain individuals (such as the elderly), or avoiding recognized points of agitation. In all cases, regulation offers a means of limiting offensive behavior that may undermine the trust-building process (Montville 1993).

Transformation in the relationship may be the result of any one of several factors. It may stem from a change in the situation itself and the conflict at hand. It can also occur when one party independently experiences a shift, resulting in a new perspective on its association with the rest of the world. Or it may come as a consequence of new learning and information generated from the relationship itself (Saunders 1990).

The evolution of a beneficial relationship and the rebuilding of trust and the capacity to trust can take on several characteristics. First, an increase in communication that leads to better knowledge and understanding tends to promote a growth in interdependence (Montville 1993). This positive development may come from the mutual experience of an ability to work together on problems that threaten both parties. But, as Saunders (1990) points out, successful cooperation on one issue does not guarantee a positive relationship nor the potential for working on other issues. Nevertheless, continual collaboration on a variety of problems can lead to increased insight and eventual trust.

Consistent interaction on shared problems can develop into a valuable capacity in its own right. The mutual benefit of collaborative problem-solving— that is, defining problems, setting objectives, developing alternative solutions, and selecting a course of action—can become an end in itself. This capacity allows the relationship to take on added value and become less strained and more stable. Given continued cooperation, fear eventually begins to subside and, over time, trust develops. As it progresses, the focus on group differences decreases to a level of healthy cross-identity tension. Ultimately, the powerful experience of transforming change can have a widespread ripple effect throughout the community and even beyond, further expanding the capacity to trust.

Reestablishing Personal and Social Morality

The fourth phase in the process of social reintegration is reconstructing the concept of *thémès*, or "what is right,"[3] and reestablishing guidelines for individual and group behavior. Social ethics include acceptable standards for appropriate contact and communication among each segment of the population, standards of honesty, forbidden grounds, responsibility to family and community, personal accountability, the role of loyalty and obligation, and methods for handling emotions such as anger, injustice, betrayal, and jealousy. The development of healthy community social standards is essential to building faith among groups and providing a foundation for social interaction. Furthermore, it can help place boundaries on specific actions, thereby limiting inappropriate or offensive behavior that can build tension and lead to resumption of hostilities.

Simply recognizing the need for such rules and order is the first step in the process. After intense disorder and violation of moral standards, there may be a tendency toward increased community-wide awareness of the dearth of legal and social guidelines. As trust gradually builds across identity lines, a more formal structure within which to develop the growing relationship can provide added reassurance and strengthen credibility. The second step, then, is acknowledging the immorality of past acts. This step actually begins in phase two, during the process of divulging grievances and mourning losses. In phase four, reviewing and admitting to violations committed serves to confirm the communal ethical foundation and reestablish norms of behavior.

Third, defining and firmly asserting a moral order can set the code of conduct as a legitimate social structure. This may be either or both an informal, verbal process of fixing limitations on individual behavior, or an institutional procedure defining legal boundaries and penalties for violation. In the case of the latter, great care should be taken to establish an impartial authority when (re)constructing the judicial system. If the population perceives the judicial system as biased or corrupt, it will fail to serve as a moral guide and may instead be viewed as an avenue for revenge, thus prolonging the cycle of hostilities. Conversely, good laws and judgments can help rid the culture of impunity and reestablish intolerance of immoral conduct. By carefully advocating atonement, moreover, these can assist in the process of forgiveness. (Arguably, real forgiveness must come from a genuine sense of remorse. Misuse of gestures of atonement can exacerbate the grief and misunderstanding; they should there-fore be used only in conjunction with personal acceptance and an authentic sense of repentance.)

The development of a legal system to help set the tone for morality ideally begins after the first three phases have been well established. If punishment by law begins too early in the process of rebuilding community cohesion, it may again be seen as revenge. Instead, it must be conducted in a spirit of commu-nity healing.

In addition to the legal system, communal law can serve as another source of moral guidelines. Given equitable treatment for all identity groups, defer-ence to traditional cultural practices can help reestablish social ethics while reaffirming shared heritage. Accordingly, respected moral authority figures, whether they be community elders, tribal chiefs, village mediators, committee members, or religious leaders, can enhance the strength of moral law.

The last step in the process of rebuilding a sense of individual and group morality is maintaining the established codes. For institutionalized ethical rules of behavior to be effective, all members of society must be held account-able for their actions. A sense of responsibility for individual behavior, then, should be part and parcel of community life, and any deviance must be regarded seriously.

Reintegration and Restoration of Democratic Discourse

The last phase in rebuilding social cohesion is the process of systematizing a diverse contribution to community affairs, which restores community spirit and helps ensure its sustainability. A healthy society accepts and integrates its diverse elements. Though not without contention, such a community has the skills and structure with which to handle disputes peacefully. This inclusive-ness supports participatory discussion that allows the community to make comprehensive decisions, plan for the future, and implement development strategies.

The process of reconstructing inclusive systems of operation in a deeply divided society, such as one recovering from identity conflict, involves several elements. First, as suggested in phase three, it necessarily entails problem-solv-ing, given the multitude of issues facing the community, such as reconstruc-tion, economic rehabilitation, and care for the marginalized members of the community (Conradi 1993). Second, to continue on the path toward reintegra-tion, the process must entail a win-win approach that accommodates at least some elements of all parties' interests (Assefa 1993). One-sided decision-mak-ing structures tend to encourage resentment and ill will. Third, it should incorporate meaningful participation from as broad a base of community members as possible to help create a cooperative vision of shared goals. Ideally, such inclusiveness encompasses individuals and groups often on the fringes of decision-making, such as women and the handicapped. Last, considering the probable extended time frame of the healing process, the focus should be on long-term effectiveness, rather than short-term results.

At the same time, certain divisive ventures ought to be avoided. According to Assefa, the win-lose formula of multiparty elections and the (often externally generated) pressure for pluralism, for example, tends to undermine any shared vision, mutual cooperation, or consensus. He explains that "although people in multi-party systems tend to recognize the maxim that 'winning is not everything,' in deeply divided societies, winning might be the only thing." He illustrates this point with the 1992 Angola elections, where lack of confidence that the political system would care for all of Angolan citizens generated a party power-play in which winner took all (1993:26–27).

Similarly, the (also often externally generated) pressure for the economic competition of a free market system can aggravate the polarization of a society, according to scholars Eftihia Voutira and Shaun Brown (1995). In the typically resource-scarce environment of a postconflict community, competition for resources is intense. Therefore, pressure for economic rivalry may be a divisive strategy for rehabilitation, potentially reopening wounds and increasing resentment and hostility.

Instead, according to Voutira and Brown, the approach to developing democratic discourse should be integrative and inclusive and encourage consensus-building as much as possible; the underlying mechanism should encourage parties to seek common ground rather than vie for position or dominance. In contrast to majority rule, Assefa's reconciliation politics uses the problem-solving method of "interest negotiation," involving continuous interaction in search of mutually agreeable solutions to issues of reconstruction, relief, development, and so on (1993). Above all, this approach focuses on cooperation, which, by definition, entails interdependence and the building of relationships.

Several instruments can help the process of reintegration and the development of democratic discourse. One mechanism used successfully, at times, early on the road to democratization is a national convention. A convention offers the potential to develop a common vision of postconflict society by soliciting a wide array of opinions and holding intensive discussions on the sensitive matter of future development. Obviously a delicate, complex, and time-consuming endeavor, a national convention nevertheless provides a forum for building consensus on critical issues (Assefa 1993). A similar process might be useful in a community setting to build a common vision of a rehabilitated society.

Another tactic is to rebuild traditional decision-making structures. Particularly in protracted conflicts, these mechanisms tend to become debilitated to the point of being inoperative and, therefore, may be absent during the initial stages of rehabilitation. As in the deference to communal law in phase four, resuscitating elders councils, religious institutions, committee formats, and citizen plenary sessions helps restore traditional custom and places emphasis on internal rather than foreign means (Rupesinghe 1991). Chapter 7 will explore this process further. It is important to note, however, that some of these mechanisms may have become (or, indeed, have always been) biased or oppressive. Correcting the inequities and empowering the institutions, as Assefa contends, may help move the society toward a more rooted, participatory, and harmonious structure.

Another forum for democratic discourse that can lead down the path toward reintegration is the (re)development of a civil society. Though civil society can play multiple roles in the relationship between the state and its citizens, its relevance here is the access it provides to the democratic process (Blair 1992). In a healthy political structure, civil society offers an arena for citizen participation in decision-making. It also provides a means by which the population holds the government accountable for its actions. A strong civil society, moreover, offers avenues for peaceful change by presenting disgruntled citizens with access to nonviolent methods of persuasion, instead of resorting to physical violence.

Conflict-ravaged communities have usually lost most semblance of civil society, which is generally the product of a strong social infrastructure. In addition to the dispersal of, and decrease in, the population itself, the means and security required to assemble members of civil society are likely inadequate. As a result, whatever political structure may exist cannot benefit fully from citizen involvement, and the population itself suffers from the lack of access to the larger decision-making structure. Revitalization of civil society can provide a means of democratic discourse and, ultimately, peaceful change. Strengthening civil society in a recovering community offers greater opportunity for wide participation and for presenting differing views in a relatively safe space.

These phases present a generic, ideal progression from a segregated, hostile population to a respectful, cooperating community committed to mutual future development and sustainable peace. The actual process of reintegration, rebuilding community cohesion, and eventual reconciliation, however, is obviously complex, convoluted, and long. There is no cathartic cure for the wounds of violence.

Nevertheless, what choice do we have as international helpers in these circumstances but to approach recovery from complex emergencies in a comprehensive, yet visionary manner? As we have seen, this entails addressing not merely physical and economic issues but also psychological and social rehabilitation. The next chapter discusses the role of the international community in the recovery process. It explores the negative impacts of external aid, proposes a new operational framework, and offers specific strategies for rebuilding community.

CHAPTER SEVEN INTERNATIONAL INTERCESSION IN COMMUNITY REHABILITATION

The problem of rebuilding houses can be solved. But the problem of rebuilding souls is difficult.

—Tajik on the possibility of sustainable peace (Anderson 1995a:11)

The international community—that is, the entire array of foreign actors interested in a country's situation—intentionally or inadvertently plays a part in the process of recovery from a complex emergency. The course taken can either mitigate or exacerbate the effects of violent conflict. The challenge in this decade of global emergencies, therefore, is to improve the actions of the international actors so as to promote a healthy society and increase the chances for a sustainable peace.

Two factors hinder this task. First, individual foreign actors may not always have sustainable peace as their highest priority, particularly when political interests are at stake, such as natural resources, ex-colonies, military allegiances, geographic location, historical relationships, and even, in places, ideology. The task, then, extends to the whole of the international community to guide the overall efforts in a positive direction. The second obstacle is the dearth of understanding about the outcome of various actions. This likely stems from our relative inexperience with complex emergencies, and from the resulting inadequate evaluation of their circumstances and our intercessions.

The conceptual framework of community-level healing outlined in chapter 6 requires an operational framework for implementing the objectives, which is the focus of this chapter. First, however, we will look closely at the current state of international aid in complex emergencies. Then we will study its unintentional—but dangerous—negative effects. Finally, we will examine selected activities along the spectrum of international aid for promoting community healing.

The Evolution of International Aid in Complex Emergencies

In the preponderance of complex emergencies since 1990, the humanitarian seat has radiated under the spotlight of international attention. Though not a phenomenon entirely novel to the nineties, their increased numbers, size, and demands have focused diplomatic, media, and public interest, particularly in donor countries, on alleviating the suffering they bring and, to some extent, addressing their causes. This development has coincided with new conditions related to complex emergencies themselves.

New International Climate

The attention has brought some change to international intercession, including the addition of several new players. Most significantly, perhaps, the UN General Assembly created two posts to respond more directly to the field demands of complex emergencies. The first was the Under Secretary-General for Humanitarian Affairs in 1991, and the second was the UN High Commissioner for Human Rights (UNHCHR) in 1994. The new reform measures proposed under the new Secretary-General, Kofi Annan, however, eliminated the Department of Humanitarian Affairs at the end of 1997 and rolled it into the Office for the Coordination of Humanitarian Affairs.

The 1990s also brought some additional resources and capacities. UNHCR's budget doubled between 1989 and 1995, for instance, and contributions from major donors more than tripled from $1.4 billion in 1984 to its peak at $4.5 billion in 1993 (U.S. Mission 1995:11, 14). Several UN agencies, moreover, have increased their capacity to respond to emergencies. The UNDP and DHA, for example, created rapid response forces, the DHA and UNHCR established revolving funds to cover startup costs, and the World Food Program (WFP), UNICEF, and UNHCR have all expanded their mandates to some degree (U.S. Mission 1995:11). In addition, the inclusion of vast military sources in the relief equation since the turn of the decade has significantly augmented the resource pool. Private funding has also been substantial, accounting for nearly 30 percent of funding for humanitarian aid in 1995 (U.S. Mission 1997:17).

Recent years, however, show a slight decline in donor funding for emergency relief, and many observers maintain that the needs still far outweigh the available resources (Loescher 1993; USCR 1995; Walker 1996). While humanitarian relief funding has increased since the beginning of the decade, foreign aid across the globe is decreasing as a result of tighter fiscal policies, increased domestic concerns, growing population strains, and other factors. This decrease tends to diminish the nonemergency programs that may prevent the conditions that contribute to complex emergencies. Among these programs are family planning, education, health care, agriculture, and water resources (Borton 1993).

The pressure to respond, compounded by the complexity of these forms of disasters and our relative inexperience with them, has forced the international community to scramble for practicable actions to resolve the crises, particularly during the first half of the 1990s. Consequently, humanitarian assistance is often used as a substitute for political action in complex emergencies. The result is what could be termed the "politicization of humanitarian aid." This is a play on terminology, in that the phrase is most frequently used in reference to the looting or diversion of relief supplies for the purpose of enhancing the political or economic position of local fighting factions (Loescher 1993:28). Here, however, I am using it to refer to international actors' themselves substituting humanitarian aid for appropriate political action. Offering visible, popular, uncontroversial relief aid is often easier than the less tangible, sticky steps involved in political intercession. As such, relief becomes the subject of political manipulation and thus "politicized."

On the other hand, the politicization of aid comes also from an apparent inadequacy of available options. The intricacies of today's emergencies make it difficult to locate the appropriate tool for the job. In fact, to many policymakers and heads of international organizations, the toolbox looks surprisingly empty. New mechanisms are needed to respond to contemporary conditions. As will be discussed, however, many options exist currently that can be applied in concert with others, which together may address the situations effectively.[1] Appropriate response becomes all the more important now that the international community is beginning to recognize that its inadequacies only serve to extend and even exacerbate the emergency (Sollis 1994).

The New Disaster Climate

The humanitarian scene is also undergoing significant evolution at the field level. Just one of the many elements the relief community now has to face is the conditions brought about by failed states. In the absence of authority, the inevitable power struggles present serious security problems for aid workers (Minear and Weiss 1993b). One does not have to look further than Liberia and Sierra Leone to see why many field professionals have grown concerned about the increased threats, assaults, and physical dangers they face in relief work. The loss of Fred Cuny not only reminds us of the risks but causes us to rethink our concept of assistance.[2]

The liability comes in part when humanitarian organizations lose control over relief resources. Such loss of control often results from diversions by the military, interference from fighting factions or government entities, looting of relief supplies, obstruction of convoys and distribution mechanisms, and so on (Anderson 1994; Minear and Weiss 1993a; Prendergast 1995). While such conditions are now common and concern for security has grown accordingly, appropriate responses have been elusive. Because of the pressure, international actors have recently made attempts to articulate new options.

At the same time as conditions in the field are becoming increasingly complex and dangerous, the number of new organizations responding to these scenes is rising dramatically (Aall 1996; Borton 1993; U.S. Mission 1997). In Rwanda, for example, NGOs poured into Kigali in August 1994 and literally overwhelmed the city. In a matter of weeks, white faces and four-wheel-drive vehicles began to dominate the cityscape, the price of housing doubled, and enterprising Rwandans began earnest appeals for jobs as office clerks, logisticians, drivers, house cleaners, or cooks.

There are several reasons for this growth. First, Western donors began to rely increasingly on NGOs for implementation of emergency aid in the 1980s, when they experienced greater difficulty working through bilateral channels and even international organizations, according to John Borton (1993), a research fellow of the Overseas Development Institute. As Borton points out, relief agencies often have greater flexibility, speed, and less rigid mandates in providing aid in areas of conflict, political instability, and disputed sovereignty. The United States, for its part, has dramatically increased the speed of its response through on-site funding of NGOs.

Second, as resources have moved from development to emergency in the zero-sum game of foreign aid, many organizations previously engaged in long-term programs have shifted to short-term relief operations. Organizations reliant on Western government financing for agriculture, public health, alternative energy, community development, small enterprise, natural resource management, and the like are receiving a small piece of the funding pie (Owen 1993). In response, they have followed the source and adjusted and augmented their skills base to react to emergency situations (Borton 1993).

Third, as startling images of ongoing crises are now broadcast around the world in seconds, the public appeal for immediate response has escalated. Concerned citizens react by starting their own organization in an attempt to alleviate the suffering as well as their own sense of helplessness (Awoonor 1993). In a benevolent gesture of goodwill, they often collect used clothing, medicine, canned food, excess medical equipment, and other unbidden transportable items and send an envoy along with the supplies to the affected country.

Finally, most countries place very few restrictions, if any, on individuals wishing to start an NGO, and even less constraints on NGOs entering a disaster-ridden country with the intention of helping. Given independent funding, whether from public contribution, wealthy philanthropists, religious fund-raising, or foundations, NGOs are generally limited only by their boards of directors and guiding principles. Most Western governments, however, require a degree—albeit minimal—of substantiation before providing financing for emergency programs.

In the absence of significant government regulation, it is widely recognized that the NGO community as a whole has had few institutional mechanisms for establishing and accepting standards of self-regulation (Minear and Weiss 1993b). As a conglomeration of independent entities, in the past NGOs have found it difficult to organize and commit to limitations on activities and agreed protocol. Much of the international NGO relief community, nevertheless, have recognized the need for standardization, and codes of conduct and best practices are currently emerging.[3] (The actual development of standards will be addressed later in this chapter.)

The consequence of the explosion of new NGOs responding to foreign complex emergencies is substantial. While there has been an impressive escalation in professionalization and capabilities among the leading organizations, the level of competence in the entire community varies widely. The increasing number of young agencies involved in any emergency and employing relatively unseasoned staff, therefore, translates into a drop in the average level of relief worker experience. On occasion in these complex, often hazardous, settings, one encounters foreigners in the field who are not only confronting their first political crisis, their first disaster of any sort, but sometimes their first experience abroad. In addition, the newer organizations have very little institutional knowledge, memory, or protocol with which to guide their employees in an appropriate response through the extremely intricate and dangerous maze of a complex emergency (Frohardt 1994; Minear 1994). The short-term nature and limited funding parameters of most responses, by definition, offer little time to build such experience in any single setting (U.S. Mission 1995). Furthermore, the general standards, procedures, and approaches that are being developed have not yet gained sufficient strength to effectively guide the notoriously independent nature of nongovernmental organizations in the field.

In short, the fragile environment can become more perilous and chaotic with the introduction of well-intentioned but inappropriate aid. Such foreign involvement can add to the difficulties of coordination, distribution of resources, housing, inflation, security, and the overall effectiveness of the international community. Cuny writes, "The arrival of massive amounts of useless relief goods, untrained personnel and volunteers, and untrained officials all add confusion to a disaster and delay recovery actions. Furthermore, the time and money spent sorting out and eliminating this unnecessary assistance cannot be recaptured" (Cuny 1983:201–202).

Because of their lack of experience, new organizations generally have even less contextual understanding of conditions specific to the complex emergency. Many observers consider this to be a problem across the board in the relief community. Inexperienced agencies, however, are at a particular disadvantage; since they have not learned lessons from related situations, they may not understand certain implications of their actions, and they may not have access to local information gained through long-term involvement in the region (Minear and Weiss 1993a). This inexperience can seriously degrade the professionalism of the international response and often offsets the positive work of others in the field. In the strong words of Fred Cuny, "In any case, international agencies rushing to the scene don't have a clue about what they are doing nor are they aware of the complexity of the political environment in which they operate. The rest of us spend a lot of time picking up the pieces after these well-intentioned, but counterproductive, agencies" (Cuny 1990:12).

Another dimension of the lack of widespread professionalism in the field is the relief community's relationship with the host country. The inundation of foreign organizations often overwhelms a nation struggling with internal problems (Awoonor 1993). Under these conditions, the government's ability to manage and oversee the foreign-run activities is usually minimal and inconsistent at best. At the same time, particularly the less sophisticated NGOs may disregard the sovereignty and desires of the authorities and people of the country in which they operate. This became a serious issue in Rwanda and, to a lesser extent, in eastern Congo when the fragile new governments eventually gained strength and began a process of NGO registration. Not a few NGOs deemed it an affront to their independence and refused to comply. Eventually, thirty-eight of these organizations in Rwanda, as well as those the authorities considered to be ineffective, were expelled from the country (Kumar et al. 1996:97).

Except in those countries basically devoid of government, an attitude of disregard for local authority often results in tension between the host country and the relief community as a whole, which can compromise the positive outcomes of assistance as well as put aid workers at risk (Minear and Weiss 1993b; Van Brabant 1998). Other postures can be equally damaging, according to Kofi Awoonor, who speaks of the "recipient fatigue" of host countries: "Humanitarian assistance is guided by moral virtue, a sense of anticipated well-being that the gesture of giving is sure to bestow on the giver. . . . A mild degree of self-righteousness propels the gesture, the feeling of 'but for the Grace of God, there go I' " (1993:74).

Awoonor goes on to berate the fund-raising efforts of NGOs as the "capitalization of mercy." Their appeal to charity for the starving dark masses of Africa and the dazed refugees, "reinforce the stereotype of underdeveloped nations who can do nothing for themselves unless the rich and the powerful intervene. . . . Are we the peoples of the so-called Third World so helpless that we can only be portrayed as eternal objects of pity?" he asks (1993:78). Indeed, the concept of charity does have strong roots in the aid community.[4] At the same time, the broad array of organizations represents an equally wide spectrum of attitudes and philosophies. Our challenge, then, is to narrow that range to include only those that demonstrate deep respect for accountability, professionalism, and high standards of operation as well as for a host country's culture. Equally important is to examine our own motivations in order to exclude pure self-interest and a condescending view of the recipients.

In the process of relief operations, NGOs, often either inadvertently or by necessity in the case of failed states, assume the responsibility of government agencies by providing health care, food, water, security, and shelter for the citizens. As a result, in conditions of the "atrophy of government,"[5] humanitarian organizations become the reigning authority. Their higher public image and local authority may become a thorn in the government's side as it creates a new power structure in the region (Amoda 1996). This was particularly evident in Somalia as the public as well as community leaders began to turn to NGOs for answers to political questions. In the Belet Wayne area, I observed that clan leaders were both resentful of and reliant on international organizations' often inadvertent influence on local decision-making. As a result of their actual and perceived power, agency representatives were the objects of intimidation and lobbying.

In defense of NGOs, there has been significant movement over the past years to rectify some of these problems and increase the level of performance in the field. Besides the development of codes of conduct and best practices, international NGOs have begun collaborating considerably more than in the past. This has created lively discussions over such difficult issues as security, accountability, limitations on aid, inclusion of gender considerations, and so on.

The Negative Repercussions of International Aid on the Conflict

Foreign aid can adversely impact host communities in a number of ways. Most relevant for this discussion is the fact that aid often inadvertently aggravates the inter-identity tension (Anderson 1994; Frohardt 1994; Prendergast 1995). Not many years ago, the common philosophy was that economic scarcity contributed to intergroup hostilities; deprivation was an ingredient to war. This reasoning prevailed during the insurrectionist period and was often used to incite movements against the dominant force.

Today, however, it is becoming increasingly clear that injecting resources into conditions of poverty often exacerbates inter-identity animosity. The Local Capacities for Peace Project (mentioned in chapter 1 and headed by Mary Anderson) has been studying this phenomenon. Anderson says, "Evidence is that aid more often worsens conflict (even when it is effective in humanitarian and/or development terms) rather than helps mitigate it" (1996a:14). There seem to be four ways in which this occurs.

Introducing Resources into a Resource-Scarce Environment

First, according to Anderson (1994) and others (e.g., Cuny 1983), rather than alleviating the competition by augmenting the total amount available, adding new supplies seems to increase the intensity of the competition. There may be a natural element of human greed after periods of scarcity that multiplies the desire for sustenance in fear of another period of drought. Satiation, it appears, is a rather rare phenomena in identity conflicts.

Introducing vast quantities of resources into a resource-scarce environment alters the economic equation. Relief commodities often become the new currency in areas inundated with assistance (Minear and Weiss 1993b). In Guinea, for instance, rice functioned as the medium for bargaining, in some cases supplanting the need for actual legal tender. When it assumes this role, relief grows in value and is pursued by any means available, becoming subject to looting, manipulation, diversion, theft, and intentional mismanagement. In Somalia, where sorghum is the traditional staple and rice is considered a luxury, the massive quantities of rice brought into the country by aid agencies during the famine in the early 1990s spawned enormous thievery and diversion. According to John Prendergast of the Center for Concern, "Internationally donated rice in Somalia reached legendary status in terms of its attractiveness to looters, whereas sorghum drew little interest" (Prendergast 1995:12). These international aid practices clearly contribute to increased instability and violence.

The insertion of commodities into an area of need, moreover, often frees local resources to be used for combat (Anderson 1994:8; Creative Associates 1997:3/143). Without the daily requirement of cultivating, searching for, and preparing food, people, transportation vehicles, and time can be dedicated to the conflict. In Somalia, where the procurement and preparation of food required significant collective effort, relief lifted a large burden off the shoulders of all community members, but particularly those of young men inclined to fight.

As a valued commodity, aid itself can become the source of competition between identity groups. When relief becomes the regional focus, it can divert energy away from traditional occupations such as those in agriculture, cottage industries, and the like (Cuny 1990). The interdependence between local populations for commerce, information, transportation, and other aspects of daily life, moreover, can deteriorate with the introduction of international relief distributions. In Afghanistan, foreign assistance contributed to the competition for aid among the *mujahidin* that continued to divide the country, and in fact became an extension of the conflict (Minear and Weiss 1993a:37).

The repercussions of this kind of rivalry are compounded when territories are divided by faction, allowing them to regulate the movement of relief supplies (Prendergast 1995). By controlling aid routes, the combatants are able to manipulate civilian populations at the mercy of outside assistance, and thus prolong the conflict (Anderson 1996a). An example was the Bosnian Serb control over incoming aid to Sarajevo. The citizens inside the city were literally under siege, which served to exacerbate the regional tension. More recently, roadblocks controlled alternately by Serbian special police or the Kosovo Liberation Army excluded whole populations from receiving humanitarian aid, and consequently increased tensions.

Inadvertent Favoritism

A second way in which foreign aid can contribute to the conflict is when relief agencies wittingly or unwittingly exhibit bias in their assistance. Opposing groups carefully scrutinize organizations for their fairness in distribution, whether it is a matter of location, amount or type of aid, or the manner in which it is allocated. Perceived favoritism can not only diminish the legitimacy of the organization itself but can also create greater resentment against the other groups, again exacerbating existing tension (Anderson 1996a). Once it is labeled as biased, an agency usually finds it difficult to reclaim a reputation of neutrality. Subsequent assistance to any group is likely to be tainted and the "favored" populations, accordingly, viewed as opposition.

Favoritism may skew not only distributions but also other actions, such as hiring practices. More often than not, in the cases I have observed, international agencies enter a foreign environment and, unaware of the intricacies of the situation and in a rush to respond, hire the most qualified, available individuals, without paying close attention to identity. The organization may not be aware that a certain identity group may dominate the capital city, has more education, is more characteristically assertive (particularly when seeking employment), or has more of the skills required by relief agencies. As a result, an inattentive relief worker may hire many more workers from one group than another and thus give the impression of bias in the agency's operation. In a Tamil section of Sri Lanka, for instance, donors established a reconstruction program in which administration of some resources was predominantly Sinhalese, leaving the Tamils with limited control over affairs in their area. As a result, the Tamils viewed every other aspect of the reconstruction program as unfair (Cuny and Cuny 1992:79–80). The identity of an agency's translators can be particularly sensitive, since the bias of the individual is perceived to have a ripple affect throughout the organization.

Targeted assistance to specific populations such as returnees or internally displaced persons may also be perceived as unfair, since such groups normally consist of members of one identity group more than another. Providing specific aid to unaccompanied minors or women is less apt to be seen as an identity-based bias, but such programs might also create resentment and tension between community members simply out of perceived favoritism.

Proportionality across identity lines, therefore, is an important principle under contemporary circumstances. The guidelines of some organizations, such as Catholic Relief Services or the American Friends Service Committee, specifically dictate providing aid to both sides of the conflict. Nevertheless, some international organizations will inevitably be accused—justifiably or not—of bias no matter how careful many are to be fair (Prendergast 1995). Cultural differences inevitably leave foreign aid workers blind to important elements of discrimination. The influence of donors can also bias NGO activities by impelling the organization to carry out the political policy of the financing establishment (Minear and Weiss 1993b).

Regardless, in conflicts where opposing groups manipulate access to humanitarian organizations, avoiding bias may be nearly impossible at times. Many of the older NGOs have been reevaluating their operating doctrines as they struggle with inherently difficult conditions in complex emergencies. Even the ICRC, known for its strict adherence to the Geneva Conventions and its laws of impartiality and neutrality, has had to withdraw from situations as a result of its inability to adhere to its principles (Minear and Weiss 1993a). As a result of this dilemma, a growing debate over intentional partiality is emerging, and organizations are reviewing the appropriateness of neutrality under conditions of clear injustice, such as one-sided massacres in Rwanda and Bosnia.

Unintentional Empowerment of Factions

Humanitarian operations can serve in several ways to sanction and even assist the fighting capacity of the groups in combat, such as when supplies diverted from intended civilian recipients physically sustain the combatants. In El Salvador, for example, assistance distributed to civilians in zones controlled by the rebel forces reinforced the rebels' political and military strength by providing them with physical sustenance. This had the added repercussion of provoking attacks by the government army on both the civilians and the rebels in the area (Minear and Weiss 1993b:33).

Additionally, the government may use hard currency introduced through aid projects to fund conflict efforts (Creative Associates 1997:3/150). When relief organizations negotiate with local factions for passage of relief supplies, employ armed elements to protect relief goods, and deal with factional heads for the release of kidnapped relief workers, they reinforce the status of the fighting elements (Frohardt 1994; Minear and Weiss 1993a; Prendergast 1995; Van Brabant 1998). Direct communication with combatants, according to Anderson, supports their claims to legitimacy—especially when a breakdown in governance increases theft and harassment of aid personnel and forces organizations to negotiate with factional leaders (1994:11; 1996a:48). Somalia offered several examples of fighting clans kidnapping, threatening, or killing relief workers. Under such circumstances, aid organizations understandably responded by enlisting local clan members to guard them. Several elements of the relief community have been scrutinizing this situation and examining alternatives.

Furthermore, the government or military can abuse international assistance to repress certain elements. In particular, development projects may be used for counterinsurgency, forced relocation, or pacification of the civilian population (Stein 1991). Pacification programs, for example, may be disguised to resettle rebel strongholds, redraw identity lines to redistribute populations of support, or to force citizens to choose sides between fighting elements (Cuny 1990). All these actions serve to promote the conflict by accepting the terms of war, bestowing legitimacy on warriors, and undermining peacetime values (Anderson 1996a).

Insisting on Conciliatory Gestures Too Early

A fourth element of relief operations that may hinder rather than help the healing process is foreigners' "forgive and forget" attitude. Donor governments and international institutions may insist that the government grant a general amnesty for all refugees or establish plurality in leadership before they will provide significant financial aid. The European Union, for example, initially set implicit conditions on its funds to the new government of Rwanda based on "enlarging the government." Doing so meant specifically including the party of those implicated in the genocide, a move that was highly unacceptable to the new government (Kumar et al. 1996:32).

Additionally, international organizations may put undue pressure on factional representatives and civic leaders to attend reconciliation conferences, problem-solving workshops, and the like. Many outside organizations proposed such conferences in Rwanda shortly after the genocide. These efforts either failed for lack of participation or, worse, forced individuals to confront each other before they were situationally and emotionally prepared, possibly reinfecting the open wounds and generally causing greater resistance.

Similarly, conflict resolution specialists may introduce training into communities and situations not prepared for outside intercession. This can be particularly dangerous since the vast majority of foreign conflict management organizations do not maintain a continual presence in the field. As a result, participants may begin the fragile process of internal healing and then have to face the daily reality of conflict alone. Further, according to Colin Rule (1993) of the National Institute for Dispute Resolution, some groups' use of techniques and approaches that are inappropriate to the ethnic, gender, and cultural makeup of participants may inflame tensions.[6]

The consequence of foreign entities' insisting on rapid reconciliation and reintegration can increase rather than decrease hostilities. The attention focused on conflict-laden issues immediately after severe loss and social upheaval may simply draw attention to and reignite the underlying animosities. Such pressure may increase intra- as well as intergroup tension. Finally, outside intercession in community dynamics may exaggerate the actual level of hostility, creating a larger conflict than originally existed (Voutira and Brown 1995).

The negative repercussions of foreign assistance should be judged carefully; many elements are beyond the relief community's immediate control and all must be weighed in balance with the positive outcomes. As long as there are situations that cause human suffering, there will be agencies attempting to alleviate it. The goal of the international community should be to reduce the negative impacts and expand the positive results by establishing concerted policies within a coordinated operational structure.

Building a New Operational Framework

The new conceptual framework requires a corresponding operational paradigm for guiding international aid programs. Such a structure might help international organizations detect and mitigate the negative effects of assistance as well as establish programs that specifically address the damaged relationships between groups and between individual community members. It incorporates designing long-term and comprehensive strategies for economic development, rebuilding social structures and institutional capacity, strengthening community cohesion, and developing civil society.

My field research and experience have led to five conclusions about community-level healing in a complex emergency. First, the return of displaced populations can offer enhanced potential for rebuilding relationships. Some returnees left sanctuaries that provided protection, supplies, and services, though not all were so well endowed. Nearly all returnees, however, risk poverty, retaliation, and rejection back in their home community and are, therefore, anxious to reinstate a degree of security. With that in mind, most re-turnees have a strong interest—at least initially—in restoring peaceful relations with fellow community members. At the same time, members who remained at home may be exhausted from fighting and in need of support and assistance in rebuilding the infrastructure and the economy. They, too, are often initially disposed toward attempting to live in peace. Together, these attitudes offer a window of opportunity to begin the healing process as displaced populations return.

Second, the problems inherent in a violence-ravaged community frequently demand immediate and concerted attention, thereby presenting opportunities for cooperative decision-making. In a postconflict environment, the often enormous needs, such as reconstruction, care of the marginalized members, reestablishing social structures, and economic rehabilitation, require practical solutions. Although conventional leadership may be absent, priorities must be set, resources assessed, and plans made to address the problems. These demands provide distinct opportunities to repair the community decision-making apparatus.

Third, international relief and development personnel already in the community offer a continual third-party presence. Because aid workers maintain a constant and potentially long-term residence in the community, they often serve as witnesses and unofficial monitors of the situation. The largest contact the international community has with the conflict—certainly at the grassroots—usually comes through relief operations. Consequently, community-based expatriate personnel tend to be relatively familiar with the local people, situation, context, and modalities, and can bridge the relief-to-rehabilitation gap by offering support for such ensuing intercessions as peace-building initiatives and human rights monitors.

Fourth, rehabilitation projects present occasions for cross-conflict communication, reintegration, and trust-building. Simply by virtue of their (ostensibly) continuous, relatively long-duration interaction over the life of a project, identity groups have multiple opportunities to reassociate with each other and relearn how to communicate across identity lines. The sheer number of possible projects multiplies this potential interaction.

Fifth, community-level reconciliation can contribute to reduced tensions nationwide and provide a broad grassroots base of support for high-level peace agreements. Widespread community healing can have a pervasive calming affect on the national temperament. As violence fails to reignite at the local level, leaders lose support for their struggles, and they may decide to engage in official settlement discussions (Meyer-Knapp, forthcoming). Conversely, accords negotiated among leaders can win support in the communities through broad-based healing tactics. Countrywide peace, in fact, *requires* community adherence; leadership-level and community-level efforts must work in tandem to bring about sustainable stability.

It is clear that the new operational structure must incorporate the big picture. As discussed in chapter 1, any useful conceptual framework should include not only a comprehensive analysis and consideration of the various factors bearing on the situation but also a larger time frame. The entire predisaster-to-development cycle must be borne in mind in designing an operational structure for rehabilitating wartorn communities. This process entails more than physical and economic reconstruction and more than the melding of preventive, relief, and development aid. It requires an even larger perspective, inclusive of an awareness of the nature and basic causes of the conflict, relief and development considerations, as well as attention to the social, political, and human rights dimensions—all of which may extend over a period of years, if not decades. Postconflict reconstruction must focus beyond the typical infrastructure, livelihood, and market rebuilding. To borrow the words of scholar Peter Sollis, it must also deal with "the hidden scars of warfare through policies and programs which support the reconstitution of the family and kinship ties and the social and cultural institutions that are critical to aiding recovery" (1994:15). Reconstruction, in short, offers the opportunity to redress previous inequities and to go beyond the status quo ante.

Strategies for Rebuilding Community

In outlining approaches for healing communities destroyed by violence, it is important to note that there are no easy answers and that each situation is unique, requiring individualized tactics. There is clearly no blanket prescription for peace. Developing peaceful relations, moreover, is an internal process, not one that can be imposed from the outside. Each step must be taken when the time is right and the participants ready.

Outsiders can, however, play an important role in preparing, supporting, and otherwise encouraging cross-conflict interaction and eventual reintegration. Providing an element of security, for example, or helping fighters disengage from the conflict can be roles for the international community. The Local Capacities for Peace Project found that while imagining reconciliation was difficult (particularly given the horrors of identity conflict), many combatants welcomed the opportunity to detach themselves from the hardship of fighting (Anderson 1996a). International actors are in a particularly good position to assist in this effort.

All efforts must be tailored to the unique conditions of each situation, based on in-depth understanding of the components making up the context and strict attention to their influence on the circumstances. Flexibility, innovation, and constant attempts to cater to specific needs are absolutely critical. In that same vein, it is also important, as Awoonor (1993) points out, to maintain a policy of working first with resources, ideas, and methods indigenous to the population before introducing outside elements. Such an approach requires eliciting suggestions rather than dictating them, investigating and increasing the local capacity, and enhancing regional competence.

A general approach to community rehabilitation might have four dimensions.

Do No Harm

First, and most fundamental, is the Hippocratic principle of "do no harm." As the title of Anderson's book (1996a) suggests, it is better to do nothing than to cause further damage. Literature by Anderson, Prendergast, and Creative Associates outline specific steps aid agencies can take to minimize the potential of causing greater injury in societies already suffering from complex emergencies. For example, both carefully selecting the site(s) to off-load relief supplies as well as carefully choosing which method(s) of distribution to use can avoid diversion of aid by military units. In Somalia, the ICRC contracted with entrepreneurs to transport relief goods throughout the country. The entrepreneurs themselves ensured the security, with the incentive of a 10 percent profit upon delivery. Looting dropped from 60 to 10 percent (Prendergast 1995:9).

Another way to minimize theft and manipulation by fighting forces (and thus to avoid increased tension) is to provide aid directly to family members rather than through an official intermediary. In recent years, the concept of supplying food relief to and through women in order to deliver needed goods straight to the mouths of the hungry, as well to diminish the risk of corruption or diversion, has received considerable attention.

Ethical Engagement

The second dimension in community rehabilitation is the concept of interceding under the guidance of moral principles. Thomas Weiss and Larry Minear, of
the Humanitarianism and War Project, suggest eight maxims as ethical guide-
posts in humanitarian operations. Known as the Providence Principles(Minear
and Weiss 1993a:19), they are:

1. *Relieving life-threatening suffering* as the primary action of humanitarian
   efforts;

2. *Proportionality to need*, that is, all action should correspond to the
   degree of suffering;

3. *Nonpartisanship* and elimination of political, sectarian, or other agendas;

4. *Independence* of all humanitarian organizations from the interference
   of home or host political authorities;

5. *Accountability* and the necessity of being transparent on all humanitarian actions to sponsors and beneficiaries (as well as other relief organizations);

6. *Appropriateness* to local circumstances;

7. *Contextualization*, taking into consideration the overall need and the
   impact of actions; and

8. *Subsidiarity of sovereignty*, that is, when disputed, sovereignty should
   defer to the needs of the suffering.[7]

The viability of some of these principles, particularly in light of identity conflicts, may be doubtful.[8] In a country consumed by civil conflict, for instance, it
is difficult to imagine the government's deference to humanitarian needs over,
in its eyes, the larger concern for national sovereignty. In addition, it is generally accepted as good practice for organizations operating in a foreign country
to communicate closely with host-government authorities. Such contact may
make the independence principle difficult to uphold.

Moreover, the desirability of complete nonpartisanship is now being called
into question in the context of such extreme cases as Rwandan refugee camps,
where humanitarian agencies found themselves indirectly supporting the
efforts of alleged genocide perpetrators to retool for a subsequent assault on the
country. "The strict interpretation of traditional precepts such as neutrality has
questionable utility for humanitarian organizations responding to current complex emergencies," affirms Mark Frohardt of the Center for the Study of
Societies in Crisis (1994:4). In fact, certain elements within the humanitarian
community have recently debated the appropriateness of heretofore strict

adherence to such principles as nonconditionality of assistance (though not of protection), free access, impartiality, freedom of movement, and no political involvement.

That said, humanitarian operations nevertheless increasingly require strong guiding principles to direct and standardize activities in the growing complexity of today's emergencies. The recent focus on best practices, thus, provides welcome guidance for all agencies, not the least of which, the new ones. Contextualization, appropriateness, accountability, equal treatment, freedom of choice, proportionality, and participation are indeed vitally important in humanitarian activities and should be taken seriously by those working in strife-torn environments.

The Holistic View

The third aspect of community rehabilitation is the importance of maintaining a comprehensive approach that contains broad analysis and integrated programs. Economic incentives should be included in the effort to reestablish water and electrical systems; environmental considerations should be a regular component of infrastructure reconstruction; and the issues fanning the violence should be first and foremost on relief professionals' minds in designing social rehabilitation programs. Prendergast (1995) argues that in analyzing a situation, an organization should look at the patterns of marginalization along class, identity, gender, and political lines. Indeed, it is necessary to consider how social relations predetermine much of the way external relief will be distributed, how communities set priorities in reconstruction, how leadership influences protocol, and how certain civic groups participate in the decision-making process.

Ultimately, a holistic approach requires use of the broadest possible resources, close coordination and collaboration between various elements working in the field, and continual reexamination in light of current conditions. The independent nature of NGOs provides them with advantages in terms of flexibility, even as it makes cooperation a challenge. "NGO experts and independent groups can get access to [disputants] and provide helpful insights, precisely because they are informal. They can analyze conflicts, find facts, and suggest creative violence-prevention measures at an early stage; they can, in principle, get into any society, start interviewing various actors, and feed the information into governments, other NGOs, the United Nations and humanitarian organizations," writes Jan Oberg, director of the Transnational Foundation for Peace and Future Research (1993:428). Humanitarian aid, for example, has been used to accompany ceasefire arrangements as well as to support indigenous dispute resolution processes (International Alert 1993). It is important to maintain a broad view of the situation and promote both top-down *and* bottom-up approaches to societal rehabilitation. Leadership-level settlement and grassroots dialogue are both enhanced when they accompany each other.

The Long-term View

The fourth and last aspect of community rehabilitation is the importance of keeping the distant future in sight. International aid workers should constantly analyze their programs for their impact on long-term development, social relations, environment, regional issues, and political affairs. Equally important, outside assistance should build self-reliance into all activities.

Each program should have an exit strategy—a carefully designed plan for leaving the community able to continue the program alone (or transitioning out of it, if it is no longer necessary). The exit strategy should include training, local leadership and participant responsibility, and nonrapacious funding mechanisms. Such a time frame, however, can rarely be determined at the outset. In fact, the exact timing of an organization's departure should be subject to constant and careful review, so that it occurs when it offers the best potential for the population. In short, aid organizations should think in terms of *sustainability* with regard to peace, economics, social rehabilitation, and reconstruction.

Limitations on Aid

These rather strict and idealistic parameters may be difficult to implement for a variety of reasons. To be candid, most new relief agencies lack personnel who are sufficiently experienced, country-savvy, culturally sensitive, appropriately skilled, and situationally grounded for the complicated role they will almost certainly be required to play. Moreover, each organization is itself limited in the breadth of its actions by its mandate, which defines and restricts its ability to maneuver in any given situation. While this is not necessarily a handicap (and indeed is quite necessary), the inflexibility of field directors in adequately adjusting protocols to meet specific needs can inhibit innovation and interagency collaboration. This goes for donor agencies as well, which are often unable to adapt to the reigning circumstances or extend their support for novel or unconventional programs.

Each situation requires creativity and broad thinking. Solutions that work in one country cannot necessarily be transferred directly to another. Finally, and perhaps most difficult, quality work takes time, and in an emergency, time is a luxury. After the height of the emergency is past, the recovery process is usually prolonged. Capacity-building, reconciliation, and social rehabilitation require tremendous patience on the part of international aid workers used to fast-paced work.

Activities and Program Components

The following is a compilation of various programs or elements within programs that can contribute to the de-escalation of tensions in the community setting. All address at least one, and many address most, of the five phases of healing outlined in chapter 6: establishing safety; communalization and bereavement; rebuilding trust and the capacity to trust; reestablishing personal and social morality; and the reintegration and restoration of democratic discourse. Some of the elements listed here are vital to every community-based program, some are activities that may be integrated into other ongoing programs, and still others stand alone as programs themselves.[9] Thus, used in concert with one another, they may contribute to a community's overall potential for sustainable peace and prosperity.

This selection of ideas is by no means comprehensive, as the possibilities are endless. While not strictly a compendium of activities, this approach *is* designed to provide an introduction to ways in which international organizations can tangibly and positively affect a conflict through field programs. Ultimately, as previously discussed, each situation requires unique answers, drawing on the creativity and innovation of individual organizations and constituents. In that regard, these suggestions might serve as a catalyst and inspiration for specific field operations.

Contextualization

Working in concert with the local context entails conducting all activities in a foreign environment based on extensive awareness of current conditions. It requires an in-depth understanding of cultural, social, and economic patterns, comprehensive knowledge of the conflict (regional, national, and local), a thorough grasp of international and humanitarian law, and a consideration of the entire situation in light of its political, human rights, social, development, and military implications. Contextualization entails researching background information on the country, including its culture and conditions; maintaining a high level of awareness of local factors; seeking and utilizing indigenous sources of information; establishing close communication with other organizations, local contacts, country specialists, and academics; and maintaining a broad perspective in the planning and implementation of all programs.

Maintaining a thorough understanding of the situational context can limit the number and size of costly and potentially dangerous mistakes by reducing the assumptions and errors caused by insufficient or false information. A closer view of a country may reveal needs not being addressed as well as opportunities to improve assistance. This can place program activities in a more realistic light and reduce false expectations based on theoretical models or those transferred from other environments. Contextualization also helps integrate humanitarian, human rights, environmental, conflict management, and development activities. An approach that focuses on understanding the fault lines of tension, on assessing areas for potential cross-identity cooperation, and on incorporating cultural or technical peacemaking capacities enhances the chances for successful reintegration by building trust; it also offers greater opportunity for using indigenous methodologies and resources.

All actors directly or indirectly involved in community rehabilitation can ultimately participate in gathering and updating their knowledge of the context. Participants in the contextualization process include (though not exclusively) country directors, program managers, relief workers, NGO partners, and donors.

In a five-step process of contextualization, the first involves a studious attempt to ascertain the various factors involved.[10] According to Peter Sollis,

> the policy-maker's view of the world is often less sophisticated than that of the poor people who must survive humanitarian emergencies. Policy alternatives conform to stereotypes about poor people's lives as simple, monotonous, and predictable. Survival strategies, however, are wide-ranging and complete. As a result, while the poor use multifaceted criteria to define their well-being, external actors reduce these to one or two measurable indicators. (Sollis 1994:14)

As external actors, therefore, our analysis should be in-depth and incorporate several contextual aspects, one of which is a consideration of the current conditions. Such an examination should include the actual state of affairs in regard to humanitarian, political, human rights, military, conflict, geographic, demographic, migration, and physical concerns. It also should include the impact of programs on these elements and should analyze their potential for peacebuilding. Another aspect concerns standards. This demands an exploration of the political system, customs, methodologies, cultural practices, and communication systems of the society; the roles and responsibilities of various groups based on age, class, gender, ethnicity, geography, religious affiliation, or status; and baseline information on health, education, the economy, living standards, and so on. The assessment should employ ethnographic and sociological sources in examining various group dynamics. Of equal importance is the historical aspect, which should look at the recent and ancient past for significant changes in the cultural, political, social, or other realms of society as a possible way to uncover the roots of the violence. A viable historical study should also explore the development of the conflict, including its various stages as well as significant political and military events.

In-depth analysis must also assess local capacities, studying the innate capabilities of the community and region. These might include the technical expertise of medical personnel, engineers, computer programmers, or logistics specialists; the local decision-making capacity of committee systems, democratic forums, or consensus formats; and sources and channels of power such as local authorities, clan-based structures, religious entities, or ethnic groups. Such a study should also consider the society's peacemaking systems, such as elders' councils, designated conflict arbitrators, informal—or formal—justice systems, or civil authorities. International actors should also review local food distribution networks, local markets and natural resources, along with indigenous coping mechanisms for famine or social upheaval. Finally, the information should note specific individuals or groups inclined toward peaceful coexistence or engaged in peace-promoting activities. This type of data collection should both measure current activities and indicate gaps that require filling.

It is critical that international organizations conduct each in-depth analysis of the context unconstrained by official or unofficial guidance or interference. Particularly in conflict environments, individual assessors should be independent and as free from bias as possible, to ensure the most accurate reading of the situation and build trust in their approach. In addition, they should engage numerous and varied sources to limit the possibility of skewed or inaccurate data.

The second step to contextualization is to base international actions on the findings. The results of the assessment should be used to inform agency programs, approaches, and techniques. By working in concert with the given conditions and modalities, organizations will be less likely to make serious errors of omission or commission, and the probability of successfully negotiating the fault lines of the conflict toward better intergroup relationships will improve.

One significant aspect of this is the role gender can play in the relief and peacemaking processes. Because women tend to shoulder the heaviest burden in postconflict reconstruction, partly as a result of gender role delineation and partly out of sheer numbers, programs should use the information gathered in the assessment to directly address the needs of women. A careful in-depth analysis in El Salvador in 1994, for example, would have found that women headed six of ten displaced families (Sollis 1994:11). Appropriate programs, therefore, might have included specific economic assistance, family-related health care, or shelter construction, and used women's roles as primary administrators of basic needs such as community drinking water, sanitation, utilities, fuel, and so forth to encourage joint community reconstruction (Sollis 1994:9). Such programs can also help reestablish social standards with respect to women's roles in society.

The third step is to maintain a balanced approach to reintegration assistance. The methods used in promoting reintegration should reflect the context in which they are conducted and thus keep an even perspective on all aspects of community rehabilitation (Vieira de Mello 1993). It is therefore important to integrate the full spectrum of environmental, human rights, relief, repatriation, military, education, psychosocial, legal, and civil factors into a cohesive strategy aimed at sustainable peaceful coexistence. This clearly calls for close and continual field coordination and well-established lines of communication. At the same time, distinctions in operational mandates must be very clear between the sectors. This is particularly an issue between military and relief operations in complex emergencies. Confusion, overlap, disparity, and inappropriate, if not dangerous, actions can result from poorly defined lines of authority.

Once a full assessment has been conducted and balanced programs have been established based on the findings, the fourth step in the contextualization process—situation monitoring—begins. Continuous evaluation will present new information, changes in conditions, significant diversions from the original format, the impact of program activities, shifts in local structural support, acceptance by the community, and the like. While it is important to maintain an independent perspective on information, collaborative, internal, and participatory monitoring has proven beneficial in creating ownership of a program and its outcome (Prendergast 1995). Evaluations should be repeated regularly and alterations made based on the findings.

The fifth step in the process is to maintain a vigilant view of the larger context. It is important not to develop tunnel vision from intense scrutiny of a community or its conditions. Indeed, it is essential to be aware of the overall eventualities indirectly affecting the situation. This means keeping informed of international trends, global and regional conditions, the political milieu, the approaches of other organizations, and the relationship of the activities to the overall rehabilitation process, particularly with respect to its progression in the five phases of healing.

Above all, keep in mind that contextualizing the situation has several conditions and qualifications that limit its effectiveness. To begin with, cultural differences are only understandable and surmountable to a certain extent. At some point, the subtleties and unknowns are beyond the scope of even the most diligent expatriate. The information available, moreover, is never completely adequate, and it is difficult to determine how much is sufficient for establishing programs. Furthermore, as foreigners to the environment, we carry with us our own set of cultural biases that often blind us to the context in which we work.

Capacity Use and Capacity-Building

The process of utilizing and increasing the local population's ability to provide for itself, manage operations, make decisions, solve problems, and locate resources is an invaluable tool for the international community. In so doing, organizations use local material resources, such as building supplies, food, and agricultural tools, and local technical services such as transportation, well-drilling, utility repair, road construction, trash removal, and excavation. They may also employ human skills in medicine, sanitation, computer programming, program management, logistics, psychology, peacemaking, animal husbandry, education, agriculture, and even urban planning, democratization, legal systems, and removal of landmines. International organizations can offer training and system development in these areas.

Building the ability of local communities to provide for themselves can decrease dependency on foreign sources by relying instead on regional specialists and supplies. It can also create alternative leadership to fighting factions by building chains of responsibility in, and receiving input from, other, noncombat lines of authority (Prendergast 1995). This ultimately removes support for fighting factions by reducing their role in decision-making processes. Increasing a community's viability and its demand for appropriate support, moreover, can increase the accountability and reciprocity of authorities as well.

Capacity-building also elevates the regional status of the community and its members through their own resourcefulness and independence. Trust develops through the increased interaction, number, and duration of cross-group contact inherent in participatory programs. This helps weaken stereotypes, create shared perceptions of a common humanity with a shared destiny, and develop a sense of community through reliance on others (Klein 1995). As a result, self-esteem and empowerment grow through participation in and responsibility for community programs (Sollis 1994:4). Developing local capacity can also contribute to sustainable peace and development by establishing mechanisms for realizing community goals, which can ultimately breed community commitment. The renewal of interdependence can, in turn, reduce the chance of a reversion to conflict.

Relying on and building local resources affects nearly all phases of psychosocial recovery. The renewed interdependence between groups, for example, enhances safety, while intergroup cooperation can promote communalization across identity boundaries. Trust gradually builds through enhanced reliance on other community members. Personal and social morality, similarly, increase as a consequence of greater community and authority accountability. Ultimately, intergroup decision-making helps develop restoration of democratic discourse and promote reintegration.

Ideally, most members of the community participate in community projects, lending skills, ideas, resources, and labor. Initially, however, there may be three—not mutually exclusive—types of participants: those partaking specifically to share their skills, resources, and expertise; those who welcome and are particularly disposed toward training and resource development; and those who are specifically looking for ways to disengage from the conflict. Discovering the first and second requires the type of contextualization assessment discussed above to ascertain the skills and resources in the area—or the interest and capacity to learn. Local organizations employed in the region can provide significant input and knowledge about the capacities of local populations.

Locating members of the third category requires noting groups and individuals who resent the conflict. These are the same people who bear the least respect for existing factional leadership and may be the most willing to build an alternative structure (Anderson 1996a). Sources might include religious institutions (which can serve as a replacement authority to military leadership), schools (which are another form of community voice), and traditional consultative structures such as chiefs, clan elders, and village mediators.

Capacity utilization and building can be both a means to an end, by using local resources efficiently to address relief or development problems, and an end in itself, as a way of building commitment and skills for a self-sufficient society. It requires three specific and diligent actions on the part of the international community: using local rather than imported skills and resources in relief and development programs whenever possible; further assessing local capacities and supporting their development and use; and promoting local decision-making, planning, and responsibility.

In so doing, international organizations can buy, employ, and rent local capacities, while partnering with local NGOs, charities, and civic, work-related, and task-oriented groups. They can also insist on indigenous participation in the design, planning, implementation, and management stages of projects, and encourage and defer to local decision-making structures and leaders. As civil society strengthens, moreover, expatriates can help design nonrapacious revenue-generating mechanisms to increase organizations' self-sustainability. For emergency response, international agencies can depend on such local structures as fire brigades and local physicians. If the capacity is lacking, they can provide skills training and offer guidance as well as resources, project assistance, and/or funding. International organizations can employ a simple seven-step process to maximize the use and building of local capacity. First, the international organization, local counterparts, and community members identify a problem or project. Second, they identify an appropriate solution to the problem and the resources required to carry it out. If such local resources are available, together they mobilize them to meet the needs. Third, they identify any gaps in capacity and any local sources that might be developed to fill these gaps. Fourth, the international organization and indigenous counterparts develop the local capacity through training, mentoring, and guidance. Fifth, if no local sources are available, they offer fundamental training and procure outside resources. Sixth, local and international entities work together in project decision-making, and, seventh, the international component gradually diminishes, and local capacities continue to manage the project.

Capacity-building requires conducting an in-depth contextualization assessment. This includes analyses of resources, needs, individual and community vulnerabilities, indigenous problem-solving methods, local civic institutions, traditional social networks, community technical committees, individuals and organizations particularly disposed toward peaceful coexistence, and local dispute-resolution systems. Participatory planning is also essential, engaging as many elements of society as possible and recognizing and supporting the resulting choices and strategies.

Ongoing training and development should include specific capacity-building activities for women, such as developing job skills, widows' associations, women's farming groups, cottage industries, and market cooperatives, and for the military and police, including training in discipline, the Geneva Conventions, Codes of Conduct for Combatants, juridical accountability, cross-cultural relations, and job skills for demobilized soldiers. Other training programs could address human rights, leadership and governance, problem-solving, democracy, technical skills, conflict management, business administration, and renewable and nonrapacious revenue generation. All capacity-building activities must be monitored for inequities, successes, opportunities, and gaps.

Capacity use and building has several drawbacks and difficulties. One limitation is that it is an inherently long-term process, and immediate, efficient results should not be expected. Because each situation is unique and evolves largely out of trial and error, developing local capabilities and resources requires enormous patience. Many practitioners view capacity utilization, let alone capacity-building, as unpractical during emergency operations.

The practice of capacity-building may entail several other difficulties as well. Supporting indigenous organizations can represent an alternative power structure, which could threaten the authorities and may therefore be dangerous. Skilled individuals are frequently drawn from government and civil society organizations to employment with the more lucrative international relief and development agencies, thereby creating a brain drain. Finally, the most successful capacity usage and building require coordination among all the actors, which may be difficult to orchestrate.

Increasing Protection

Improving physical security (usually inadequate in postconflict societies) is the first of the five steps to recovery. Doing so entails working through structures such as peace-keeping forces, military units, local brigades, and community members, using civilians and nonviolent tactics for safeguarding communities and, in the case of returning migrants, working with the UNHCR. Increasing the level of protection can bring respite from violence, allowing the first phase of healing to take place. Reducing fear and trepidation, then, can promote community interaction between groups and offer opportunities for communalization and trust-building. Furthermore, a program of protection can begin to eradicate the culture of impunity, and to establish legal structures for ensuring justice. This contributes to the reestablishment of social morals. Physical security is crucial to the implementation of long-term development programs that require a stable environment. Improved local confidence can, in turn, lead to an increase in local commitment to and investment in community rehabilitation and, at the same time, enhance the prospects for international financial investment.

While all members of society may be indirectly concerned with and undoubtedly benefit from protection programs, active participants generally include local police forces, individuals involved in the judicial system, military officials, government authorities, civil society organizations, and possibly demobilized soldiers. International participants include foreign militaries, peacekeeping forces, bilateral agencies, international relief agencies, and private foundations.

The fundamental goal of a protection program is to improve the overall security at the community and national levels. Several strategies might work in this regard, though presumably all in tandem provide the best results.

Maintaining an international presence is often invaluable. Expatriates interspersed among hostile groups tend to serve as witnesses and monitors of the situation, thereby suppressing the level of violence. As eyes and ears for the international community, foreigners working with relief and development agencies, conflict management groups, and human rights organizations throughout the country maintain constant awareness of grassroots occurrences. Diplomatic missions visiting various locations could prove helpful in this respect, as well. The ICRC plays a special role in its interaction with detainees. The essence here is not the reporting of inflammatory incidents but the sheer presence of foreigners in the communities. Further, international organizations, because of their putative noninvolvement and available resources, can offer a safe space for cross-conflict meetings, individuals fearing persecution, local leadership pursuing peace initiatives, or others in need of sanctuary and protection.

A more formal aspect of using an international presence to increase security in unstable regions is the role of official security operations. Units such as observer missions, peacekeeping forces, and foreign militaries always deploy under specific rules of engagement—that is, they are authorized to use force only under a specified level of threat. Some may function strictly as a protective element, and not as a fighting unit, in an effort to induce a greater level of assuredness among the population. Other operations simply serve as an official third-party "eyes and ears" on security issues. Still others may be more aggressive in their effort to protect, as in the case of Somalia, where the rules of engagement were liberal.

An additional aspect of security is the establishment of safe havens, zones of tranquillity, and special protection areas inside hostile regions. These offer areas of refuge for the persecuted, displaced, or abandoned, in which there has been an agreed-upon ceasefire. International forces established within the zones theoretically ensure the absence of fighting. Bosnia is an example in which safe havens were initially effective but backfired when the internal ceasefire was violated.

Another official channel for security is UNHCR's role as protector of returning refugees and, in some cases, of IDPs and even local residents. In Tajikistan, for example, UNHCR's presence in the communes receiving returnees acted as an assuaging force, providing security for some and admonition to others. Another option for international protection is the use of Open Relief Centers. Such centers offer protection and material assistance, particularly for displaced persons but also for local residents and returnees (Stafford 1993; UNHCR 1993a). Open Relief Centers have been used effectively in a number of countries, including Rwanda and Sri Lanka.

Human rights monitoring missions, such as those deployed in Central America, Haiti, and Cambodia, provide another form of external protection. The newly created UN High Commissioner for Human Rights became operational by establishing its first official field program in Rwanda following the 1994 conflict. Its function, in part, was to provide international vigilance on human rights issues, in an attempt to decrease the number of protection violations.

Unofficially, there is a growing global interest in alternative protection arrangements. For example, witness programs typically post individuals and teams in areas of particular tension, and accompany individuals thought to be in serious danger. The more sophisticated operations may instigate conflict resolution efforts in a community or between individuals. Such programs have been implemented with relative success in Central America.

One important method of improving security is reducing the incentive for disruption. Since the high value of relief supplies invites malfeasance, decreasing the desirability of relief goods can avoid attracting the interest of fighting factions. This can be done through minimizing food distributions in favor of nonfood items, educational materials, and subsistence aid, which generally hold much lower value than food (Prendergast 1995). International organizations should also avoid using relief arms of military factions as counterparts in distributions. Such relief elements, though possibly legitimate, have other, higher motivations and may use the material aid to subjugate civilians or intentionally cause instability. Minimizing dislocation is also important since displaced populations and their supplies are more vulnerable to protection problems, such as manipulation and looting, than are resident populations (Prendergast 1995).

While foreign entities can play an important tempering role in hostile environments, establishing independent sources of order and an internal capacity to provide security fulfills long-term safety needs. International organizations can refine and routinize police force training, help fund and guide military demobilization programs, and provide military training to establish discipline as a fundamental element of military conduct. Strengthening formal internal protection units can ultimately diminish the level of misconduct and abuse of power and instead create disciplined units focused on protecting the civilian population.

The development of an equitable justice system can also play a critical role in eradicating a culture of impunity. (Re)establishing a rule of law, defining areas of responsibility, building experience and training into court and legal procedures, and expanding the number and level of trained and accountable judges, magistrates, lawyers, court officials, and police officers could play a major part in increasing security and reestablishing social ethics. International organizations can help fund and provide technical assistance in rejuvenating the judicial system. This kind of institution-building can potentially result in a well-formed and stalwart system of justice that can endure political turmoil and promote a strong sense of ethics in a society.

Externally, truth commissions, war crimes tribunals, and other international investigations into violations of international law can have a pacifying influence and contribute to the reestablishment of social ethics. Serious allegations of crimes against humanity can affect not only the individuals implicated but the status of a country itself. Arrests and convictions of war criminals remove the individuals and their influence from society; truth commissions give voice to victims of human rights violations; all of these condemn acts of aggression to the global public in a process of reestablishing social morality. This international attention may serve to mollify victims and cool down an otherwise hurt and angry population, thereby increasing the level of security.

Programs attempting to increase protection in an inherently insecure environment, however, can be riddled with uncertainties and problems. The introduction of external forces is often seen as an invasion and an affront to national sovereignty. Peacekeeping forces and the like can, in fact, increase tension by introducing another element of physical force into the equation. It has been well noted that attempting to abate force with force can simply endorse the notion that strength and the threat of violence are the best means for resolving issues. Yet alternative tacks such as witness programs are often unprofessional, lack consistency and standards, and fail to coordinate with other international aid elements.

Extensive controversy exists over the appropriateness of training military and police units. Many believe that training may simply increase the potential of already powerful forces in a society, preparing them for greater violations. Others contend that a well-disciplined armed force can introduce accountability and pride into a socially corrupt system, thereby instilling order. Certainly, abuse of power remains a legitimate fear.

There are other potential dangers to the protection approach. One is that rebuilding a society's judicial process may eventuate in a corrupt system that virtually paralyzes the country and further emboldens violent factions. Another lies in the fact that international organizations are inevitably labeled with biases, justifiably or not, that can jeopardize their protective attributes if put into the wrong context. UNHCR's presence in a community, for example, if seen as discriminatory toward one group or another, can endanger recipients by inviting retaliatory attacks by opponents. Yet another pitfall is that a country's reliance on an international presence to impart an element of stability is limited by time and can develop into dependence.

Furthermore, war crimes tribunals and other official investigations based on international law are usually slow to begin, commencing long after the worst of the violations have been committed. The assuaging influence, therefore, may have lost some force as the country sinks into martyrdom when the crimes have seemingly gone unnoticed. The preventive capacity of these official channels may, consequently, be limited.

Collaborative Community Rehabilitation

Reconstruction projects can incorporate components that help facilitate reintegration by engaging and benefiting a broad spectrum of community members. Organizations implementing collaborative community rehabilitation projects employ participatory project management methods, carefully select the project location and nature, and ensure that direct beneficiaries represent diverse community membership. A project, for example, may include joint decision-making in its design and management; it may target marginalized individuals of all identities, thus easing the burden of the whole community; or it may be located in an area accessible and beneficial to all groups.

Rehabilitation assistance with both physical and social objectives can advance many of the five phases of psychosocial healing. Through tangible, community-based projects, it can draw displaced populations back home, attracting them with both community renewal and improved social relationships, thus beginning the healing process. Reconstruction programs invariably provide employment for some members of the community, which not only boosts the local economy, thus rewarding the community for efforts at reintegration, but increases the sense of individual and communal security (Anderson 1994).

Collaborative projects, moreover, can help rebuild intergroup trust through cross-conflict interaction over an extended period of time (OTI 1995). Such programs can also develop community problem-solving skills by involving all identity groups in the design, development, and management of the program (OTI 1995). Under certain conditions, this may also contribute to communalization. Joint decision-making can discourage the concentration of resources of any one group and promote empowerment and recognition of minorities by involving them equally in the project. This promotes the democratization phase. Ideally, whole-community collaboration reduces social and political isolation and promotes interdependence, which benefits the entire community.

All elements of society can participate in collaborative community rehabilitation, depending on the project. Minimally, however, a project includes members of all identities, both genders, a variety of ages, and all social ranks. International participants can be NGOs, the United Nations, development, bilateral, philanthropic, relief, or institution-based organizations.

The fundamental objective of this methodology is to improve intergroup relationships while contributing to the reconstruction of community infrastructure or economic rehabilitation. Direct physical engagement in reconstruction activities can serve as a relatively safe step toward committing to the future of a community. Project selection for collaborative rehabilitation can incorporate several aspects—the location, type, or methodology of the project—emphasizing one over the others, or integrating them all.

LOCATION OF PROJECT

Reconstruction programs ostensibly renew dysfunctional community structures and increase employment. The selection criteria for appropriate communities in which to implement a project should be based not only on economic and physical needs but on social factors, such as the tranquillity of the area, an indication from the community of its desire to improve relations, the self-motivation for community renewal, and the agreement of leaders of all parties to support and collaborate on the project.

An example of this is "spot reconstruction," a concept adopted by Fred Cuny in Sri Lanka. Spot reconstruction specifically targets villages located in low-conflict zones—often with mixed representation—with reconstruction aid in support of formal peace initiatives. It focuses on areas of minimal conflict and mixed groups, such as those containing recent returnees or urban areas with large numbers of voluntarily resettled displaced persons (Cuny 1989; Cuny and Cuny 1992). In Cambodia, small-scale projects were introduced into villages known to have sizable returnee populations, in an effort to facilitate integration (Rogge 1992). This type of whole-community approach to improving village infrastructure can raise the general living standard, presumably reducing competition for resources as well as creating new foci of activity apart from the conflict.

TYPE OF PROJECT

The form a reconstruction project takes can also encourage cross-group collaboration. In selecting projects to promote reintegration in Bosnia, for instance, USAID's Office of Transition Initiatives (OTI) developed operational guidelines for project selection. These included projects that bridge ethnic divides in mixed communities or develop bridges between ethnically distinct communities; involve both sides in the implementation process; ensure that results benefit both sides; promote reintegration and interdependence; involve multiethnic labor forces; promote groups outside the conventional lines of authority; and benefit a broad constituency such as the disenfranchised and the apathetic (OTI 1995). Thus, project selection in this context is based on the intended benefit of all conflicting parties as a way of developing a mutual interest and point of collaboration among adversaries. Road reconstruction, repair of telephone lines and public utilities, and rehabilitation of shared social ministrations such as hospitals and schools are good project candidates.

Another consideration is projects that require the benevolence of adversarial parties for the benefit of all, with the intention of initiating the trust-building process. In several conflict-ridden situations, for example, international NGOs instigated housing reconstruction projects for returning refugees and displaced persons that required the labor and even material contribution of the community residents. This personal investment in the fate of the returnees resulted in their greater overall accommodation, and the gesture of goodwill on the part of the community was a large first step in restoring trust.

A third consideration is the potential for the project to increase local stability. Quick Impact Projects (QIPs) can work in this capacity as an incentive for greater cooperation at the community level. QIPs are "small-scale micro-projects that require a modest, one-time investment and must be carried out locally" (Fagen 1993:33). Usually implemented during the fragile "swing" period when refugees and internally displaced persons return home, QIPs, with their high potential for rapid results, often provide an immediate boost to the whole community. In Cambodia, for instance, QIPs facilitated returnee reintegration through water and sanitation improvement, agriculture, fishing, and income-generation activities (Vieira de Mello 1993).

In Tajikistan, one QIP proposal was to establish a weaving brigade among women of one ethnic group and a wool manufacturing enterprise among women of another, requiring collaboration for mutual benefit (Anderson 1995a:30). These types of community efforts offer an immediate return on cooperation, encourage reintegration as well as rehabilitation, and provide a bridge between relief and development. "The presence of QIPs unquestionably has enhanced movements toward reconciliation," writes Patricia Fagen, head of the UNHCR office in El Salvador (1993:33).

A fourth related point is the project's potential for supporting economic recovery. Beyond immediate aid in the form of QIPs and initial resettlement kits, such as seeds and tools for agriculture, projects focusing on economic rehabilitation can both improve local conditions and shift attention away from the conflict toward livelihood regeneration. As Cuny emphasized, credit, in particular, is critical to stability, since it is often necessary for any substantial rehabilitation (1983; Cuny and Cuny 1992). Moreover, both a willingness to accept a loan and a willingness to risk the offer, indicate trust in the future.

Foreign organizations can establish a milieu of commitment and reliance through credit incentives and joint small enterprise programs. They can encourage or mandate certain kinds of interaction as a condition to funding. Small business start-up credit or small-scale revolving loan funds, for example, may be granted more readily to those proposing cross-conflict partnership, those hiring across identity lines, or those intent on locating in mixed identity areas, high-tension zones, or areas traditional to other groups.

METHODOLOGY

The way in which a program is selected, designed, implemented, and managed will also affect community relations. International organizations that intentionally employ staff who represent all groups, identify diverse project participants, hold joint meetings, insist on cooperative decision-making, and orchestrate shared management and maintenance of projects can ultimately invite long-term, intergroup interaction.[11] Foreign agencies can specifically gear programs to intergroup interaction by designating roles for individuals of mixed identity makeup and requesting tasks requiring growing levels of trust.

In reconstruction projects, foreign agencies using local purchase for materials should consider explicitly buying across conflict lines. In doing so, they can thereby establish confidence in the manufacturing, delivery, and quality of goods produced by the various groups. In-kind donations of labor and materials from all beneficiary groups further necessitate cross-conflict communication and demonstrate goodwill. In Bosnia, for instance, an International Rescue Committee water project that benefited both groups in the community stipulated bi-ethnic construction and management as well as labor and material contribution (OTI 1995).

Another innovative model of this approach is that of the African Community Initiatives Support Teams (ACIST) in Rwanda. Teams supported by international NGOs and made up of Africans and non-Africans worked within communities on local improvement initiatives such as agriculture, small enterprise, artisanship, education, cultural arts, and sports. Because they emphasized grassroots conceptualization and participation at the lowest level of society, and required community contribution of labor and resources, they necessitated whole-community interaction and decision-making (CWA-ACIST 1995–96).

As with every approach to responding to complex emergencies, a collaborative community rehabilitation program has its downside. An intensive focus on economic development, for instance, may undermine the slower and more subtle social development, thereby creating a lopsided society vulnerable to renewed conflict. That is, without a balanced approach of addressing with equal fervor such issues as care of the disenfranchised, psychological recovery, deprogramming of demobilized soldiers, social welfare, and rehabilitation of dispute management systems, the reconstruction effort may simply lead to greater conflict.

Moreover, since international aid introduces tremendous power into an area, the channels used for its distribution affects traditional roles, authority, and relationships (Anderson 1996a). NGOs and their staff, for example, can become the supreme local command, usurping community leaders and reengineering community relationships. Similarly, because skills and resources between identity groups are often different, equal distribution of responsibility and allocation of funds may be nearly impossible. Skilled labor for specific tasks, for example, often rests primarily with individuals with certain credentials that may be more common in one group than another. A concerted effort to pay attention to identity makeup, however, could in fact increase divisions between groups by reinforcing awareness of differences. Save the Children Federation in Tajikistan, for example, found that "staff who have both enough closeness to the situation to have credibility and enough distance to be seen as non-aligned and disinterested may be better able to play localized reconciling roles than those who represent different alliances" (Anderson 1995a).

Rehabilitation projects can also fall prey to violence in areas still embroiled in conflict. This may be literally the result of an outside attack on the community, as has happened repeatedly in Sudan, or the work of embittered insiders resentful of the project or its supporters. Ultimately, the challenge of integrated program management may simply prove to be too difficult or too early for some mixed communities. It may, in fact, exacerbate tensions among community members and lead to further deterioration in community relations (Anderson 1995a).

Conflict Management

In this context, conflict management involves community-level activities that attempt to directly and positively affect inter-identity relationships, and to enhance the prospects of peaceful coexistence among community members. This usually entails increasing the instances of positive cross-conflict contact, which can ultimately promote many phases of the healing process.

Conflict management activities can alleviate tension simply by providing a voice to underlying grievances that otherwise may not be articulated. This can initiate the communalization and bereavement process which, for cultural or other reasons, might not commence on its own. International participants in such a program often serve as external monitors, which can reduce the number of violations and thereby enhance the sense of security, particularly in the initial phases of recovery. The international organization can provide a neutral, safe space for participants to explore the root causes of the conflict and begin to rebuild working relationships, develop trust, and ultimately request forgiveness.

Programs incorporating a conflict management focus can legitimize, support, and give power to individuals and groups working in concert toward better inter-identity relationships. As community leaders, they, in turn, can begin to redraw the lines of moral behavior, creating boundaries for tolerance of hostile acts. Certain conflict management activities, such as incorporating peace education into the school curriculum, can directly teach moral behavior. Others have the potential to employ and build decision-making capacities or, through the process of reintegration, help restore the voice of the ostracized to the community system. Use of conflict management skills in the reconstruction of infrastructure, moreover, can facilitate whole-group decision-making and enhance the democratization process. These skills have a potentially long-lasting effect that can remain as a resource for the prevention of future conflicts.

In the host country, participants in a conflict management program might include government officials, local authorities, national NGOs, academics, professionals, educators, community members, elders, business leaders, media reporters, representatives of work-based groups, and religious, civic, and social leaders. Expatriates involved can include academics, conflict management specialists, diplomats, international NGOs, foundation personnel, and UN representatives.

A more integrated approach to conflict management is beginning to emerge (Minear and Weiss 1993a:36; Montville, forthcoming:4). The fields of humanitarian assistance and conflict management are simultaneously converging, from different angles, on issues of community-level violence in identity conflicts. The concept of "field diplomacy,"[12] which integrates conflict management skills into long-term community-based programs, for example, is developing, at least in theory. Several humanitarian and human rights organizations are beginning to apply aspects of conflict management in their programs. The vision of close collaboration, however, is still in the distance, as very few relief, development, or conflict management activities have actually bridged the gap.

The study of British conflict resolution NGOs, mentioned in chapter 1, illustrates the conflict management approach. The study found that the NGOs do not normally intervene directly in the conflict, but instead try to indirectly affect behavior and "promote a general ethos of well-being." Specifically, the study concludes, "they see their role as building networks and facilitating the transformation of group dynamics amongst people who might in the future play a role in conflict resolution interventions" (Voutira and Brown 1995:19). The researchers divided the NGOs into three categories offering three different approaches. The first consisted of those working at the top level and using the UN vocabulary. They relied on international bodies and government funding, conducted short field trips, and organized high-profile conferences. Their basic premise was that misunderstandings generated conflicts.

The second group was NGOs whose main purpose was to influence public opinion. For this purpose, they conducted broad-based field research, encouraged citizen diplomacy and grassroots awareness, and attempted to influence leaders. They used development vocabulary and relied on membership, public, church, and some government funding. Their assumption was that conflicts resulted from obstruction of the free flow of information across identity lines. The last category was comprised of organizations that targeted conflicts at the grassroots level. Their vocabulary was that of peace activism and they relied on information from the grassroots, the techniques developed by the other two models, and funding from membership and foundations. Their main premise was that conflicts were the result of human rights violations. None of the NGOs, however, established field programs attempting to help rebuild relationships and resolve fundamental issues over an extended period of time (Voutira and Brown 1995).

Community-based conflict management in complex emergencies can be divided into three basic approaches, each containing specific activities:

1. MOBILIZING THE COMMUNITY FOR CONFLICT MANAGEMENT

This involves marshaling local leaders and community members in community-level efforts of crisis management and possibly prevention. When members of the local population become major stake-holders in the rehabilitation process, they generate broad-based will and accountability toward peaceful coexistence.

Peace committees. Foreign organizations can advocate, help establish, and empower local peace committees. Made up of noncontentious, mutually respected, and diverse community representatives, peace committees can help counter rumors and exaggerations, serve as go-betweens for international agencies and the local community, and mediate between contentious individuals and groups or between groups and the government. They can also advocate nonviolent solutions to potentially violent conflicts, support local peace initiatives, and provide incentives and support for local authorities to advocate conciliatory actions. In so doing, they often help improve the sense of local security and take significant steps toward reestablishing codes of ethics. Both in Nicaragua and South Africa, peace committees have had substantial success. Similar in many ways, ethnic reconciliation commissions have been established in Bulgaria, the Czech Republic, and Poland.

Indigenous mechanisms for conflict resolution. Virtually every society has some mechanism for dispute settlement, such as mediation by elders, meetings among local leaders, settlement by a designated peace official, popular justice, legal procedures, or arbitration (Rule 1993). Although these mechanisms may exist in identity conflict contexts, they often disintegrate along with the social order. International organizations, thus, may attempt to rehabilitate and strengthen existing indigenous dispute resolution systems. This could involve recognizing, providing support for, and encouraging the revitalization of the elders' council, the role of the traditional peacemaker, the justice circle, the tribal court, and representative committees, or the mediating role of women's organizations. It clearly requires intensive investigation into local methods, cultural practices, and nuances as well as enlisting the support of, and empowering, groups, individuals, and organizations in the area that are inclined toward reconciliation.[13]

International agencies can further serve as catalysts for revitalization by initiating and facilitating meetings, offering incentives, lending facilities or resources, and increasing protection by acting as impartial witnesses. Several NGOs have worked at this level. In southern Sudan, for example, international organizations played the initial role of go-between in restarting a traditional dispute-settlement process. This entailed extended communalization, and then provided support in the form of food, funding, transportation, and documentation (Lowrey 1995). In Burundi, an international NGO attempted to revitalize the traditional peace process at the commune level by restoring the role of traditional mediators as an official, legal, and binding system for local dispute resolution (Refugees International 1995).

2. PROMOTING DIALOGUE

Activities involved in the promotion of dialogue attempt to generate a willingness and ability to understand opposing views, develop conditions of trust, transform group dynamics, and acknowledge the mutuality of legitimate needs, rights, and obligations. The primary focus is on the process itself rather than specific outcomes.

"Conflict transformation" workshops. Although they use a variety of names and models, generically, these are interactive sessions held by third parties for

members of conflicting groups in an attempt to improve understanding. Participants usually include societal and religious leaders, academics, and professionals representing a variety of perspectives. The third party is normally an NGO, professional organization, religious group, or academic institution, or possibly a bilateral or multilateral organization, foundation, or philanthropic association. The third party's objective is to encourage cross-conflict sharing and begin to conceive of a peaceful, mutually interdependent existence.

One specific example is the "problem-solving workshop," pioneered by scholar John Burton. In the workshop, participants analyze a conflict and its psychological and emotional dimensions, gradually gain a better perspective of both parties' fears, needs, priorities, and constraints, and ultimately move into the realm of collaborative problem-solving (Gutlove 1992:10; Montville, forthcoming:114).

Public forums. An open discussion forum, which may be hosted by a local entity and supported by an international organization, offers communities the opportunity to consider various issues and problems, candidly and as a whole. The objective is to bring out various, perhaps previously unheard or potentially mediating views, offer a safe meeting-ground for cross-conflict interaction, and ideally, come to agreement on proceedings. The discussion might address technical issues (such as the reconstruction of water systems, hospitals, roads, and houses, the care of the unaccompanied children, assistance for widows, burial sites for the war dead, and the opening of schools) or more contentious problems (land ownership, new leadership, council membership, and political affiliations). It may also entail broader opinions and attitudes toward the more complex and visceral aspects of the conflict, such as rights and responsibilities of displaced persons, community response to group violence, local perspectives on national issues, and new ethics for individual conduct.

International organizations can help establish ground rules, procedures, and methods for handling disagreements, as well as provide guidance and facilitation during the initial discussions. Optimally, this will develop into a healthy decision-making process that could be used as a format for rediscovering unity, discussing differences, and developing a common vision, all of which contribute to intercommunal reintegration. Communities in Nicaragua and Tajikistan have conducted such public forums with relative success.

Sustained dialogue. These efforts attempt to redefine the relationship between conflicting parties and work through the underlying contentious ingredients. Sustained dialogue generally involves third-party commitment over years of intermittent interaction in an effort to come to long-term solutions. The extended time frame enables participants to explore the deep-seated roots of the contention, to communalize and to mourn, and, ultimately, to develop trust and moral recovery. Throughout their protracted—though not resident or uninterrupted—engagement with local populations, facilitators encourage sharing and exploring the experience of violation and loss. Generally, participation begins with interested individuals and expands to include higher authorities.

The Kettering Foundation is a leader in sustained dialogue. It employs a six-step approach that begins with an extensive background study of the parties in conflict. It then develops interdependence and a process for continuing interaction. This leads to a scrutiny of the power relationships and sets limits on certain behavior, eventually evolving into new perceptions of each of the opposing parties (Saunders 1993b). The Kettering Foundation has been holding bimonthly discussions using this format with conflicting factions in Tajikistan since 1993. The Institute for Multi-Track Diplomacy also carries on long-term programs in more of a training format, notably in Cyprus and the Middle East. In its periodic meetings, it focuses on basic principles of interpersonal communication, providing conceptual tools to analyze and deal more effectively with conflict-related issues, developing skills to express needs and interests more clearly and to understand those of others (Klein 1995).

Conflict management training. A more common approach is that of improving skills and methods for handling conflict nonviolently. A conflict management institution, private foundation, conflict resolution professional, or NGO usually conducts the training session, which is held in a setting removed from the visible battle. Participants normally include representatives of the disputants or, at a minimum, members of the various antagonistic groups, usually professionals, intellectuals, academics, and leaders. However, training may also include managers of significant social services such as unaccompanied children's centers and educational institutes, as well as community officials, religious organizers, civil society leaders, and tribal or ethnic leaders.

Such forums attempt to develop greater understanding of the conflict and improve the dispute-handling capacity of antagonistic groups. A conflict management skills training usually spans no more than several days and may be repeated or continued in several ensuing sessions. The format of these sessions does not generally engage the process but, rather, emphasizes the value of, and techniques of initiating, new forms of communication. Conflict management training content usually includes presentation of the issues of contention from various points of view, communication skills learning and rehearsal, collective reflection, techniques in mediation and negotiation, and possibly conflict analysis.

The philosophies and variations of conflict management are unlimited. Some methods are elicitive in their approach, others more prescriptive; some go so far as to try to establish a new paradigm of interaction. Moreover, the application is potentially expansive. International relief and development agencies might offer their expatriate and national program staff conflict management training, workshops on specific issues such as human rights, or internal seminars on related topics, such as traditional dispute resolution methods. Such in-house training can broaden the skills of the participants as well as develop community-level understanding of the issues. Programs can also address specific components of civil society, such as managers of large businesses or journalists. On the other side of the border, conflict management training may be presented to refugee communities with the intention of developing greater facilitation and communication skills for use both within the camps and upon repatriation. An interesting example of a more comprehensive approach to conflict management training is the Nansen Group in Kosovo. Begun by a Scandinavian NGO, Kosovo citizens attend three seminars in conflict management as a basis for membership in the group. Following this orientation, participants can engage in any number of cultural, education, or social programs, each of which is conducted by one Albanian and one Serb.

3. PROMOTING UNDERSTANDING THROUGH SPORTS, THE ARTS, AND PROFESSIONAL ACTIVITIES

Cultural and physical programs can help reacquaint individuals in conflicting groups, change perceptions, stereotypes, and images, and renew respect through integrated, mutually interesting activities. Interactive activities of cross-conflict appeal can create an atmosphere of shared learning and cooperation.

Sports. Athletics in particular are a medium through which various international groups have attempted to break down the cultural divide by bringing conflicting parties together in a spirit of mutual gain and enjoyment. Over time, such repeated activities can help develop intergroup trust. This can be especially apropos in conflict and postconflict conditions when intense boredom has set in, little entertainment exists to remove the image of conflict, and young men in particular occupy themselves with nefarious activities. In Bosnia and Somalia, for example, several NGOs and bilateral agencies have supported cross-conflict athletic matches, reconstructed sports arenas, and funded equipment.

The arts. Art, music, dance, and drama offer modes of intergroup interaction and appreciation. Many have found that even in the divisive setting of identity conflict, cultural presentation often remains highly esteemed and can serve to revitalize cultural traditions. This can be critical to healing a tormented community (Maynard 1997). In Croatia and Bosnia, CARE uses theater and dance to help schoolchildren integrate emotional and conceptual understanding of the regional conflict. By acting out a hypothetical dispute and eventually transforming it to a state of peace, the children experience both the emotions of conflict and the process and satisfaction of resolution.

The arts represent an important method of expressing the shared experience of crisis as a form of communalization. This can be particularly useful in helping children to externalize and share traumatic events through activating the imagination and social awareness. Through these programs participants engage in creative, wholesome activities that encourage them to participate and share, rather than withdraw. Foreign organizations can support projects in the arts through revitalization of professional organizations, encouragement of local arts center projects, and support of children's school and community-based programs.

Professional and recreational activities. Professional and recreational organizations also offer opportunities to communicate across conflict barriers on subjects of common interest, and to begin to renew trust. These groups may be work-related or even union-based, such as railroad workers' alliances or nurses' coalitions, or philanthropic associations, such as committees for the restitution of historic monuments. They may also be professional associations, such as psychologists' or teachers' boards, hobby groups, such as ham radio or chess clubs, or leisure groups, such as sewing or singing leagues. In this respect, the focus is not on the development of the group, as in rebuilding civil society, but in renewing specific integrated activities. In Bosnia, for example, OTI funded the printing and distribution of an academic journal and the reopening of a karate club (OTI 1995).

Unfortunately, the limitations to concerted international efforts at conflict management can be substantial. Perhaps the single largest obstacle is the time inherent in coming to terms with the contentious issues. Healing from the wounds of violence, as we have seen, requires enormous dedication and patience, neither for which the international community is known. The rapid pace of the Western world seems to create—perhaps justifiably—an innate impatience in donor responses to complex crises. This coincides with short-sightedness in foreign policy, which can result in lack of financial commitment to long-term and less tangible programs such as conflict management. Furthermore, the unglamorous, uncertain, and often dangerous character of life in a remote community immersed in a complex emergency understandably does not attract international conflict resolution specialists, thereby resulting in few resident, community-based conflict management programs. For these reasons and perhaps others, the focus of foreign intercession is usually brief and without substantial follow-up, which tends to prevent comprehensive exploration of the roots of conflict and can leave participants without a cohesive strategy or durable support. Bosnia, for example, is replete with individuals who have been trained in conflict management by any number of international organizations during and after the conflict. Somewhat abandoned as the rehabilitation phase proceeded, no structure exists to support their facilitation skills and many have not used them since.

A comprehensive approach, once again, requires close coordination between all entities working in the region, including human rights, diplomatic, humanitarian, and development agencies. Thus far, concerted cooperation between groups has been relatively rare. The inherent lack of collaboration at the grassroots level results specifically from the fact that humanitarian and development organizations live and work directly in the community, whereas most conflict management and diplomatic activities, and to a lesser extent human rights, occur in a removed setting. Thus, the opportunity for sharing programs and opportunities is limited.

Another problem, as the study of British conflict resolution NGOs illustrates, is that none of the three types of programs examined deals specifically with armed combatants. While there is good reason to engage academics, officials, professionals, religious leaders, and the like in conflict management efforts, the personal and grassroots nature of identity conflicts, I believe, demands that the common civilian fighter also participate in conflict reduction. By limiting the process to more intellectual elements, the exclusion of small militia bands, armed young men, and neighborhood gangs removes a vital component of the fighting force from the discussion. Moreover, conflict management training sessions, in particular, tend to attract individuals already inclined toward peacemaking and may ignore the attitudes of the common citizen.

It is also essential to consider the broad range of cultural assumptions that naturally accompany international intercession in foreign conflicts. Such issues as direct versus indirect manner of conduct; attitudes toward cooperation, competition and conflict, orientation toward tasks, authority, social rank, status and caste, modes of communication, and time management; and attitudes toward third parties, vary enormously between cultures (Moore 1993). More fundamental is the Western assumption of a universal response to, and recovery process from, exposure to violence. Though an area of interest to many in the conflict management field, not enough is known yet about the cross-cultural implications of Western concepts, the transference of techniques, or even the benefits, risks, or appropriateness of discussing feelings or expressing loss in different cultures. Although many organizations endeavor to use primarily responses and activities elicited from local participants, the spectrum among the international programs is wide. By all accounts, avoiding introducing foreign methods into a culture, without consideration of identity and cultural differences, is imperative.[14]

Influencing Public Consciousness

Public impressions can be shaped through formal education structures, informal instruction programs, and media outlets to affect attitudes and perceptions across society. International organizations can support reforms in educational curricula and teaching methodologies, help initiate integrated learning programs, and promote the dissemination of nonbiased, constructive information through radio, television, and public education programs. Using such public forums to influence public consciousness can counter negative propaganda being expounded through social networks or through clandestine or even official media channels; help reverse escalating prejudices through specific activities aimed at developing cross-identity appreciation; and introduce factual information that sheds new light on confusing or conflicting precepts of identity groups. This can have a positive influence on nearly all phases of the healing process.

One benefit of such forums is their ability to enhance security through broadcasts of information on the location and extent of violence and protection mechanisms. Open discussion of the issues directly contributes to the communalization process, while public media can offer programs that support bereavement. By presenting various opinions and perspectives on issues of conflict in an open dialogue across identity boundaries, public education programs can help guide moral recovery while ridding forums of biased and harmful material. They can also present new guidelines for moral behavior and acceptable social standards. A public forum for discussion of national and communal issues, moreover, can enhance the democratization process and give voice to the otherwise unheard.

The use of educational and media outlets could include those involved in formal schooling, such as teachers, students and administrators, or staff and participants in informal programs at community and activity centers, as well as professional journalists, radio and television station managers, journal and newspaper editors, columnists, show hosts, and the general public. International organizations involved in such activities could include foreign journalists, reporters, and media specialists, educators and administrators, conflict specialists, NGOs, and bilateral and multilateral institutions.

The first approach to creating a public forum concerns reforming the curriculum and teaching techniques. Formal school curricula, including textbooks, teachers' guides, educational devices, and visual aids, may be riddled with biases or influenced by previous regimes' partiality. Redressing the material can not only improve the teaching platform but also demonstrate an unwillingness to contribute to segregation or prejudice. Included in the revision of educational texts and teaching curricula can be the insertion of material promoting mutual cooperation. Additionally, teachers can use tools for generating discussions and eliciting responses in the classroom aimed at increasing awareness and changing prejudicial behavior.

International organizations can suggest, promote, and support such efforts. UNICEF and the UN Educational, Scientific and Cultural Organization (UNESCO), for example, have supported peace education programs within school systems in Lebanon and Rwanda in which all prewar educational materials were scrutinized for biased and unethical influence and were subsequently replaced with stereotype-reducing curricula that support moral development. Teacher training was conducted to elicit and encourage methods of cross-group sharing as well as discussion of moral principles and appropriate, nonprejudicial behavior with students (Hansen 1995; Kumar et al. 1996).

Peace radio and television comprise a second approach. Public media programs can range from those with broad-based appeal broadcasting nonbiased, mutually interesting, and beneficial information or entertainment, to those directed specifically at undermining or confronting the conflict by addressing stereotypes, issues of conflict, and historical events. NGO, bilateral or multilateral organizations, or independent institutions can conduct such programs in partnership with local broadcasters and editors.

Foreign entities can not only offer general financial support, material resources, counsel, and program material but also entreat public and government or authority endorsement. Further, they can help develop programming and public interest in debates, presentations, and interactive networks on important ethical topics. In this way, media programs can promote healthy intergroup relations by airing various views on issues of rehabilitation, publicizing successful intergroup cooperation and programs rebuilding community relations, and presenting discussions on topics of civic import. Bosnia, Burundi, and Rwanda all have organizations supporting alternative radio broadcasts, and include multiethnic staffing as well as alternative information forums promoting healthy dialogue and messages of integration and peace (Kumar et al. 1996).

Those involved in influencing the public consciousness may face several obstacles. First, tacit public opposition to pervasive oppressive attitudes may endanger the promoters. Editors, show hosts, and educators could risk physical harm by presenting contrary views in public forums. At the same time, personal danger might inhibit the participation of necessary partners such as school administrators, journalists, or public personalities. If the threat were extreme, it could minimize public participation, since listening to a radio station, reading a journal or textbook, or attending a class others deem as controversial might be grounds for harassment.

The fact that schoolrooms constitute an environment removed from the rest of society limits the effect educational reform can have on a student. Thus, the social pressures placed on children outside the classroom by family members, peers, social institutions, and society as a whole might simply reduce the effectiveness of school education (Voutira and Brown 1995:27). In addition, studies show that mass media appeal is more effective at strengthening already-held views than changing them, and better at developing basic understanding of new notions than persuading the adoption of such notions (Montville, forthcoming). To have a significant effect on public opinion, moreover, the media must be multifaceted, credible, consistent, and persistent, which is often difficult in postconflict societies.

Psychological Rehabilitation

Helping to heal those psychologically traumatized by exposure to extreme violence can take the form of trauma training, direct aid, or community-based communalization programs. Because memories of violence and bloodshed tend to remain fresh in the minds of affected populations, they can not only hurt individuals but undermine intergroup harmony and cooperation. Highly traumatized individuals such as widows, disabled soldiers, unaccompanied children, and sexually abused women can continue to harbor resentment and anger toward former adversaries (Maynard 1997). Their presence, furthermore, serves as a community reminder of past offenses. Therefore, programs addressing psychological trauma can benefit the individual as well as the community as a whole.

Psychological rehabilitation programs have many potential merits, not the least of which is improving the state of the severely traumatized, allowing them to care for themselves and, ultimately, to contribute to society. This can reduce the guardianship burden on society and free resources for community-building. By assisting the severely traumatized, rehabilitation activities can lower community-wide fear and distrust while increasing individual skills in preventive psychological maintenance in times of extreme violence. Indirectly, this can contribute to an increased sense of security. Rehabilitation programs can enhance the second phase of the healing process through communalization and mourning as an integral part of psychological recovery. Joint care of the traumatized, if done cooperatively, can help improve community relations and rebuild trust. Further, programs that promote women's recovery from rape improve the overall condition of women as well as their contribution to society. Rape information campaigns that increase awareness of the effects of violence can also contribute to reestablishing moral codes of conduct.

Complete rehabilitation of the psychologically traumatized ultimately allows them to partake in community discussions, thus contributing to the democratization process.

Those involved in psychological rehabilitation could include government officials, primary caregivers (such as teachers, unaccompanied children's center workers, family members of the traumatized, and health center workers), women's groups, medical professionals, psychologists, and social workers. Internationally, rehabilitation can involve NGOs, UN agencies, psychological associations, and bilateral agencies.

The primary activity in psychological rehabilitation entails training. The objective of trauma training sessions is to provide caregivers with information on the nature and signs of mental distress, encourage its early recognition and treatment, and suggest ways to approach caregiving. A new phenomenon to most societies, training generally covers the causes of psychological disturbance, identification of susceptible individuals, the typical symptoms and psychological nature of the disorder, and the dangers of prolonged neglect. Training also usually includes a discussion of the activities that can mitigate negative effects, such as the value of grieving, communalization, treatment routines, and the role of specific individuals in the care process. In Rwanda, several international agencies, most notably UNICEF, engaged in such training aimed primarily at trauma in children, and consequently involved primary caretakers, teachers, and health professionals. International organizations may work in partnership with local NGOs or professionals as a way of more closely involving local custom, culture, and language.

Psychological rehabilitation can also be enhanced through direct aid. Trauma counseling itself poses many difficulties across cultures and may, in fact, be an inappropriate activity conducted by an outside entity. International agencies can, nevertheless, support it through local avenues such as funding, training, and technical assistance to psychologists and social workers who work directly with victims of psychological trauma. Women's health care centers, for example, can train and employ local medical professionals in psychological trauma counseling of rape victims. Moreover, such facilities can offer special health care programs or establish groups specifically oriented toward women's psychological needs, as they did in Rwanda (Kumar et al. 1996).

Another form of direct aid involves not psychology but conflict management. Field diplomacy—that is, the long-term, resident engagement of conflict specialists in local contentions—offers potential for improving the communalization and bereavement process, which is an inherent part of psychological healing. In this vein, through community-wide programs sponsored by conflict specialists, members have regular opportunities to discuss experiences and feelings, obtain psychological and physical support, and begin to reconcile their lives with the suffering and losses they have endured.

One of the major objections to psychological intercession in foreign cultures is the danger of imposing Western values and procedures on others. The growth of interest in the psychological affects of war on civilians emanated from Western study of combat veterans (Shay 1994). Many programs that began with this background may not have taken cultural factors into consideration in their application abroad. It is difficult if not impossible for outsiders to fully understand cultural nuances. In approaching psychological problems head on, Western programs may even cause further damage to the delicate social structure, including health centers, school systems, or unaccompanied children's programs, by imposing activities that contradict traditional healing patterns.

Until recently, programs addressing psychological issues had received relatively little attention in the larger relief community. Those involved in more tangible sectors such as food, health, and water frequently denigrated the role of psychological programs, perhaps partially out of misunderstanding due to lack of exposure. This, however, is gradually changing as such postconflict settings as Bosnia, Rwanda, and Liberia present noticeable violence-related trauma and our knowledge of its effect on overall recovery grows. Nevertheless, understanding and acceptance of the role psychological assistance plays in the larger international assistance effort is still inadequate.

Rebuilding Civil Society

Reconstructing civil society entails reestablishing "civic space" in which "individuals and their associations compete with each other in the pursuit of their values" (Voutira and Brown 1995:5), free from overwhelming identity group or state influence. Civil society is comprised of active, voluntary organizations, social coalitions, and corporate associations representing different interests and concerns, which serve as both critics and grantors of civil liberties within a democracy (Blair 1992). In the course of political upheaval, civil society usually breaks apart, therefore, no longer serving as a control or guide to government. The reconstitution of this influence is an important link in rebuilding a democratic, sustainable, reintegrated society. Developing a civic space requires reestablishing such organizations as NGOs, environmental groups, unions, media, business and professional associations, human rights organizations, youth and women's leagues, academic institutions, special interest groups, community health associations, and cooperative credit societies. It also entails helping them find their voice in the new political and social context and to begin to play an active role in reshaping the state of affairs.

An inclusive civil society can provide a voice to the disenfranchised, war-weary, and those with special interests and help disengage them from the conflict by offering them an occupation for their time and an alternative outlet for venting disagreement. During the conflict, many such groups and individuals may have become separated. Through interaction in such civil society activities as association meetings, organizing, advocacy, public information campaigns, and fund-raising, they have the opportunity to become reacquainted. This can contribute to the trust-building phase of recovery. Moreover, by using nonviolent means of advocating change and presenting ruling authorities with guidance, controls, and demand for accountability, civil society institutionalizes the process of democratization and nonviolent conflict management. Through this type of diverse public pressure, a strong civil society can promote long-term stability, thereby reinforcing the tenets of democracy.[15] In this manner, civil society can have direct influence on reestablishing social standards of conduct.

Theoretically, all sectors and individuals of a society can have a voice through participation in civil formats. Similarly, virtually every interest can be incorporated in some aspect of civil society. International agencies engaged in the rebuilding process could include international NGOs, bilateral aid organizations, private foundations, and special interest groups and their international civil society counterparts.

Since civil society is, by definition, a citizens' forum, outside entities cannot actually conduct the process or provide the voice. International organizations can, however, suggest, guide, and offer consultation, funding, and encouragement. They can also offer support for civil society initiatives through their daily relief and development activities. For example, establishing a food distribution system that meets the needs of the population with as few diversions as possible may lead NGOs to channel goods through a network of women. This, in turn, may develop into an organization that becomes the voice for women's issues in the community and perhaps across the country.

The Kettering Foundation's work in Tajikistan illustrates how the development of civil society can promote the peace process. During the foundation's sustained dialogue, participants began to discuss their desired components of postconflict Tajik society. As a result, several participants who saw the need for greater civic responsibility established organizations for citizenship education. The Kettering Foundation supports this effort through civil society fellowships and workshops, and through assistance to Tajik university professors in designing courses on conflict prevention, resolution, and civil society development (Saunders 1996b).

Another example in the advancement of civil society is the work of the U.S. Agency for International Development (USAID). Directly or through partner NGOs, it funds projects that range from building and strengthening democratic institutions, supporting NGOs, and making improvements in the administration of justice, to supporting small business associations, trade union development, and citizen participation. It also contributes funds for training in market-based economies, education in the rule of law and human rights, and the development of natural resources and environmental policy (Blair 1992).

Mercy Corps International, an international NGO, helps other countries develop their civil society through its own grassroots development activities. By working closely with farmers, educators, women's groups, health care workers, and local merchants, it assists local citizens to define their needs, establish a plan for meeting their needs, and organize themselves and encourage others to participate. It also helps them to recognize appropriate and inappropriate government leadership, and strengthen their collective voice to have their desires heard. It has aided regional development committees in Honduras, for example, articulate their needs to mayoral, congressional, and presidential candidates and hold them accountable to their campaign platforms.

Several limiting factors are apparent in civil society development. To begin with, third-party, particularly Western, encouragement of civil society development may be more of an imposition of foreign standards of democracy than a contribution to internal interest (Amoda 1996). Civil society, as mentioned, is inherently an internal function, demanding devotion and persistence on the part of a country's citizens, and is not something that can be bestowed by outsiders. Another limitation is that development of civil society is intrinsically a long-term process that demands years of patience and support. As with conflict management, international interest often wanes after a short period of time, potentially leaving NGOs, associations, and other groups alone in their pursuit of increased civic capacity. Furthermore, civil organizations frequently bear the mark of elitist institutions and therefore may exclude the participation of the lower classes. Indeed, engaging in civil society activities can be more conducive to educated individuals with a certain amount of leisure time. The nature of many such organizations presumes, in fact, a degree of literacy and professional experience. This is by no means universal, however.

Given the immense unknowns and rapidly changing circumstances, the international community faces some of its biggest challenges ever in today's complex emergencies. Still, its arsenal of options, extensive as it may presently be, is growing and is unlimited. What now lies ahead is global collaboration on a scale as yet unseen in the international community. Coordinated strategy, collective innovation, and cooperation of effort will be required of us in the years to come in order to deal with the enormity of the problem of complex emergencies. The next and last chapter attempts to outline some of these areas for international action and offers specific mechanisms to address them.

CHAPTER EIGHT **THE NEXT PHASE IN INTERNATIONAL AID**

Development in the context of postwar reconstruction cannot simply be a question of rebuilding physical infrastructure, supporting the growth of productive capacity and generating new wealth. It must also be a matter of dealing with the hidden scars of warfare through policies and programs which support the reconstitution of the family and kinship ties and the social and cultural institutions that are critical to aiding recovery.

—Peter Sollis (1994:15)

International assistance to communities torn apart by complex emergencies has made notable progress since the end of the Cold War. This advancement is, in part, due to the contributions of new disciplines and an overall growth of appreciation for the intricacies involved. Today, there are programs that address psychological trauma, peacekeeping units that coordinate with relief workers, and human rights monitors who live side by side with doctors and logisticians in remote locations. Still, the international community's greatest challenges lie ahead. On the near horizon, it confronts further crises requiring a proactive, comprehensive, and coordinated strategy under growing financial and attention constraints.

While a collaborative response plan is possible in theory, the reality of global politics and human nature does not support a systematic, united, and preestablished approach. Judicious response is predicated on recognizing the situation, obtaining adequate resources, generating the political will to act, implementing appropriate and coordinated actions as well as on such situational factors as gaining country access. Agency desire for control and autonomy, individual aspirations, bureaucratic power plays, and basic apathy, however, tend to subvert such cohesive plans of action. For these reasons, conflict prevention strategies, a logical response to the proliferation of complex emergencies, are repeatedly ignored.

Nevertheless, the international community must continue to develop a range of viable actions to address complex emergencies. Prevention, early reaction, orchestrated programs, and the transition to rehabilitation and development all need proactive attention simply because it is the right thing to do. As Larry Minear states, "What the system lacks is not energy but vision, not good will but discipline. It is a time for tough-mindedness rather than warm-heartedness, for soul-searching rather than hand-wringing" (1994:13).

The conceptual and operational frameworks outlined in the preceding chapters attempt to define a structure for international intercession in complex emergencies. This chapter sets the approaches outlined thus far into an agenda for future action. First, it offers considerations that can affect the ability and way in which the international community intercedes. Next, it explores a systems approach to global intercession, suggesting several areas to amend. Then, it suggests reforms necessary to adapt general strategies to current conditions. And finally, it offers a vision of future international intercession.

International Assistance: Some Important Considerations

As the international humanitarian community redefines its role in complex emergencies, it must struggle with a number of factors that restrict its effectiveness, such as compassion fatigue, the appropriateness of international aid, and its limitations.

Compassion Fatigue

Public sentiment in foreign countries may simply grow numb from the continual bombardment of information about suffering people in foreign lands. Compassion fatigue can compromise any plan of action developed by international actors, no matter how noble. To date, concern for others has been the driving force behind much of the West's outlay of billions of dollars and enormous energy assisting foreign disasters (the extensive influence of national interests, colonial ties, and natural resources, notwithstanding). Observers point out, however, that this moral obligation to the well-being of others that incites much of the international response may not sustain itself through many more intensive identity conflicts (Owen 1993). Many international experts have already highlighted compassion fatigue as a reason for the slow reaction to Rwanda and the lack of effort in the early years of Bosnia's conflict. Some postulate that it is the limiting factor in our involvement in Kosovo. I tend to think that the reason for the inactivity in these examples rests more in a multiplicity of political and identity factors than in real donor fatigue. Nevertheless, sustained responses to complex emergencies undoubtedly require not only material resources but emotional resources as well.

Unlike some observers who see growing indifference as tragic disregard for our fellow human beings, I see it, in part, as a result of modern reality. As population pressures increase and the world becomes more interdependent, the West may be gradually coming to terms with an aspect of life that has become somewhat foreign to the more industrialized nations: physical suffering. The daily struggle for existence, frequent exposure to dying, and even war have been absent from the personal experience of most Westerners in the past fifty years. Poverty, sickness, physical malformation, pain, and death tend to be despised, hidden, avoided, and even shunned. When public images of such suffering appear on television, therefore, our response is a desire to eradicate them.

To much of the rest of the world, death and suffering are more familiar—though equally unwelcome—parts of everyday life. The apparently unstoppable global population growth may well force a higher level of pain on the world in the near future, as a result of food shortages, environmental destruction, population pressures on urban environments, natural resource demands, competition for space and access to land, and violent power struggles. The West may, therefore, inevitably be gradually exposed to greater pain and suffering.

What this means for international responses to foreign emergencies is more difficult to articulate. Ideally, growing interdependence, communication technology, and migration pressures may force a more comprehensive global strategy for handling world crises. Prevention would rest less on domestic financial or political factors than on a universal understanding of the need for international collaboration. Responses would be generated out of a comprehension of the larger picture, both regionally and globally. Considerations might include international resources and implications of actions on the local and worldwide scenes. Such a holistic approach, however, would also incorporate the limitations of international response, a greater tolerance for suffering, and host country accountability in favor of larger, more comprehensive goals. David Owen advocates "mutual obligations and responsibility" (1993:58), which, at times, may require participants in inter-identity conflicts to address the consequences of their actions themselves.

Appropriateness of International Assistance

A second factor to consider in reviewing the role of foreign aid in complex emergencies is the effectiveness of the assistance system itself. Beyond the micro-level issues discussed in the preceding chapters, such as effect on the economy and intergroup hostilities, international aid has its own impact on society. Policymakers and scholars are increasingly questioning the viability of foreign intercession—or at least aspects thereof—for improving conditions in receiving countries (Anderson 1996a; Awoonor 1993; Kumar et al. 1996; Leaning 1993).

The simultaneous decline in development assistance and increase in disaster aid in the 1990s points to a changing international picture. On the one hand, development has arguably been relatively ineffective in the past thirty years. USAID, for example, came to this realization in the Greater Horn of Africa.[1] The fruit of years of development efforts in most of the ten countries that comprise the Greater Horn (Somalia, Sudan, Ethiopia, Djibouti, Eritrea, Rwanda, Kenya, Uganda, Tanzania, and Burundi) have been repeatedly destroyed by civil strife. The extraordinary amount of food assistance did nothing to reduce the growing numbers of famines in the region (Creative Associates 1997).

Development literature is also full of case studies of foreign-born programs that do not consider the cultural or local context, sometimes backfiring and making conditions worse. Despite the programmatic success of lowering mortality rates, improving water systems, increasing agricultural production, or developing commercial law standards, development aid has also had negative affects. Examples include unintentionally creating dependency, decreasing local resource capacity, reengineering social structures, diminishing cultural importance, and creating a resource problem by introducing foreign techniques and products. Despite its doubtless positive influences, international assistance nevertheless has developed a stigma of general failure.

On the other hand, the increase in funding for relief as a function of a decrease in development aid is due, in part, to the existence of complex emergencies. These emergencies draw organizations previously dedicated solely to development, as well as new ones, onto the relief scene, bringing into question the legitimacy of their activities. One consequence is the uninvited arrival of "do-gooder" organizations in a country to deliver goods not necessarily needed and in a manner conflicting with local custom, for the sake of relieving the benefactor's conscience. Although such inappropriate actions are not universal, they have influenced the image of relief organizations. Conflict management also has a reputation for bringing inappropriate techniques into a foreign environment and entering the scene uninvited (Moore 1993).

Moreover, the stigma of charity can be seen as oppressing recipients and reducing their self-reliance (Awoonor 1993). Aid agencies attract empathy and money by picturing withered young children receiving bowls of cereal from the munificent foreigners. Assistance to refugee communities, as discussed in chapter 3, can create "DP apathy," which in turn makes repatriation more difficult and reliance on outside assistance upon return more necessary.

Somalia raises another question about the appropriateness of aid. Although the international military intervention was said to have saved 100,000–125,000 lives (Sommer 1994a:2), it also left the country in protracted turmoil. The debate here is not over the viability of interceding in famines, but over ignoring long-term needs for short-term gains. While I leave the lively "to intercede or not to intercede" debate to other, more qualified policy analysts, I believe it is important for the international community to weigh carefully the implications of its actions.

Limitations on Aid

A third factor in considering intercession is the constraints of the international system in addressing crises. The expectation that outside assistance of any kind will ultimately be of benefit is not only misleading but potentially dangerous. It contributes to the kind of statement emanating from Liberia during its brutal uprising in the spring of 1996: "We are killing each other! Where is the international community?" To provide another illustration, in 1996 I participated in a group of humanitarian specialists gathered to discuss the situation in Somalia. The question from one who worked in the country and was acutely aware of its deteriorating stability was, "What will the relief community do to prevent the development of another all-out conflict?" These two instances illustrate the assumption that "the international community" (often used to refer to relief organizations) not only will respond but has the responsibility to respond to all crises. More fundamentally, it assumes that the response will positively affect the deteriorating social conditions.

My reply is twofold. First, accountability as a basis for individual action seems to have disappeared somewhat, perhaps a function of the abundance of development assistance since the mid-1950s. It is crucial, I believe, that each component of the global community take responsibility for its actions, whether it be initiating conflicts with its neighbors or providing assistance across borders. Second, it is equally important that each action be kept in perspective. Relief aid, after all, is essentially meant to help keep people alive. It does not solve political problems nor, by itself, does it increase security. In the former Yugoslavia over the past four years (i.e., since 1994), food and material aid were used regularly as a substitute for political action. In the same vein, foreign military presence, or even the foreign conflict management specialists, should not be expected to resolve internal conflict by themselves.

Having said that, I believe that the international community desperately needs to expand and refine its response toolbox. We need a methodical, comprehensive approach to foreign intercession in complex emergencies, incorporating the widest possible elements. I suggest we establish a systems approach, refine and restructure specific elements, and fine-tune our methodology in the field.

A Systems Approach to Intercession

"Unlike other regimes," writes Minear, "the international humanitarian relief system is not framed by a body of law, principles, and norms; implemented by an institutional apparatus; and enforced by sanctions to assure accountability" (1994:2). It works on a much more informal basis, using lateral, voluntary collaboration (as opposed to hierarchical and dictatorial), with no governing body, and few rules, regulations, recourses, standards, or even common methodologies. However, the growing complexity of the humanitarian context—including greater security risks, diversions of supplies and expansion of NGOs—now calls for some degree of formalization. The establishment of a more systematized structure is necessary both to address the new issues facing the relief community today and to deal with the magnitude of the requirements in the world in an efficient and organized manner.

At present, there appears to be little coherent international rationale for responses to emerging or existing emergencies as exemplified in the disjointed approach to the Kosovo conflict. Similarly, there is no real systematic framework for analysis of the situation and no consistent global decision-making forum. To the contrary, most responses seem to follow certain patterns of communication (proposals for intervention, for example, in the UN Security Council, or meeting of the Inter-Agency Standing Committee), yet remain fundamentally uncoordinated and somewhat arbitrary.

Expanding the international reliability and capacity to deal with identity conflict and complex emergencies, I think, takes creativity, innovation, and a rare degree of interaction among many elements of whole bodies politic. Communication must expand in many directions, including between organizations—particularly UN agencies; between different types of organizations, whether it be UN agency, NGO, military, or diplomatic; between categories of response from peacekeeping to conflict management to human rights; and certainly between the levels of application (that is, field, policy, or academics). In my experience, adjusting activities based on in-house reflection alone can make only limited strides. This kind of comprehensive exchange reflects the reality of whole bodies politic. Developing it requires a systems approach to addressing the scope, time frame, preparedness, and coordination of international assistance.

Scope

The first aspect of regulating and expanding our capacity to address international crises is to include a broader geographic and population range. International actors should examine the entire spectrum of issues particular to each population, from the community level to the region. Looking more closely at the ethnicity of the fighters in certain areas, for example, might illuminate opportunities or, conversely, eliminate options based on ethnic tendencies.

At the same time, the international community should tend to refugee needs while attempting to address the reasons for flight (Loescher 1993). The importance of this is gradually being acknowledged in the international community. The Joint Evaluation of Emergency Assistance to Rwanda, for example, cited the experience of Rwanda, where refugee situations were ignored by those working inside the country, and population particulars were neglected in some of the returnee operations (Kumar et al. 1996).

The second aspect of expanding the scope of international response is to increase the number of the disciplines employed. Using a wide variety of expertise offers the broadest input into an appropriate response. For example, the typical field coordination structure for humanitarian crises should be expanded to include the sectors of conflict management and human rights (Cohen 1996). In that way, those involved in health care, for instance, can integrate their assessments, work, and findings into human rights operations. At the same time, their work can incorporate conflict management considerations.[2]

Unfortunately, many policymakers and field practitioners are reluctant to delve into the more controversial and ambiguous areas such as psychological trauma, conflict mitigation, and even human rights protection. Unlike the conventional sectors of water, sanitation, health, shelter, and food relief, these are less quantifiable, and their success may not be immediately apparent. With little data on the effectiveness of crisis prevention, for example, many donors are hesitant to invest time and money. Nevertheless, it is critical that they do so. It is in these programs, I believe, that the real future of a stable world order lies. At the same time, improved means of ascertaining, evaluating, and verifying the efficacy of various approaches is needed. For this the world needs to draw on the skills of sociologists, psychologists, and anthropologists who are experts in qualitative analysis. Like all other elements, this process must be an international and interagency effort.

Time

A systems approach to intervention should include a broad time frame. Consideration of a disaster should not begin when an emergency is declared, but when the first signs of trouble begin to appear on the horizon. In fact, an even better approach would be to develop connections and monitor the situation *before* there is any sign of contention. Actual conflict prevention, however, is not a consistently achievable endeavor. Despite some international reluctance and a realistic skepticism about their use in a political world, prevention efforts, nevertheless, compose an important end of the international intercession time frame.

At the other end of the spectrum, reductions in morbidity and malnutrition rates do not signal the end to a crisis. Follow-through of international assistance to rehabilitation and political and social reconstruction is vital to sustainable peace. Beyond this time-consuming process, there need to be development efforts that help support a peaceful society. The systems approach should encompass this full range of interaction with the affected populations across a wide span of time from prevention to long-term development.

The international efforts in Bosnia are an example of the lack of an expansive time frame. Many observers claim that international reaction to prevent the escalation of hostilities was too slow. In particular, the warning signals acknowledged in the early stages were not heeded, and it was not until years into massive "ethnic cleansing" that the international community launched real efforts. When the United States first committed troops to the region, however, it was with a predetermined end date. Regardless of changes in conditions or needs at the time of demobilization, the United States' military contribution to a sustainable peace was initially limited to one year.

Most Bosnia experts are intimately aware of the enormous rehabilitation needs of the country, both politically and socially. Human rights, which have been devastated, for instance, must be reestablished. The culture of impunity must be eradicated and institutional capacity rebuilt within the justice system. Reestablishing safety, communalization, redevelopment of trust and social ethics, and democratization all require enormous amounts of time, yet the international attention span is insufficient for these to come to fruition.

Donor investment in complex emergencies tends to peak dramatically just after the crisis itself reaches its peak. It then falls abruptly and tapers off to a lower level (USGAO 1992). International concerns typically become the most serious after the outbreak of violence, and diminish after the ceasefire. Donor investment in an emergency, I believe, should expand from the usual six-to-twelve-month time frame to a more intensive five-year investment. As the conflict develops, interest would exist in the periods of stable peace, and concerted efforts would build during the increasing instability. Optimally, international intercession would help to keep tensions from rising to the crisis point. The same amount of resources, then, could be used to reduce the extent of an outbreak, recover more rapidly, and build the national capacity to prevent and handle future problems. This capacity could include international strategic planning, national contingency planning, and regional prevention planning. Such a long-term strategy, according to Loescher, could also relieve immigration pressures on Northern countries, brought about by the massive refugee flows at the heart of the crisis (1993:168).

Preparedness

A systems approach to intercession logically involves early recognition of problems coupled with appropriate response. An important part of this approach is the need to incorporate preparedness planning, which would include predetermining an appropriate responsive action. The question then becomes, "What degree of humanitarian suffering under what conditions should justify what form of international action, by whom, through what operational mechanisms and with what precise objectives?" notes Francis Deng (1993:161). I would only add to his list, "When?"

I suggest an approach much like that used in the United States in fighting forest fires. All sections of each U.S. Forest Service Ranger District in a national forest are mapped according to terrain, elevation, fuel types, exposures, structures, roads, streams, anthropological sites, mines, and wildlife habitat. They are then analyzed according to their history of forest fires at various times of the year and monitored for fuel moisture content to maintain awareness of current volatility. A plan is drawn up for each section, predetermining the organizational response to a fire in a certain area, given specific fuel moisture and time of year. Under some conditions, the fire will be allowed to burn untended, as a natural method of brush disposal. Others may be monitored by airplane once a day. Still others may be corralled away from specific habitats or areas but otherwise left untouched. Of course, some may be extinguished altogether. In this way, planners are thoroughly aware of the conditions, have a tentative plan of action, can prepare for fire outbreaks, and use an appropriate methodology.

Granted, fighting forest fires and confronting complex emergencies are not directly analogous. For one, those drawing up the fire response plans actually have jurisdiction over the forests. Nevertheless, I believe some lessons can be learned from this approach. First, understanding the context is of utmost importance. Hence early, complete, and continual contextual analysis (as discussed in chapter 7) is important. This can be accomplished via more systematic monitoring, greater attention and care to potential trouble spots, and improved early warning and context information-sharing.

Second, developing concerted plans of action prior to outbreaks or even the development of trouble spots is important to addressing needs quickly and appropriately. Such plans require gathering or at least determining available resources, allowing greater specification and preparation. It also permits better understanding of the context on the part of the responding agency. Third, predetermining a plan of action, even if not followed exactly, can encourage much greater innovation and flexibility and help avoid automatic, uniform responses to all complex emergencies. Finally, if a range of alternatives existed initially, responses and resources can be adjusted more easily.

The drawback to this firefighting methodology is that it requires much greater attention and allocation of funds and resources to preparation, something many international organizations are reluctant to indulge in. Some might argue that it could also lead to self-fulfilling prophecies: too much attention given to minor hostilities might indeed exacerbate the problem.

Coordination

A final element in the systems approach is coordination, an essential element of disaster response. In a situation drawing hundreds of organizations of many varieties, collaboration is needed simply to eliminate overlaps for the sake of efficiency in the zero-sum game of humanitarian relief. Better coordination (a cry invariably heard in reference to every disaster) can serve several other functions as well.

First, as outlined above, it is important for cohesive planning over an expanded time frame. Conflict mitigation efforts need to be incorporated into development planning and diplomatic policy, for instance. The de-escalation in the emergency phase, as another example, should be closely choreographed with an increase in rehabilitation efforts. Second, coordination is vital for shared programming among the various sectors, from peacekeeping to food distribution to refugee repatriation. Cross-pollination ensures not only comprehensive strategizing but also the development of new ideas and collaborative efforts across sectors.

Third, such communication should occur among all international actors, including the donors themselves. Although various coordinating bodies exist, actual collaborative strategizing, in my opinion, is relatively rare. Because many NGOs are dependent on donor financing, their programs often reflect the will of their financier. It is important, therefore, that they share information, understand the availability of resources, communicate various interests, and, optimally, develop a cohesive strategy.

Finally, the international community should improve its communication with the affected population, country professionals, local authorities, and the host governments. Such coordination is indubitably a difficult task, given political agendas, agency efforts to maintain neutrality, cultural differences, and a host of other variables. Nonetheless, living and working in a foreign context demands acute attention and communication with the local citizens who are the hosts of the country, objects of the effort, and most informed about their own needs.

Under the rubric of "coordination" I might add two other elements. One is that interagency communication is more than simple sharing information on current activities. It also includes forward thinking. While current activity coordination has attracted a fair amount of attention in the past five years, strategizing, planning, and problem-solving have not. What is needed, I believe, is for all involved organizations, both in country and foreign, to develop think tank/problem-solving groups that can strategize on specific problems and focus on the larger picture.

The other element is standardization. Relief agencies use many different methods and technologies to address complex emergencies. While strict regulation is neither possible nor desirable, greater uniformity in approaches to capacity assessment, baseline information-gathering, relations with authorities, media, contextualization, security, institutionalization of human rights, local procurement, and hiring practices could minimize negative impacts and improve the appropriateness of international intercession. This is beginning to take place among international NGOs. In my experience in the field and at headquarters, coordination is a delicate thing. We need enough to harness the energy, but not so much as to thwart creativity.

The International Structure: A Need for Modification

One of the major tasks for devising a more appropriate and effective international system of intercession is to adjust and reorganize some of what we already have. For decades, observers have been calling for changes in the international regime, and various institutions have responded to some degree and at different times. In light of the increasing requirements levied on the international community as a result of the growing complex emergencies, however, I think yet another look at the system is warranted. My suggestions here are general and brief and meant primarily to focus attention on certain aspects of reform. In each area, experts have developed recommendations far beyond the scope of this book.

Mandates

Operational precepts that define an organization's boundaries become sacrosanct in the field. They not only determine the requisite actions to be undertaken but limit their range to a specified population, geographic boundary, activity, or time frame. While somewhat adaptable to varying situations, many such precepts nevertheless need fundamental modification to fit today's conditions.

In question are the mandates of such organizations as UNHCR, which frequently must expand its parameters to address today's conditions. Other UN agencies, as well, face reorganization in order to streamline international assistance. Though I am not prepared to debate or advocate specific changes in the UN system, I join with others in stating that the large, bureaucratic, competitive structure of UN relief agencies desperately needs to be reformed for the sake of efficiency and effectiveness.

The challenge for the community as a whole is not to point fingers, but to carefully examine the strengths and weaknesses of each institution. Scholars of all sorts have recognized the need for a clearer division of labor based on the inherent or potential capabilities of each organization (Hathaway 1996; UNHCR 1993a). Many observers, for example, have identified the need for developing or assigning a UN organization to protect, care for, and collect data on internally displaced persons, returnees, and victims of conflict. Despite the fact that technical responsibility for IDPs lies within domestic jurisdiction, the demand for such a protectorate as well as a declaration of legal principles is mounting (Cohen 1996). Hence, the principle of sovereignty appears to be gradually succumbing to the reality that outside intercession may be necessary to preserve human rights. Still far from universal acceptance in international circles, the potential for designating a specific agency to care for citizens inside their country of origin is, nevertheless, evolving (Cohen 1996; Deng 1993; Girardet 1993; Ruiz 1993; UNHCR 1993a).

Another problem related to mandates is the care of refugee children. In part the responsibility of both UNICEF (as children) and UNHCR (as refugees), their specific needs are occasionally neglected altogether in the battle over obligation. Similarly, women's issues in emergencies constitute another area that needs clarification. Their concerns are extremely important, given the role of women in society, the injuries they sustain in identity conflicts, and their vulnerability in complex emergencies. Nevertheless, few UN agency mandates specifically address women's issues. Yet another problem area is human rights. Though the inception of the UN High Commissioner for Human Rights was a significant step in this direction and has brought greater operational capacity to the field, the issue of protection is still less than adequately addressed.

I would stretch the discussion of mandates to include mission objectives, specifically those of foreign military forces in humanitarian operations. As with UN agencies, the lines of obligation are often unclear, though here there are no mandates upon which to rely. The experience of many of my colleagues, and my own as a military liaison to humanitarian operations in several complex emergencies, has been that such confusion can and has led down dangerous paths. Without delineating areas of responsibility to exclude decisions pertaining to relief operations, military functions sometimes operate independently and outside their area of knowledge. Military forces should be limited to logistic and security assistance and operate in strict and continual communication with humanitarian components. To its credit, the U.S. military has made impressive efforts to understand the relief environment and improve its operations in humanitarian emergencies. Nevertheless, as with UN agencies, issues of division of labor still appear to require close scrutiny.

Funding Mechanisms

Many argue justifiably that it is not only UN mandates that require serious reevaluation and, in some cases, restructuring. The inadequacies of various funding mechanisms also contribute to overall ineffectiveness. For instance, in the UN, the reliance upon voluntary contributions through an appeal process for relief operations can exacerbate interagency competition, delay response, reduce continuity, and limit such activities as organizational development (Borton 1993).

Another problem is that donor funding for the full spectrum of early response through repatriation and social rehabilitation is inadequate. Partly the result of a lack of perspective, insufficient funding thwarts the implementation of such efforts as long-term, community-level field diplomacy. This kind of program becomes the victim of a shortening, rather than lengthening, international attention span.

The current focus on relief requirements over long-term development needs, though understandable given the immediacy of modern complex emergencies, should nevertheless be reevaluated for its overall effectiveness. As John Borton of the Overseas Development Institute contends, the immense power of Western governments "to influence the pace and direction of change within the international relief system" (Borton 1993:15) suggests that a prominent focus of any such evaluation lies within donor agencies. It would behoove donors to review their own organizational structure for priority of funding in light of the needs generated in today's conditions.

Such a review might result in eliminating certain branches and building new ones or merely redirect energy toward programs that will most likely help build sustainable peace. Though donor structures often reorganize, the suggestion here is to reformat using longer-term, more comprehensive objectives within the larger conceptual framework. One commendable example is USAID's creation of the Greater Horn of Africa Initiative, which attempts to address the root causes of complex emergencies in the region and redirects traditional development funds to that end.

Regional Structures

Other opportunities lie in the development of regional organizations. Many argue for restructuring the international system to rely more heavily on regional institutions, not only political entities such as the Organization for African Unity (OAU) and the Organization of American States (OAS) but other resources such as the All Africa Council of Churches, the Association of Southeast Asian Nations, and the Nairobi Peace Initiative. As Western countries draw down their funding for international intercession, regional organizations and institutions could fill the gap. Though limited in their own ways, using more local capacities helps develop skills, resources, and institutional competence to address future issues within a geographic region.

The United States, for example, passed the African Conflict Resolution Act of 1995 to support the development of Africa's capacity to avoid and manage conflict on the continent. The act was intended to bolster the efforts of the OAU begun in 1993 to build a conflict prevention mechanism. Loescher suggests, as well, that regional organizations can be strengthened to participate in human rights monitoring. Such a change could contribute to "consciousness-raising" with regard to humanitarian, human rights, and democratic principles, and could, perhaps, reduce the impact of intercession on national sovereignty (Loescher 1993:190).

Restructuring the system to increase the use of cross-mandate approaches could allow much greater flexibility to address specific needs on a regional level. A cross-mandate approach is one in which all interested parties "pool their resources and work in close collaboration to provide community-based assistance" to all persons in need (Mechal and Simkin 1992). Instead of the usual geographic and operational restrictions, a cross-mandate approach offers greater flexibility to develop new options based on local and regional requirements.

Information Systems

Yet another challenge facing the international community is to improve information flow. While this is necessary simply because of the rapid technological changes in communication systems, it corresponds with a growing need for better intra- and interorganizational information-sharing. Improvements in technology have had a substantial influence on communication over the past five years alone and promise to affect it further in the future (Stephenson and Anderson 1997). The use of the Internet as a medium of information exchange has spawned such developments as ReliefWeb, an on-line disaster-information system housed in the UN. ReliefWeb has the potential to have application in data collection, information-sharing, response coordination, strategy development, contextualization, and standardization. UNHCR's Reflink similarly offers an electronic database that gives users access to current academic and policy research about refugees and related subjects. Multitudes of other organizations offer information through their web pages. The growing use of e-mail list serves on various subjects and geographic areas of concern is further increasing the information flow among individuals and organizations.

The influence of such communication technology is evident in the crisis in Kosovo. In 1997, students protesting conditions in Kosovo received global attention as they publicized reports of the demonstrations on the Internet. In subsequent months, as conditions deteriorated and violence erupted, information has continued to pour through the electronic medium to list serve recipients around the world. The use of cellular telephones has further impacted the Kosovo emergency by helping organizations locate populations in need, compile information about current conditions, and coordinate relief efforts. As communication options continue to grow around the world, one of the challenges will be to refine and organize the data for the most efficient use. Another will be to define the method and protocols for information use. Issues of equal access—particularly in remote or underserved areas of the world—and information security are also on the agenda.

An encouraging sign of increased cross-agency information flow is the establishment of the Framework for Coordination, which links UN peacekeeping, humanitarian assistance, political affairs, and (more recently) development and human rights departments in a joint decision-making structure based in the UN Secretariat. Through the Framework, desk officers in each department share data on conditions in specific countries and link response actions in an effort to prevent the outbreak of violent conflict and complex emergencies. This type of cross-fertilization among organizations needs to be developed further throughout the relief community.

Another necessary improvement in data collection is the building of objective needs-based indicators to help understand deteriorating situations. The objectivity of any analysis of a complex and politically volatile situation can be questionable. Nevertheless, there is a general consensus on the need to increase the even-handedness of the international community's responses to crises. Restructuring could not only entail developing common indicators but enlarge the sources of information upon which to base the indicators. An expanded information structure should include some nonsensitive intelligence sources. To date, this kind of formal exchange has been small (albeit growing), and official inclusion might entail overhauling parts of the intercession coordination and information structure to include the intelligence community.

Weapons Export

A final area that requires immediate international community redress is that of small arms manufacturing and sales. The abundance of light weapons in circulation, which includes pistols, rifles, grenades, machine guns, antitank and antiaircraft rockets, mines, and mortars, contributes not only to the number of casualties in identity conflicts but also to a readiness to use them. A significant common denominator in today's armed violence is this abundance of lethal weapons. "It is the flow of small arms and light weapons that is most relevant to the incidence of internal conflict and the outcome of recent wars," claims arms researcher Aaron Karp (Morrison 1995). According to Karp, of the thirty major armed conflicts in progress, small arms were the major weapon in all but four (Dikshit 1995:41).

The inordinate amount of small arms distributed during the Cold War inundated the third world with the capacity to create and sustain armed conflict. Information on the exact numbers is unavailable since, during that time, only the transfer of larger weapons systems was regulated. Moreover, the recirculation of weapons throughout the world has made them impossible to track.

Despite the changes in global politics, the manufacturing and exportation of such weapons has not diminished but, many believe, has increased inordinately. Both Russia and the United States are still big players, according to weapons expert David Morrison, who states that Russian firms are attempting to gain more of the global market share. Where once they supplied 90 percent of all the weapons imported by the Angolan government between 1987 and 1991, they now also do business with anticommunist rebels (Morrison 1995). They have even reportedly expanded their weapons trade to their Chechen opposition during the conflict (Landay 1995; Morrison 1995). The United

States, for its part, still has a big hand in weapons deals as well, ranking fifth among the countries with small arms industries (Landay 1995).

However, the image of superpower—or even industrial power—dominance over the arms trade is outdated in the post–Cold War era, as other countries get involved. By 1994, nearly three hundred companies in over fifty countries were producing small arms, according to the United Nations Institute for Disarmament Research. A large part of this 25 percent increase in ten years is claimed by China, which has the world's largest small arms industry (Landay 1995). South Africa, too, has become a major exporter, generating $187 million in profits in 1993 (Morrison 1995). In fact, in 1995, South Africa declared its intention to increase arms exports by 300 percent by the year 2000 (Cock 1995).

One of the worst offenders in the proliferation of violence is land mines. Over 110 million mines are spread across the globe in over sixty countries. In nine of the most serious infestations, land mines cause eight hundred deaths a month (Singh 1995:ix) and indiscriminatley maim tens of thousands of others, most of them unarmed civilians (Girardet 1994:7). More are planted cheaply and easily each year, for a cost of $10–$20 each, with some costing as little as three dollars. Now made of plastic, they are virtually impossible to detect, save with hand-held prodders. Therefore, clearing them costs between $300 and $1,000 per mine (Girardet 1994:22). As with other light weapons, the Western industrial nations are not the only or even the largest manufacturers of mines. In fact, China, India, and the former Soviet Union have been the biggest exporters of conventional antipersonnel mines in the early 1990s (Bond 1994:7).

The result of extensive circulation of countless light weapons throughout the world is not only actual violence but the perpetual fear of renewed conflict once a semblance of peace has been achieved. The presence of abundant weapons is undoubtedly contributing to the deterioration of stability in Angola. Not only government armies and recognized opposition groups pose a threat, but other political extremists, criminals, self-defense units, poachers, hunters, mercenaries, and private security forces now have access to arms (Cock 1995:91–96).

Although several countries in recent years have made attempts to address the larger issue of small arms, the strong political and economic interest attached to the arms trade make it a highly charged debate. In 1995, in fact, the United States approved new guidelines formalizing the use of U.S. embassies and agencies to market military hardware and expanding access to regional markets (Landay 1995). Nevertheless, the growing recognition that small arms contribute directly to internal turmoil and increase the lethal power of disputing identity groups seems to be growing. The U.S. Congress, for example, has written legislation attempting to establish a code of conduct for U.S. arms sales, among other things banning sales to foreign entities who violate human rights (Landay 1995).

Land mine reduction efforts are receiving greater attention. The designation of the Coordinator of the International Campaign to Ban Land Mines as the Nobel Peace Prize recipient in 1997, and the Canadian-sponsored forum aimed at gaining international agreement on steps toward their eradication, put the issue at the top of the international agenda. Human rights and humanitarian organizations' campaign to halt their use has also had an impact on the media and public opinion. Though these significant actions indicate a probable turning point in the acceptance of mines as a common weapon, their ultimate demise is still bogged down in political and technical quagmires. The new proposals to require metal inserts or self-destructing devises, for example, are considered too expensive and are therefore unlikely to be used by those intent on terrorizing a population or blocking supply routes. The United States' resistance to joining the Canadian-led effort is another distressing indication of the probable difficulty of eliminating this scourge in the near future.

Although the weapons market is lucrative for those who sell arms, its human cost is dear. Curbing arms sales, which are a primary contribution to international crises, should be foremost on the humanitarian mind. As we move into the next millennium, this and other difficult issues facing the international community will have to be confronted head on.

A Vision of the Future

Looking back at the eight years since the end of the Cold War, one can argue that the global response to complex emergencies has progressed in some significant ways. Equally apparent, however, is the need for further changes. In the years to come, I envision the international community refining its understanding and attitude toward intercession to encompass the broader picture and incorporate the realities of today's changing global dynamics.

In this vision, scholars, practitioners, and policymakers will combine efforts and expertise to create reality-based programs that more closely reflect the needs of the community threatened with, or engulfed in, identity conflict. These efforts will be determined by consistent and active monitoring of the country's conditions (increasingly by regional organizations, which offer insight into potential trouble spots) as well as assessment of its humanitarian, human rights, or other needs. Early in the process, actors from all points in the range of whole bodies politic will lend their skills to prevent the deterioration in inter-identity relationships. They will select from the broadest possible array of approaches, ranging from noninterference to diplomatic means to economic incentives to humanitarian aid, based on intimate knowledge of the local conditions and capacities.

Later in the development of a complex emergency, the international community will view the entire scene in its full context and offer appropriate, proportional assistance. Organizations and international actors will work under standards and ethical principles to avoid exacerbating tensions. Safety zones, Open Relief Centers, and cross-mandate approaches will become standard in providing protection to IDPs and returnees. Refugees and resident citizens alike will be treated even-handedly by such programs as conflict management skills training and attempts to reestablish moral codes.

Reintegration assistance in the middle and later stages of a complex emergency will become a significant aspect of many organizations' work, involving the use and development of local capacities, and efforts to begin the process of communalization. International NGOs will partner with local ones, building skills and resources as well as civil society. Issues of gender and identity will be incorporated into all programs, attempting to bridge the gap and encourage reintegration. In this vision, the international eye will not turn away when the crisis begins to abate. To the contrary, the camera will continue to portray images of the global and local community, each working toward a sustainable, peaceful society.

With such idealism, perhaps we can roll into the twenty-first century with new parameters for international intercession in complex emergencies. Lest I become lulled by my own wishful thinking, the words of Fred Cuny come to mind: "It is too innovative; they will never buy it." Nevertheless, even without Fred's own visionary leadership, perhaps some collective vision can serve as a common focal point for refining our global capacity in complex emergencies.

NOTES

Preface

1. Though no single definition exists for the term *complex emergency*, it is commonly understood to entail a breakdown in political, economic, and physical order and includes civil conflict, large-scale population displacement, economic disintegration, life-threatening hunger and/or disease, human rights violations, and at least partial political and/or social collapse. Such dire circumstances require massive international assistance.

1. The International Humanitarian Context

1. Figures for conflicts vary somewhat, complicated by definitions, changes in conflict status over the course of the data collection period, and criteria for collection.

2. The term *complex emergency* did not actually come into common use in the humanitarian community before the end of the Cold War. Sometimes, such disasters born of political and social conflict have been called "slow-onset" or "man-made" emergencies. These figures refer to emergencies that put more than 300,000 lives at risk.

3. The conventional definition of a refugee is a person who is compelled to leave his or her country due to fear of persecution, armed conflict, or civil strife and whose life or security would be endangered if he or she returned. (See chapter 3 for further discussion of these definitions.)

4. "Others of concern" could include besieged populations, returnees, vulnerable sectors, resident victims of violence, or seriously marginalized populations.

5. In selecting this term, I refer to *Webster's Unabridged Dictionary*, which defines "intercede" as, "1: to interpose in behalf of one in difficulty or trouble . . . [and] 2: to mediate; attempt to reconcile differences between two people or groups." However, it has been pointed out that this is an American understanding of the term "to intercede," connoting a nonpartisan, benevolent action. British usage of the word imparts a different understanding, implying interfering *on behalf of one side* and is often used in reference to the Catholic Church. For lack of a better term, I nevertheless find it acceptable in this context, given an understood American interpretation.

6. An interesting study of British NGO conflict resolution programs conducted by the then Overseas Development Administration and the Refugees Studies Programme concludes, "The effectiveness of operations . . . is not so much one of 'disciplinary affiliation' (psychology, sociology, or international relations), size or budget of the NGO, but the level at which intercessions are addressed [high, mid, or grassroots]" (Voutira and Brown 1995:26).

7. The comments of Sarah Burns, a UNDP representative, as given at a United Nations Association meeting March 6, 1996, in Washington, D.C.

3. Forced Migration: A Consequence of Conflict

1. The term *flee* is a misnomer in those instances where citizens are forcefully relocated by military or government authorities.

2. The term *displaced populations* here is used in the broad vernacular of all those removed from their homes, meaning both refugees and IDPs. Internally displaced persons specifically denotes those who have not left their country of origin.

3. The Organization of African Unity (OAU) offered what is considered the most significant and comprehensive regional treaty on refugees, in part by expanding the definition to include contingencies beyond the "well-founded fear of persecution." According to the 1969 OAU Convention, the term for refugee also applies "to every person who [qualifies], owing to external aggression, occupation, foreign domination or events seriously disturbing public order in either part or the whole of his country of origin or nationality" (United Nations n.d.:9). Later, the Cartegena Declaration of 1984 on the treatment of Central American refugees echoed the OAU's expanded definition.

4. For various reasons, however, not all qualifying refugees receive assistance. This in part explains the discrepancy in the figures of overall displacement, and those under the care of the UNHCR.

5. "Others of concern" are "those who are in a refugee-like situation, that is, those who are outside their country of origin, but who have not been formally recognized as refugees," as well as other specific categories receiving assistance from UNHCR (UNHCR 1996:1).

6. This statement could be arguably qualified with an acknowledgment of the uncelebrated plight of resident war victims, who by all reckoning account for the greatest proportion of war-related indigence and suffering and who, by virtue of their ubiquitous and indistinct nature, receive little international recognition or assistance. The lack of identification and distinction creates a catch-22 situation in which little is done to ameliorate their plight for want of adequate understanding of their conditions and needs.

7. According to the U.S. Committee for Refugees annual compilation of statistics on displaced populations, at the end of 1997 there were 13.5 million refugees and 17 million internally displaced persons (USCR 1997). Exact figures for the number of displaced populations in the world today are, needless to say, impossible to obtain. This is in part a function of definition and in part faulty and less than

diligent record-keeping by host and home governments, and by local and international agencies. It is also the result of intentional figure inflation for political purposes or to obtain increased assistance or funding; it may also reflect attempts to deny the existence of refugees in country.

8. The principle of *non-refoulement*, which states that forcible return or expulsion to a life-threatening situation is strictly forbidden, is stipulated in both article 33 of the 1951 Convention relating to the Status of Refugees and article 3 of the 1984 UN Convention Against Torture and Other Cruel, Inhuman or Degrading Treatment or Punishment.

4. The Process of Returning Home

1. The term *repatriation* is somewhat indistinct in that to some it means returning to the home community, while to others it is simply returning to the home country.

2. USCR figures are drawn from multiple sources, reflecting the inherent ambiguity of refugee statistics.

3. This example of Thailand's assistance and generally hospitable nature toward Cambodian refugees is in sharp contrast to its forced expulsion campaign in June 1979 (Rogge 1992).

4. Interestingly, a host of multilateral and bilateral donors are now establishing institutional mechanisms to address postconflict issues—the U.S. government's Office of Transition Initiatives and the World Bank's Post Conflict Unit, among them.

5. Communities in Conflict

1. In a limited survey conducted in three *préfectures*, of the 241 women medically screened, 60.5 percent had survived single, multiple, or protracted rape, 29.5 percent were pregnant, and 34 percent presented symptoms of sexually transmitted disease as a result. This was not necessarily representative of the entire Rwandan population (Kumar et al. 1996:66).

2. An estimated 21 percent of all Rwandan families have had foster children, according to a Food and Agriculture Organization/World Food Program survey conducted in August 1995 (Kumar et al. 1995:66).

6. Rebuilding Community Cohesion

1. Assefa suggests that such a holistic conception is founded on four values and principles: (1) the absolute necessity of identifying and resolving root causes, (2) the importance of justice and fairness in the process of dispute settlement, (3) the underlying commonality of interests and objectives between disputing parties, and (4) the fundamental role of restructuring relationships in resolving conflict (1993:5–6).

2. The ongoing debate over terminology reflects the changes and growth in the field. Some experts maintain that the word *resolution* connotes an unrealistic

absolute denouement of the underlying contention and hence use *transformation* instead. The latter refers to an evolution in the antagonistic relationship ostensibly toward a—possibly heated but—nonviolent interaction. The words *management* and *mitigation* are also used here, acknowledging the seemingly intractable and deep-rooted nature of identity conflict, along with the necessity of coming to terms with the situation.

3. Jonathan Shay (1994) uses the concept of *thémès* in *Achilles in Vietnam: Combat Trauma and the Undoing of Character* to describe the deep-seated ethics, which, regardless of culture, when violated elicits an intense mental learning.

7. International Intercession in Community Rehabilitation

1. One excellent resource for tools is a manual by Creative Associates prepared for the U.S. government, *Preventing and mitigating violent conflicts: A revised guide for practitioners* (1997).

2. The concern over security for aid workers has increased in the mid-1990s to include training courses on security management and preparedness measures, new safety protocols in many agenices, and more sophisticated threat assessments. For more discussion, see Van Brabant (1998).

3. For a list of recent works related to the development of a code of conduct, see Minear and Weiss 1993a:89–90. Also, as of this writing, the Sphere Project, probably the most comprehensive effort to date supported by a wide array of international relief agencies, was finalizing its publication on a humanitarian charter and minimum standards for humanitarian assistance. The project is scheduled to be completed by late 1998.

4. Cuny gives a good insider's overview of the motivation behind providing humanitarian assistance to foreign disasters and the lack of professionalism in the relief system at that time (1983:110, 125–37).

5. A phrase aptly coined by Professor Eghosa Osaghae, head of the political studies department of the University of Tanskei, South Africa, at a conference on "Empowering NGOs for Conflict Resolution in Africa," sponsored by InterAction, Washington, D.C., March 26, 1996. Personal notes taken from lecture.

6. Rule offers a good critique of Western dispute resolution and its assumptions and practices in foreign cultures in questioning dispute resolution (1993:407–12).

7. Articulating guiding principles for humanitarianism in and of itself is valuable, particularly as the situations become more complex and the number of inexperienced players entering the scene rises. To some extent, however, one might question the validity of the underlying assumption. Relief of physical life-threatening suffering, though undoubtably important, perhaps should not be the *absolute highest* goal of humanitarianism. Such abhorrence for physical suffering may be more of a Western construct than a universal one. It may be our own suffering derived from the ache of overindulgence and privilege, the painful guilt of inaction, and an injured sense of virtue that we are trying to alleviate. Taking the broadest

possible view, there may in fact be higher moral goals, which at times demand that we submit to a larger degree of suffering in lieu of a greater and more encompassing end. For a broader discussion on the moral dilemmas and responsibilities facing relief agencies, see Slim (1997).

8. To Minear and Weiss's credit, however, they do not merely propose these principles as ideals, but present substantial discussion as to their application in complex emergencies. See Minear and Weiss (1993b).

9. In *Humanitarian Action in Times of War*, Minear and Weiss outline a functional checklist for agencies working in war zones that offers specific suggestions on how to analyze a situation and orchestrate activities according to their Providence Principles (1993a:45–54).

10. Both Prendergast (1995) and Anderson (1996b) have good discussions on context analysis.

11. Interestingly, research on interethnic community relations in the United States found that involvement in common projects reduced conflict and improved the climate between newcomers and long-term residents (Voutira and Brown 1995:25).

12. A phrase used by professor Luc Reychler, University of Leuven, in Leuven (Louvain), Belgium.

13. For more discussion on the disintegration of internal mechanisms and phases of response, see Rupesinghe (1991).

14. For more on dispute resolution mechanisms in different cultures, see Rule (1993:409).

15. John Moyibi Amoda (1996) offers a good discussion on the nature of civil society in Africa, arguing that, as much as it might exist as a tenant of democracy, it does so solely as an aspect of the evolving nature of Western societal influence.

8. The Next Phase in International Aid

1. As a result of this recognition, USAID established the Greater Horn of Africa Initiative, which attempts to take a holistic approach toward development, including in it conflict resolution, prevention, food security strategies, civil society development, and other more comprehensive and innovative schemes.

2. Research conducted by Diane Paul begins the discussion on integrating human rights protection into humanitarian relief efforts. See Paul (1998).

REFERENCES

Aall, Pamela. 1996. Nongovernmental organizations and peacemaking. In C. Crocker and F. O. Hampson, eds., *Managing global chaos.*

Africa Rights. 1994. Humanitarianism unbound? Current dilemmas facing multi-mandate relief operations in political emergencies. Discussion Paper no. 5. London: Africa Rights. Photocopy.

Ahlström, Christer. 1991. *Casualties of conflict: Report for the World Campaign for the Protection of Victims of War.* Uppsala, Sweden: Department of Peace and Conflict Research, Uppsala University.

Amoda, John Moyibi. 1996. Cultivating non-governmental organizations (NGO) cultures in Africa: Matters of contexts. Paper presented at the Workshop on Empowering NGOs for Conflict Resolution in Africa, sponsored by InterAction, Washington, D.C., March 26.

Anderson, Mary. 1994. International assistance and conflict: An exploration of negative impacts. Case Studies Series no. 1. Cambridge, Mass.: Local Capacities for Peace Project.

——. 1995a. Food for work for rebuilding homes in Khatlon Province, Tajikistan: A project of Save the Children Federation. Case Studies Series no. 4. Cambridge, Mass.: Local Capacities for Peace Project.

——. 1995b. Relationship between humanitarian assistance and conflict and remedial steps that might be taken. Paper delivered at symposium on Humanitarian Aid and Conflict in Africa, sponsored by the USIP, October 2. Photocopy.

——. 1995c. Norwegian Church Aid and Norwegian Refugee Council Afghanistan/ Pakistan Project: A case study. Case Studies Series no. 5. Cambridge, Mass.: Local Capacities for Peace Project.

——. 1996a. *Do no harm: Supporting local capacities for peace through aid.* Cambridge, Mass.: Local Capacities for Peace Project.

——. 1996b. Humanitarian NGOs in conflict intervention. In C. Crocker and F. O. Hampson, eds., *Managing global chaos,* 343–54.

Arnison, Nancy C. 1993. The law of humanitarian intervention. In H. Cleveland, ed., *New strategies for a restless world,* 37–44.

Assefa, Hizkias. 1993. *Peace and reconciliation as a paradigm.* Nairobi: Majestic Press.

——. 1995. *Megabat,* or "Opening a space to allow another in" Class presentation in

Philosophy and Praxis of Reconciliation, July 19–29 at Eastern Mennonite University, Harrisonburg, Va.

Awoonor, Kofi. 1993. The concerns of recipient nations. In K. Cahill, ed., *A framework for survival: Health, human rights, and humanitarian assistance in conflicts and disasters*, 63–81.

Beer, F. A. 1981. *Peace against war*. San Francisco: W. H. Freeman. Cited in Christer Ahlström (1991), *Casualties of conflict*, 8.

Blair, H. 1992. AID, civil society, and development: An evaluation concept paper. Washington, D.C.: USAID. Photocopy.

Bock, Joseph. 1995. The Harmony Project of the St. Zavier's Social Service Society, Ahmedabad, Jujarat, India. Case Studies Series no. 1. Cambridge, Mass.: Local Capacities for Peace Project.

Bond, Lawrence. 1994. A farewell to arms: At work with the French bomb disposal squad. *Crosslines Global Report* 2, no. 1: 1–5.

Borton, John. 1993. Recent trends in the international relief system. *Disasters* 17, no. 3: 2–17.

Boutros-Ghali, Boutros. 1992a. *An agenda for peace*. New York: United Nations.

——. 1992b. Empowering the United Nations. *Foreign Affairs* 71, no. 5: 89–102.

Brown, Ashley (ed. in chief). 1985. *War in peace*. New York: Marshall Cavendish.

Brown, Bess. 1992. Whither Tajikistan? *RFE/RL Research Report* 1, no. 24: 1–6.

Buckly, Stephen. 1995. Rwandan refugees fearful of return. *Washington Post*, August 26, A1, A16.

Chabasse, Philippe. 1995. Anti-personnel mines: The war without end. In F. Jean, ed., *Populations in danger 1995*, 105–110.

Cahill, Kevin, ed. 1993. *A framework for survival: Health, human rights, and humanitarian assistance in conflicts and disasters*. New York: Basic Books and the Council on Foreign Relations.

Carnegie Commission on Preventing Deadly Conflict. 1997. *Preventing deadly conflict: Final report*. New York: Carnegie Corporation.

Chambers, Robert. 1993. Hidden losers? The impact of rural refugees and refugee programs on poorer hosts. In R. Gorman, ed., *Refugee aid and development theory and practice*. Westport, Conn.: Greenwood Press.

Cleveland, Harlan. 1993. A restless world. In H. Cleveland, ed., *New strategies for a restless world*, 5–11. Minneapolis, Minn.: American Refugee Committee.

Cock, Jacklyn. 1995. A sociological account of light weapons proliferation in Southern Africa. In J. Singh, ed., *Light weapons and international security*, 87–126.

Cohen, Roberta. 1994. International protection for internally displaced persons— next steps. Focus Paper no. 2. Washington, D.C.: Refugee Policy Group. Photocopy.

——. 1996. Protecting the internally displaced. *World refugee survey: 1996*. Washington, D.C.: USCR.

Conradi, Loramy. 1993. Grassroots peacework in Nicaragua. *Peace Review* 5, no. 4: 437–45.

Creative Associates. 1997. *Preventing and mitigating violent conflicts: A revised guide for practitioners.* Manual prepared for the Greater Horn of Africa Initiative, U.S. Department of State and USAID. Washington, D.C.: Creative Associates.

Crocker, Chester and Fen O. Hampson, eds., with Pamela Aall. 1996. *Managing global chaos: Sources of and responses to international conflict.* Washington, D.C.: United States Institute of Peace.

Cuny, Frederick. 1983. *Disasters and development.* New York: Oxford University Press.

———. 1989. Spot reconstruction: The programming of reconstruction and development assistance to support peace initiatives. Intertect. Photocopy.

———. 1990. The Georgetown University Symposium on Displaced Persons: A review of the proceedings. April. Photocopy.

--, module prepared by. 1991. *Displaced persons in civil conflict.* Geneva: UNDP/UNDRO Disaster Management Training Program.

Cuny, Frederick and Christopher Cuny. 1992. The return of Tamil refugees to Sri Lanka, 1983 to 1989. In F. Cuny, B. Stein, and P. Reed, eds., *Repatriation during conflict in Africa and Asia,* 23–101.

Cuny, Frederick, Barry Stein, and Pat Reed, eds. 1992. *Repatriation during conflict in Africa and Asia.* Dallas, Tex.: Center for the Study of Societies in Crisis.

CWA-ACIST, 1995–96. Quarterly reports of Church World Service's African Community Initiatives Support Teams. Dutch Interchurch Aid.

D'Angelo, George. 1997. Preventing complex emergencies: The Framework for Coordination, a United Nations process. Ph.D. diss., the Union Institute.

Deng, Francis M. 1993. *Protecting the dispossessed: A challenge for the international community.* Washington, D.C.: The Brookings Institute.

Deng, Francis M. and Larry Minear. 1992. *The challenges of famine relief: Emergency operations in the Sudan.* Washington, D.C.: The Brookings Institute.

de Waal, Alex. 1993. War and famine in Africa. *IDS Bulletin* 24, no. 4: 33–40.

Dewey, Arthur. 1993. The military role in emergency response. In H. Cleveland, ed., *New strategies for a restless world,* 45–50.

Dikshit, Prashant. 1995. Internal conflict and the role of light weapons. In J. Singh, ed., *Light weapons and international security,* 41–49.

Donini, Antonio and Norah Niland. 1994. Rwanda: Lessons learned, a report on the coordination of humanitarian activities. Geneva: UNDP.

Dougherty, J. and R. Pfaltzgraff, Jr., eds. 1981. *Contending theories of international relations: A comprehensive survey.* 2d ed. New York: Harper and Row.

Duany, Wal. 1994. Jikany-Lou Nuer Reconciliation Conference, Akobo, South Sudan, July-October 1994. Report prepared for briefing for the African Bureaus of the Department of State, National Security Council, Congressional Committee on Africa and the nongovernmental organization community, November 15–18, 1994, Washington, D.C.

Duffield, Mark. 1996. The symphony of the damned: Racial discourse, complex political emergencies and humanitarian aid. *Disasters* 20, no. 3: 173–93.

Fagen, Patricia. 1993. Peace in Central America: Transition for the uprooted. In *World refugee survey: 1993.* Washington, D.C.: USCR.

Fagen, Patricia Weiss and Joseph Eldridge. 1991. Salvadoran repatriation from Honduras. In M. A. Larkin, F. Cuny, and B. Stein, eds., *Repatriation under conflict in Central America,* 117–86.

Fahey, Joseph. 1993. Conflict creation. *Peace Review* 5, no. 4: 413–16.

Farah, Abdulrahim. 1993. Responding to emergencies: A view from within. In K. Cahill, ed., *A framework for survival: Health, human rights, and humanitarian assistance in conflicts and disasters.*

Frohardt, Mark. 1994. Managing the political dimensions of humanitarian assistance. Paper prepared for the Office of U.S. Foreign Disaster Assistance. Washington, D.C.: Center for the Study of Societies in Crisis. Photocopy.

Georgetown University. 1993. Challenges and opportunities in the decade of repatriation: The role of NGOs. Report of a conference held at Georgetown University, Washington D.C., June 16–17.

Girardet, Edward. 1993. What we need is a High Commissioner for war victims. *Crosslines Global Report* 1, no. 1 (August): 16–18.

———. 1994. Outlawing landmines—an issue for the 90s. *Crosslines Global Report 2,* no. 1 (January–February): 5–9.

Gluck, Kenny. 1995. International assistance to civilians: The Abkhaz-Georgia civil war. Case Studies Series no. 6. Cambridge, Mass.: Local Capacities for Peace Project.

Guatemala Partners. N.d. Learning from refugees: The achievements of Guatemalan refugees as protagonists in their voluntary repatriation. Washing-ton, D.C.: Guatemala Partners. Photocopy.

Gurr, Ted Robert. 1970. *Why men rebel.* Princeton: Princeton University Press.

———. 1993. *Minorities at risk: A global view of ethnopolitical conflicts.* Washington, D.C.: USIP.

Gurr, Ted Robert and Barbara Harff. 1994. Report of the Maryland Workshop on Early Warning of Communal Conflicts and Humanitarian Crises: Conceptual, research, and policy issues. University of Maryland, March 27. Photocopy.

Gutlove, Paula, with Eileen Babbit, Lynne Jones, and Joseph Montville. 1992. Towards sustainable peace in the Balkans: A report on a pilot effort to introduce conflict resolution theories and techniques. Cambridge, Mass.: The Balkans Peace Project. Photocopy.

Hakovirta, Harto. 1986. *Third world conflicts and refugeeism: Dimensions, dynamics, and trends of the world refugee problem.* Helsinki: Finnish Society of Sciences and Letters.

———. 1987. An ethical analysis of refugee aid and the world refugee problem. Amsterdam: Workshop on Duties Beyond Borders.

Hansen, Greg. 1995. SAWA/education for peace: Uniting Lebanon's children and youth during war. Case Studies Series no. 8. Cambridge, Mass.: Local Capacities for Peace Project.

Harff, Barbara. 1993. A theoretical model of genocides and politicides. Paper prepared for the Maryland Workshop on Early Warning of Communal Conflicts and Humanitarian Crises, University of Maryland, November 5–6. Photocopy.

Harris, Laura. 1994. The impact of ethnicity, labeling, and rumors on durable solutions to refugee flows: Developing strategies for the avoidance of ethnic conflict. Photocopy.

Hathaway, James. 1996. Can international refugee law be made relevant again? In *World refugee survey: 1996.* Washington, D.C.: USCR.

Hogan, Mark. 1992. A quest for living space: Repatriation efforts among assisted displacees in South-Central Sudan. In F. Cuny, B. Stein, and P. Reed, eds., *Repatriation during conflict in Africa and Asia,* 381–426.

Horowitz, Donald. 1985. *Ethnic groups in conflict.* Berkeley: University of California Press.

Human Rights Watch. 1995. Georgia/Abkhazia: Violations of laws of war and Russia's role in the conflict. *Human Rights Watch* 7, no. 7: 3. Cited in Kenny Gluck (1995), International assistance to civilians: The Abkhaz-Georgia civil war. Case Studies Series no. 6. Cambridge, Mass.: Local Capacities for Peace Project, 10.

Human Rights Watch Africa. 1997. Zaire: Attacked by all sides—Civilians and the war in Eastern Zaire. *Human Rights Watch Africa* 9, no. 1.

Huntington, Samuel P. 1993. The clash of civilizations? *Foreign Affairs* 72, no. 3 (Summer): 22ff.

Independent Commission on International Humanitarian Issues. 1986. *Modern wars: The humanitarian challenge* (p. 25). London: Zed Books. Cited in Gil Loescher (1993), *Beyond charity,* 13.

International Alert. 1993. Conflict in North Caucacuses and Georgia. Report of a meeting held in London. London: International Alert. Photocopy.

International Peace Research Association. 1990. *Peacebuilding and development in Lebanon.* Final conference report. IPRI/UNESCO, 48. Cited in Greg Hansen (1995), SAWA/education for peace: Uniting Lebanon's children and youth during war. Case Studies Series no. 8. Cambridge, Mass.: Local Capacities for Peace Project, 5.

Intertect. 1993. Assessing emergencies involving civilians displaced by conflict. Document prepared for the UNDP. Dallas, Tex.: Intertect.

Jackson, Stephen. 1995. Trocaire integrated rehabilitation program, Gedo, southwestern Somalia. Case Studies Series no. 3. Cambridge, Mass.: Local Capacities for Peace Project.

Jean, François, ed. 1995. *Populations in danger 1995: A Médecins Sans Frontières report.* London: MSF.

Johnston, Philip. 1993. Relief and reality. In K. Cahill, ed., *A framework for survival: Health, human rights, and humanitarian assistance in conflicts and disasters.*

Kamukama, Dixon. 1993? *Rwanda conflict: Its roots and regional implications.* Kampala Uganda: Fountain Publishers.

Keegan, John. 1993. *A history of warfare.* New York: Knopf.

Keen, David. 1997. A rational kind of madness. *Oxford Development Studies* 25, no. 1: 67–76.

Klein, Donald. 1995. The four c's of change towards conflict resolution. A working paper. Photocopy.

Knorr, Klaus and James N. Rosenau, eds. 1969. *Contending approaches to international politics.* Princeton: Princeton University Press.

Kumar, Krishna, D. Tardif-Douglin, K. Maynard, P. Manikas, A. Sheckler, and C. Knapp. 1996. *Rebuilding postwar Rwanda.* Study 4 of *The international response to conflict and genocide: Lessons from the Rwanda experience,* ed. Joint Evaluation of Emergency Assistance to Rwanda. Odense, Denmark: Steering Committee of the Joint Evaluation of Emergency Assistance to Rwanda.

Laegreid, Turid. 1995. Mismanaging the Rwandan tragedy. Discussion paper for the Workshop on the Joint Evaluation of Emergency Assistance to Rwanda. Photocopy.

Landay, Jonathan. 1995. Boom in the trade of small arms fuels world's ethnic and regional rivalries. *The Christian Science Monitor,* April 5.

Larkin, Mary Ann, Frederick Cuny, and Barry Stein, eds. 1991. *Repatriation under conflict in Central America.* Washington, D.C.: Georgetown University, and Dallas, Tex.: Intertect Institute.

Leaning, Jennifer. 1993. When the system doesn't work: Somalia 1992. In K. Cahill, ed., *A framework for survival: Health, human rights, and humanitarian assistance in conflicts and disasters,* 103–120.

Lederach, John Paul. 1992. Beyond prescription: New lenses for conflict resolution training across cultures. Working draft for InterAction's *Sharing common ground: Culture in Canada.* Washington, D.C.: InterAction. Photocopy.

——. 1994. Building peace: Sustainable reconciliation in divided societies. Submitted to Tokyo: United Nations University.

Loescher, Gil. 1993. *Beyond charity: International cooperation and the global refugee crisis.* New York: Oxford University Press.

Lowrey, William. 1995. Sudan case study: Jikany-Lou Nuer indigenous peace process. Report for the USIP summer seminar, Approaches to Peace in a Changing World, Washington, D.C., June 21. Photocopy.

Maynard, Kimberly. 1993. Tajikistan: Will we heed the warning? *Central Asian Monitor* 5: 11–16.

——. 1994. Humanitarian prospects for Tajikistan. Washington, D.C.: Refugees International. Photocopy.

——. 1997. Rebuilding community: Psycho-social healing, reintegration, and reconciliation at the grassroots. In K. Kumar, ed., *Rebuilding societies after civil war: Critical roles for international assistance,* 203–226. Boulder, Colo.: Lynne Rienner.

McNeil, Donald, Jr. 1996. Somali clan leader who opposed U.S. is dead. *New York Times,* August 3.

Mechal, Simon and Peter Simkin. 1992. Memorandum of understanding on the implication of the cross-mandate concept. November 6. Photocopy.

Meyer-Knapp, Helena. Forthcoming. *Cease fire!* Photocopy.

Mills, Kurt. 1995. Nationalism, ethnic conflict, and self determination: The challenge for sovereignty and human rights. Paper presented at the annual International Studies Association conference. Photocopy.

Minear, Larry. 1994. The international relief system: A critical review. Paper presented at Parallel National Intelligence Estimate on Global Humanitarian Emergencies, Washington, D.C., September 22, 1994. Photocopy.

——. 1995. Reconciliation across borders: An experiment in Croatia. Case Studies Series no. 2. Cambridge, Mass.: Local Capacities for Peace Project.

Minear, Larry and Thomas G. Weiss. 1993a. *Humanitarian action in times of war.* Boulder, Colo.: Lynne Rienner.

—-, module prepared by. 1993b. *Humanitarian principles and operational dilemmas in war zones.* Geneva: UNDP/UNDRO Disaster Management Training Program.

Montville, Joseph. 1993. The healing function in political conflict resolution. In D. Sandole and H. Van der Merwe, eds., *Conflict resolution theory and practice,* 112–27. Manchester: Manchester University Press.

——. 1995. Complicated mourning and mobilization for nationalism. In J. Braun, ed., *Social pathology in comparative perspective: The nature and psychology of civil society,* 159–73. Praeger.

——. In press. Reconciliation as reäl politïk: Facing the burdens of history and political conflict resolution. In H. Geong, ed., *From conflict resolution to peacebuilding.* Fairfax, Va.: Institute for Conflict Analysis and Resolution, George Mason University.

Moore, Christopher. 1993. "Have process, will travel": Reflections on democratic decision-making and conflict management practice abroad. *National Institute for Dispute Resolution Forum* (Winter): 1–12.

Morrison, David. 1995. Small arms, big trouble. *National Journal* 18 (March): 712.

Naisbitt, John. 1994. *Global paradox: The bigger the world economy, the more powerful its smallest players.* New York: Morrow.

Newland, Kathleen. 1993. Ethnic conflict and refugees. *Survival* 35, no. 1: 81–101.

Nordlander, Ylva, ed. 1993. *States in armed conflict: 1993.* Report no. 38. Uppsala, Sweden: Department of Peace and Conflict Research, Uppsala University.

Norwegian Refugee Council. 1992. Repatriation during conflict. Oslo: Norwegian Refugee Council.

Oberg, Jan. 1993. Conflict mitigation in former Yugoslavia. *Peace Review* 5, no. 4: 423–36.

Ogata, Sadako. 1993. The plight of refugees: Issues and problems affecting their humanitarian needs. In K. Cahill, ed., *A framework for survival: Health, human rights, and humanitarian assistance in conflicts and disasters,* 293–98.

Ortega, Marvin and Pedro Acevedo. 1991. Nicaraguan repatriation from Honduras and Costa Rica. In M. A. Larkin, F. Cuny, and B. Stein, eds., *Repatriation under conflict in Central America.*

OTI (Office of Transition Initiatives). 1995. OTI pilot project update on Bosnia. Washington, D.C.: OTI. Photocopy.

Owen, David. 1993. Obligations and responsibilities of donor nations. In *A framework for survival: Health, human rights, and humanitarian assistance in conflicts and disasters*, 52–62. New York: Basic Books and the Council on Foreign Relations.

Paul, Diane. 1998. *Beyond monitoring and reporting: The field level protection of civilians under threat*. New York: Jacob Blaustein Institute.

Pease, Kelly-Kate and David P. Forsythe. 1993. Humanitarian intervention and international law. *Austrian Journal of Public and International Law* 45: 1–20.

Physicians for Human Rights. 1997. Investigations in Eastern Congo and Western Rwanda. Washington, D.C.: Physicians for Human Rights.

Pierpaoli, Yvette. 1995. Reconciliation and reintegration of displaced in Burundi: Use of traditional dignitaries for return of displaced. Washington, D.C.: Refugees International. Photocopy.

Prendergast, John. 1995. Minimizing negative externalities of aid: The ten commandments. Paper presented at symposium on Humanitarian Aid and Conflict in Africa, sponsored by USIP, October 2. Photocopy.

Ransdell, Eric. 1994. The wounds of war. *U.S. News and World Report*, November 28, 67–75.

Reed, Wm. Cyrus. 1997. Refugees and rebels: The former government of Rwanda and the ADFL movement in Eastern Zaire. Washington, D.C.: USCR.

Refugees International. 1995. Burundi: Peace, one hill at a time. *Refugee and Relief Alert* (Spring): 4–5. Washington, D.C.: Refugees International. Photocopy.

Roberts, Adam. 1993. Intervention and human rights. *International Affairs* 69, no. 3: 429–49.

Rogge, John. 1992. Return to Cambodia: The significance and implications of past, present, and future spontaneous repatriations. In F. Cuny, B. Stein, and P. Reed, eds., *Repatriation during conflict in Africa and Asia*, 103–195.

Rotfeld, Adam Daniel. Introduction: The emerging international security agenda. In Stockholm International Peace Research Institute, *SIPRI Yearbook 1997: Armaments, disarmament, and international security*, 1–14. Oxford: Oxford University Press.

Roy, Oliver. 1993. The civil war in Tajikistan: Causes and implications. A report of the study group on the prospect for conflict and opportunities for peacemaking in the southern tier of former Soviet Republics. Washington, D.C.: USIP.

Ruiz, Hiram. 1993. Repatriation: Tackling protection and assistance concerns. In *World refugee survey: 1993*. Washington, D.C.: USCR.

Rule, Colin. 1993. Questioning dispute resolution. *Peace Review* 5, no. 4: 407–12.

Rupesinghe, Kumar. 1991. Internal conflicts and their transformation: An interview with Dr. Kumar Rupesinghe. By Stephanie Loomis at the symposium on Ethnicity, Social Justice, and Development: Implications for the Social Professions in Working with Diverse Populations, at the Center for Advanced Study of International Development, Michigan State University.

——. n.d. Humanitarian agencies and armed conflict. Discussion paper. International Alert. Photocopy.

Saunders, Harold. 1990. An historic challenge to rethink how nations relate. In V. D. Volkan, D. Julius, and J. Montville, eds., *The psychodynamics of international relationships*, vol. 1, *Concepts and theories*, 1–30.

——. 1993a. The concept of relationship: A perspective on the future between the United States and the successor states of the Soviet Union. An occasional paper for the Mershon Project on Alternative Futures for the United States and Post-Soviet Relations. Photocopy.

——. 1993b. Enlarging U.S. policy toward ethnic conflict: Rethinking intervention. Paper prepared for symposium on Ethnic Conflicts: Threat to Domestic and International Peace, cosponsored by the National Defense University and the Joint Center for Political and Economic Studies, November 9, Washington, D.C. Photocopy.

——. 1996a. Letter written to Cyrus Vance. January 8, 1996. Kettering Foundation, Dayton, Ohio.

——. 1996b. Prenegotiation and circum-negotiation: Arenas of the peace process. In C. Crocker and F. O. Hampson, eds., *Managing global chaos*, 419–32.

Scheffer, David, Richard Gardner, and Gerald Helman. 1992. Post–Gulf War challenges to the UN collective security system: Three views on the issue of humanitarian intervention. Washington, D.C.: USIP.

Scimecca, Joseph A. 1993. What is conflict resolution? *Peace Review* 5, no. 4: 391–400.

Search for Common Ground. 1995. An initiative to help prevent ethnic warfare and promote reconciliation in Burundi. Washington, D.C.: Search for Common Ground. Photocopy.

Seifulaziz, Milas. 1992 (June). Background to the Somali conflict. Photocopy.

Sen, Amartya. 1990. *Public action to remedy hunger*. New York: The Hunger Project.

Shay, Jonathan. 1994. *Achilles in Vietnam: Combat trauma and the undoing of character*. New York: Athenaeum.

Shiner, Cindy. 1996. Liberian warfare: Surreal and deadly. *Washington Post*, May 5, A26.

Singh, Jasjit, ed. 1995. *Light weapons and international security*. Dehli: Indian Pugwash Society and the British American Security Information Council.

SIPRI (Stockholm International Peace Research Institute). 1996. *SIPRI Yearbook 1996: Armaments, disarmament, and international security*. New York: Oxford University Press.

Slim, Hugo. 1997. Doing the right thing: Relief agencies, moral dilemmas, and moral responsibility in political emergencies and war. *Disasters* 21, no. 3: 224–57.

Sollenberg, Margarita and Peter Wallensteen. 1997. Major armed conflicts. In SIPRI, *SIPRI Yearbook: Armaments, disarmament, and international security*,

17–22. New York: Oxford University Press.

Sollis, Peter. 1994. The relief-development continuum: Some notes on rethinking assistance for civilian victims of conflict. *Journal of International Affairs* 47, no. 2: 451–71.

Sommer, John. 1994a. *Hope restored? Humanitarian aid in Somalia, 1990–1994.* Washington, D.C.: Refugee Policy Group.

——. 1994b. Political dimensions of humanitarian assistance: The case of Somalia, 1990–1994. Washington, D.C.: Refugee Policy Group. Photocopy.

Sorenson, John. 1992. Afghan refugees in Pakistan: Prospects for repatriation. In F. Cuny, B. Stein, and P. Reed, eds., *Repatriation during conflict in Africa and Asia,* 243–87.

Stafford, Douglas. 1993. New strategies: A view from Geneva. In H. Cleveland, ed., *New strategies for a restless world,* 20–24.

Stanton, Kimberly. 1993. Pitfalls of intervention: Sovereignty as a foundation for human rights. *Harvard International Review* 16, no. 1: 14–16.

Stein, Barry. 1991. The actual and desirable link between programmes of *ad hoc* assistance to return movements and long-term development programmes for the local areas where refugees return. Paper presented at symposium on Social and Economic Aspects of Mass Voluntary Return of Refugees from One African Country to Another. Sponsored by UN Research Institute for Social Development, March 12–14.

Stein, Barry and Frederick Cuny. 1991. Introduction. In M. A. Larkin, F. Cuny, and B. Stein, eds., *Repatriation under conflict in Central America,* 1–10.

——. 1992. Introduction. In F. Cuny, B. Stein, and P. Reed, eds., *Repatriation during conflict in Africa and Asia,* 9-22.

Stephenson, Robin and Peter Anderson. 1997. Disasters and the information technology revolution. *Disasters* 21, no. 4: 305–334.

Stoltenberg, Thorvald. 1993. New strategies: A view from Norway. In H. Cleveland, ed., *New strategies for a restless world,* 16–19.

Tandon, Rajesh. 1991. Civil society, the state, and roles of NGOs. *IDR Reports* 8, no. 3.

United Nations (UN). 1945. Charter of the United Nations.

——. N.d. *Human rights and refugees.* Human Rights Fact Sheet no. 20.

United Nations, General Assembly. 1951. *Convention relating to the status of refugees.* General Assembly Resolution 429 (V).

United Nations, Secretariat. 1994. UN Secretary-General's report on Rwanda.

United Nations Children's Fund (UNICEF). 1992. *The invisible emergency: A crisis of children and women in Tajikistan.* Report of a UNICEF/World Health Organization (WHO) Mission 21. February. Photocopy.

United Nations Security Council. 1991. Security Council Resolution 688.

UNHCR (United Nations High Commissioner for Refugees). 1993a. UNHCR's role in protecting and assisting internally displaced people. Central Evaluation Section Discussion Paper.

——. 1993b. *The state of the world's refugees: The challenge of protection.* New York: Penguin Books.

——. 1995. UNHCR at a glance. Geneva: UNHCR. Photocopy.

——. 1996. *Refugees and others of concern to UNHCR: 1996 statistical overview.* Geneva: UNHCR.

——. 1997. *The state of the world's refugees: A humanitarian agenda.* Oxford: Oxford University Press.

USCR (U.S. Committee for Refugees). 1995. *World refugee survey: 1995.* Washington, D.C.: USCR.

——. 1996. *World refugee survey: 1996.* Washington, D.C.: USCR.

——. 1997. *World refugee survey: 1997.* Washington, D.C.: USCR.

USGAO (U.S. General Accounting Office). 1992. AID has been responsive but improvements can be made. *Report to the Chairman, Legislation and National Security Subcommittee on Government Operations, House of Representatives.* GAO/NSLAD–93–21.

USIP (U.S. Institute of Peace). 1992. Conflict and conflict resolution in Mozambique. A conference report for Discussions from Dialogues on Conflict Resolution: Bridging Theory and Practice. Washington, D.C.: USIP.

——. 1994. Restoring hope: The real lessons of Somalia for the future of intervention. Special Report. Washington, D.C.: USIP.

——. 1995. The war in Tajikistan three years on. Special Report. Washington, D.C.: USIP.

U.S. Mission (United States Mission to the United Nations). 1995. *Global humanitarian emergencies: 1995.* New York: U.S. Mission to the United Nations.

——. 1996. *Global humanitarian emergencies: 1996.* New York: U.S. Mission to the United Nations.

——. 1997. *Global humanitarian emergencies: 1997.* New York: U.S. Mission to the United Nations.

Uwiringyimana, Leonard. 1993. The history of Rwanda: An ancient feudal system versus the present democratic system. Photocopy.

Van Brabant, Koenraad. 1998. Cool ground for aid providers: Towards better security management in aid agencies. *Disasters* 22, no. 2: 109–125.

van Creveld, Martin. 1991. *The transformation of war.* New York: Free Press.

Vieira de Mello, Sergio. 1993. Humanitarian issues in conflict-resolution: The Cambodia example. Background paper for the Conference on Conflict and Humanitarian Action, sponsored by International Peace Agency, Princeton University, October 22–23. Photocopy.

Volkan, Vamik D., Demetrios Julius, and Joseph Montville, eds. 1990. *Psychodynamics of international relationships,* vol. 1, *Concepts and theories.* Lexington, Mass.: Lexington Books.

von Clausewitz, Carl. 1976. *On war.* Edited and translated by M. Howard and P. Paret. Princeton: Princeton University Press.

Voutira, Eftihia and Shaun Brown. 1995. A cautionary tale: A review of some non-governmental practices in conflict resolution. Report for the Economic and Social Committee on Overseas Research of the Overseas Development Administration (ODA) and Refugee Studies Program. Photocopy.

Walker, Peter. 1996. Hunger and food security: The future of food aid. *Crosslines Global Report* 4, no. 21: 17–19.

Wallensteen, Peter and Karin Axell. 1993. Conflict resolution and the end of the Cold War, 1989–93. In Nordlander, ed., *States in armed conflict*, 7–23.

Watson Institute for International Studies. 1997. Historian challenges collective memory of Vichy/Algerian eras. *Briefings* (November): 14. Providence, R.I.: Brown University.

Weine, Stevan. 1996. Bosnian refugees: Memories, witnessing, and history after Dayton. *World Refugee Survey 1996*, 28–34. Washington, D.C.: USCR.

Winter, Roger. 1990. Ending exile: Promoting successful reintegration of African refugees and displaced people. Washington, D.C.: USCR. Photocopy.

Zinser, Adolfo Aguilar. 1991a. Repatriation of Guatemalan refugees in Mexico: Conditions and prospects. In M. A. Larkin, F. Cuny, and B. Stein, eds., *Repatriation under conflict in Central America*, 57–114.

———. 1991b. Refugee repatriation in Central America: Lessons learned from three case studies. In M. A. Larkin, F. Cuny, and B. Stein, eds., *Repatriation under conflict in Central America*, 187–212.

Zolberg, Aristide, Astri Suhrke, and Sergio Aguayo. 1989. *Escape from violence: Conflict and the refugee crisis in the developing world.* New York: Oxford University Press.

INDEX